Forty shades of Steam

The story of the Railway Preservation Society of Ireland

Joe Cassells and Charles Friel

Colourpoint

Joe Cassells is a native of Belfast and has taught in Coleraine for the whole of his professional career. A member of the RPSI since its foundation, he is a regular contributor to its journal, *Five Foot Three*, and the author of *Steam's Silver Lining*, an earlier publication about the Society's main line tours. Joe's railway interests centre on photography and locomotive performance recording, and his roots are firmly fixed in the age of steam. Active in the Kirk Session of his local Presbyterian church, he is also a member of the Presbyterian Historical Society. Away from the railway, he finds great relaxation in listening to church music, and is a contented explorer of old churches, whose architecture forms a growing part of his extensive slide collection.

Charles Friel has been interested in railways for as long as he can remember. He was born in Enniskillen, within sight and sound of both the GNR and Sligo Leitrim but later moved to Portadown. He joined the RPSI within a few days of its formation and has always been actively involved. He has been, at times, its Publicity Officer, and Editor of *Five Foot Three*. While Editor, he began collecting photographs of Irish railways and that collection has contributed to many publications. He has organised the Society's Belfast meetings since 1974. Since 1978, he has been the Society's Official Photographer (which means he's allowed to take and supply photographs of Society activities entirely at his own expense!). He has written Colourpoint's books on *Merlin* and *Slieve Gullion* and co-authored *Fermanagh's Railways* with Norman Johnston. A career civil servant, he is a senior management training consultant. He is married to Christine and they have two sons, James and Edward.

6 5 4 3 2 1

© Joe Cassells and Charles Friel
   and Colourpoint Books 2004

Designed by Colourpoint Books, Newtownards
Printed by W&G Baird Ltd

ISBN 1 904242 26 X

Colourpoint Books
Colourpoint House
Jubilee Business Park
21 Jubilee Road
NEWTOWNARDS
County Down
Northern Ireland
BT23 4YH
Tel: 028 9182 0505
Fax: 028 9182 1900
E-mail: info@colourpoint.co.uk
Web-site: www.colourpoint.co.uk

Cover photographs:

Front: The Society's flagship engine is No 171 *Slieve Gullion*, last survivor of the famous S class 4-4-0s of the Great Northern Railway (Ireland). Here she is seen pounding up through Whiteabbey station on Thursday 15 May 1980. The train is the empty carriages, from Whitehead to Dublin, for the Society's 'South Kerry' railtour the following weekend. Details of this, and of all of the trains illustrated in this book, are set out in the second half of the text.

Rear: Ex-Dublin and South Eastern 2-6-0 No 461 raises the echoes – and revives memories of her own glory days – as she leaves Waterford for Kilkenny with the 'Gall Tir' tour on 9 May 1998. No 461 was shedded here at the end of her CIÉ career.

All photographs are by Charles Friel unless otherwise stated.

The authors wish to thank Robin Morton and the 'RPSI 40' Committee for steering this project and all those who have contributed to the book with research, proof-reading, forewords, introductory articles and photographs. The table of films involving RPSI trains was compiled by Philip Lockett and the lists of rolling stock by James Friel.

Contents

Lord O'Neill adjusting his own locomotive *Shane* from the lineside, before a run on the Shane's Castle Railway. This engine now operates on the Giant's Causeway and Bushmills Railway.

Foreword

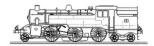

I cannot remember exactly when John Harcourt, the first Chairman of the RPSI, approached me about the post of Patron, but I do clearly remember it happening. I also remember that I had absolutely no difficulty in saying 'yes' with alacrity!

According to my diary for 1964, the Inaugural Meeting took place at 7.45 pm on Wednesday, 30 September, although unfortunately it does not record the venue.

Five Foot Three No 1, issued in 1966 with a cover price of two shillings, included a foreword from me and the opening paragraph read as follows:

> The Railway Preservation Society of Ireland was formed in September 1964. It has been my pleasure to act as Patron of the Society since its inception, and I look forward to many happy years in this capacity.

Forty years on, I can certainly look back and remember many happy occasions associated with the Society. I think the great strength of the RPSI is that, although conceived in the North, it was always seen as an all-Ireland body. During the early years, we were free from the political problems which developed from 1968 onwards, but at no time did these troubles intrude on the affairs of the Society, apart from occasional unforeseen closures of the main Belfast-Dublin line. Indeed, the fact that Dr Garret FitzGerald has acted as Vice-President of the Society for many years, underlines the all-Ireland dimension.

This dimension has also meant that we have enjoyed very good relations with both Northern Ireland Railways (now part of Translink) and CIÉ (now Iarnród Éireann). Indeed, it would not have been possible to operate the regular programme of tours throughout the island without their support, and quite often the use of their engineering facilities. We have also had the valued co-operation of the Ulster Folk and Transport Museum, who have allowed occasional exchanges of stock and notably made the GNR Compound, No 85 *Merlin*, available for restoration.

I cannot mention *Merlin* without being reminded of the late Lord Dunleath, who sadly died at the early age of 59, but had been a very active Vice-President for many years before. The restoration of No 85 was to a large extent the result of his enthusiasm for the project and, equally importantly, the funds which he made available to support it. Many of us will remember his enjoyment of the official launch at Whitehead and subsequent trips to Dublin. Speed was one of his pleasures in life, both on rail and road; indeed, he was a skilled driver of vintage cars.

The Society has grown from a small band of enthusiasts into a large and successful organisation which runs a varied programme of tours throughout the country every year. Although a small team of full-time employees is now retained, nothing would have been possible without the commitment of an enormous amount of time by volunteers, some of whom must have spent, and spend, a significant proportion of their lives at Whitehead.

Unfortunately it is becoming increasingly demanding to keep our rolling stock in a condition where it is acceptable to the regulatory and insurance authorities. Our historic wooden-bodied coaches are now unacceptable on NIR and we have had no alternative but to renovate a set of ex-NIR and BR Mark 2 coaches, in order to continue the programme of tours. However, the Society has entered into this process with a will and the restoration programme is now well in hand.

I said earlier that I could recall many happy memories of the first 40 years of the Society's existence. For many years I was a regular participant in the two-day (now three-day) tours. I always tried to sit in the ex-Great Southern and Western 12-wheeler which once ran on the old Cork-Rosslare boat express. When first acquired by the RPSI, it was still in reasonable condition, although there was an all-pervading smell of mushrooms and a flat on one wheel, which I think it retained throughout its active life with the Society. One hopes that one day it will be restored but, alas, probably only as a museum piece.

Looking back over the years at the various events, certain occasions stand out. In October 1966 we had our first run with a preserved engine – No 171 – which I suppose was the start of our tour programmes. In September 1968, I undertook a complete tour of the Irish railway system, finishing up on the first RPSI two-day tour with 186 and 4. The main tour would have been far more interesting ten or fifteen years earlier, alas! A tour in May 1975, with Nos 186 and 171, took in the soon to be closed 'Burma Road', which I remember as being particularly enjoyable. The year 1978 saw the two J15s in (English) South Eastern Railway green livery for filming *The First Great Train Robbery*. They took us to Wexford in 1978 and were on the 'Croagh Patrick' tour in 1979, which was another highlight.

May 1982 saw Nos 171 and 184 on the 'Thomond' tour, when we spent time at Attymon Junction considering the future of the West of Ireland Railway Society. In May 1984 my wife and I undertook our first 'chase' during the 'Galway Bay' tour – a pattern we have followed from time to time since.

Perhaps my favourite memory was 30 June 1984, which was my own 50th birthday special, albeit nearly ten months late! We travelled

from Antrim to Portrush where the assembled company disported themselves on the beach in traditional style, returning to the train in time for a Cornish cream tea and a rapid run back to Antrim behind No 4. The train included the ex-Great Northern Railway Directors' Saloon which I had helped to restore a short time before. This is a most attractive vehicle, and featured on many of our trains for a time. Alas, due to its timber frames, it can no longer be operated and must be a museum piece from now on. It has already spent time in the rail collection at Cultra.

My last involvement with the three-day tour was in May 1998 when I chased for a short time between Rosslare and Rathdrum, in the company of Sir William McAlpine of *Flying Scotsman* fame and Mr Robert Guinness of the Straffan Steam Museum. There is no doubt in my mind that the route through the Wicklow mountains between Avoca and Rathdrum is one of the most attractive surviving stretches of track in the country. I am only sorry that I never went to Valentia!

Looking ahead, a lot will depend on the attitude of the two administrations in Ireland to the future role of the railway system. Since very few railways are now really profitable in the ordinary commercial sense and need to be seen as a social service they are subject to the whims of governments and the overall level of prosperity. At the moment, a lot of money is being spent in the Republic of Ireland but one has considerable concern about the Northern Ireland system, which appears to be under threat in some areas. However, new rolling stock is expected shortly which should give it a lift.

Steam railway preservation is still thriving in the United Kingdom and one can only hope that we will be able to maintain and develop the reputation which the Society has built up over the first 40 years.

The Lord O'Neill
President

Introduction – The best of times

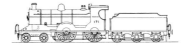

Why a book on the RPSI? Mainly to mark an important anniversary – but also, for some of us, to reflect on an important part of our own lives. The people who have contributed to this book form a representative cross-section of a huge number of members who, over four decades, have given their time and their skills freely to keep working steam alive in Ireland. Those who have maintained our operational bases, kept our engines and carriages on the road, organised our operations, staffed our trains, negotiated with the railway companies and done all the administrative work, should all find their work commemorated in these pages. I trust that they will be reminded not only of their many hours of hard labour, but also of the many hours of pleasure their work continues to give to a growing number of travellers on our main line trains.

My own contribution is to tell the story of our main line steam operations over almost forty years, and Charles Friel's is to illustrate them. I found this a particularly congenial task, since my interest has always been in the operational performance of steam engines on main lines.

On the day the Society was founded, steam was still regularly at work in Northern Ireland, but by late 1969 steam passenger trains had been more or less eliminated from Northern Ireland's railways. In 1970, steam was phased out altogether from company service. Many predicted that this marked the end of steam in Ireland, but thankfully the prophets of doom were confounded, as this chronology of nearly forty years' operations testifies.

With the goodwill of Ireland's two railway operators, Northern Ireland Railways and Iarnród Éireann, the story is still very much ongoing. Others in this book have justly paid tribute to the understanding and tolerance of those in railway management, whose primary purpose is to run their own trains but who are still prepared to accommodate ours. I want to add a word about the men who are equally indispensable – the drivers, firemen, locomotive inspectors and guards without whom there would be no trains at all.

There were the older men who were delighted to get a last breath of steam before their own retirement – just a few names must stand for the many who felt privileged to drive and fire our engines. In the north, I think of Harry Ramsey and Davy McDonald, delighted to be given No 4 for a week of ballast working in 1984 as part of her running-in programme. For them, every day on a steam engine took them back to the railway of their boyhood days, and every run with No 4 was a run with one of 'our own' engines again. "If Harry and me had this engine every day, we'd burn no coal at all", was Davy's proud comment at the end of the week.

I remember Rab Graham, a consummate footplate artist, more than happy to be whisked from Portrush to Whitehead by car on a day that No 171 failed on the 'Portrush Flyer'. Not a bit fussed about losing his mid-afternoon rest at Portrush – much more concerned that No 4 should be got from Whitehead in good time for a punctual run back to Belfast. There was the legendary Bobby Quail of Belfast, always insisting on examining his engine himself before, during and after every run he did, and only too happy to pass his vast knowledge on to the coming generation of NIR trainees. Willie McCaughley, survivor of many a hard day on the Great Northern in the 1950s, and well into his sixties, was as happy to fire as he was to drive.

In the south, I think of driver Matty Purcell of Mullingar, climbing on to No 186 after years away from a steam footplate and, within a few miles of starting, finding himself 'handing the door' for his firemen in the way he'd always done. Then there was that splendid character, Joe Murphy of Inchicore, whose experience in firing the works test train in the early 1960s extended to both Great Northern and Southern engines, and who thought that an NCC Jeep was the best thing he'd ever stood on.

I think of driver Jack O'Neill of Waterford who came up to Belfast on a day off to ride behind No 186 in the late 1960s, found himself on the footplate with two NCC men who really appreciated the rugged simplicity of a J15, and began an association with the Society that lasted until after his retirement. Other great characters included Dick Millea, Nicky Moore, Mick McGuinness, Morgan Darcy, Joe Byrne, P Colbert, 'the Heeler' Dunne, the genial Tommy Blackwell and one fine old man, still game for a turn with the shovel, even though – as he said himself – "sure I'm only a 'pricker' fireman". These are only a very few of many whose names must stand for all those who loved those last flings with steam before their own retirement.

There were the inspectors of the past, among them Frank Dunlop, Chief Locomotive Inspector of NIR, who made our engines part of his life – and none more so than the endlessly perplexing *Merlin*. There was also Inspector Ned Comerford of Inchicore who knew that his generation of enginemen was passing, encouraged the two young Renehan brothers, Tony and Dan, to take an interest in learning steam, and had the satisfaction of seeing them become the first of a new generation of steam enginemen trained in the diesel era.

And there are, thankfully of course, the new generation of men who have been willing to learn the skills of firing and driving that most unforgiving piece of machinery, the steam engine. As I write, there are presently only three regular steam drivers in Ireland – Dan and Tony Renehan of Connolly and Inchicore in Dublin, and Noel Playfair of York Road in Belfast. But there is a very encouraging band of young men, north and south, whose skills with the shovel are already extensive, and who are ready and willing to progress to the other side of the footplate as the opportunity presents itself. Nor can we forget the traction inspectors, the guards and, unseen but sympathetic, the signallers who make sure that the trains get a decent path. This book is for all of these people too, and the names I have mentioned must stand for literally hundreds of railwaymen, past and present, who have worked on our engines.

Fifteen years ago, I rashly thought that I had produced the definitive account of all the Society's operations. How wrong I was! Fortunately a number of kindly people took the time and trouble to set me right on what I had omitted and distorted and, more recently, RPSI secretary Paul McCann challenged me to complete the story up to the anniversary year of 2004. With the benefit of past experience, I will not dare to suggest that the work is exhaustive or infallible – I can only present it as a reasonably complete account of all our trains, and commend it to readers with the wish that they will spend many happy hours reliving days spent on our special trains.

Joe Cassells

The RPSI – The story so far

The Railway Preservation Society was formed in Belfast on 30 September 1964. The inaugural meeting at the Presbyterian Hostel was organised by a group of railway enthusiasts who vowed that working mainline steam in Ireland should not be consigned to the history books.

At the time, the storm clouds were gathering. Steam had ended on CIÉ, while the decision had been taken to close the Warrenpoint branch and the 'Derry Road', the Great Northern line from Portadown to Londonderry.

Steam engines and traditional carriages were being withdrawn from traffic and going to the scrap yards in increasing numbers. Apart from the collection already mustered by Belfast Transport Museum, it looked as if nothing was going to be saved for posterity.

Despite many difficulties, the determination of those founding members paid off. From humble beginnings, the Society went on to secure and restore to full working order some of the last remaining examples of Irish steam locomotives, along with a collection of vintage railway carriages of the steam era.

Thanks to the generous and continuing co-operation of Northern Ireland Railways and Iarnród Éireann, the RPSI's steam trains, complete with buffet car, are now a regular sight on the Irish railway network.

The RPSI has brought steam back to every point on Ireland's rail network – to places as far apart as Limerick and Lisburn, Cork and Coleraine, and Bangor and Ballina. The spectacle of a living steam engine brings pleasure to those with happy memories of train journeys of yesteryear and thrills a new generation more familiar with travel by road and air.

Every year, the Society operates more than thirty steam trains, tailored to appeal variously to the general public and the dedicated enthusiast. Altogether, they carry thousands of passengers every year. The Society, which

A 'Candid Camera' moment at Portrush on 5 April 1969, when NIR steam trains were still operating. Here several prominent Society members are contemplating travelling to Derry with an empty carriage train. In the foreground, left to right, are Drew Donaldson, RM 'Mac' Arnold, Derek Henderson and Norman Foster, while in the background is Leslie McAllister. No 4 has just arrived with the 12 noon relief from York Road (crewed by Rab Graham and Gerry Phelan).

enjoys charitable status, has evolved from a small group of enthusiasts to a significant organisation with 1,100 members and a turnover of £140,000 per annum.

Over the years, the Society has amassed a collection of ten steam locomotives, three diesel shunters and many historic carriages. The Society's headquarters are at Whitehead, Co Antrim, where it has developed a locomotive workshop and built carriage sheds. The RPSI also has a base at Mullingar in Co Westmeath.

The RPSI operates trains to all parts of the Irish railway system, but most of its operations are centred on Belfast and Dublin. The major event of each year is the three-day or 'International' steam tour, which takes place on the second weekend of May and traditionally heads for a far-flung railhead in the Republic. The railtour, which has been a popular fixture in the RPSI calendar since 1968, always attracts strong support from enthusiasts in Britain and further afield. The RPSI was notable for pioneering the use of photographic run-pasts, lineside buses, train splitting and false starts.

However, increasingly, the Society has become involved in the operation of steam trains geared more towards the general public. The forerunner for this switch in emphasis was the 'Portrush Flyer', which began in 1973, and is now the longest running preserved steam excursion train anywhere in the world.

Given that it was Easter 1970 when NIR ran its final steam passenger trains, steam is now a novelty for a new generation. Thanks in part to the influence of Thomas the Tank Engine, crowds of excited children now enjoy the RPSI's annual 'Easter Bunny', 'Hallowe'en' and Santa steam train specials. For a slightly older generation, a steam train provides an unusual outing as well as a welcome change from the car. Hence in mid-summer, the 'Steam and Jazz' trains from Belfast and the Mullingar barbecue trains from Dublin have created a new market.

The 'Portrush Flyer' is now complemented in the Republic by the 'Sea Breeze', a similar type of day excursion steam train trip from Dublin

to Wexford and Rosslare, which runs in the summer months.

The Society has also helped the Irish film-making industry by providing authentic steam trains for several major movies and a multitude of television programmes and advertising commercials.

Among the highlights were *The First Great Train Robbery*, filmed in 1978 and starring Sean Connery, Lesley-Ann Down and Donald Sutherland. The RPSI's train has also featured in television's *The Irish RM* in 1983 and the movie *Angela's Ashes*. A crowning moment came in 1993 when the Society collaborated with the BBC for the shooting of one of Michael Palin's 'Great Railway Journeys' – *From Derry to Kerry*. Then, in 1995, the RPSI was to the fore in the production of *Michael Collins*, the movie which starred Liam Neeson and Julia Roberts.

Although the Society initially considered attempting to preserve a working branch-line, such a concept has been overshadowed by the availability of mainline running. But to compensate, members can get their hands on the regulator and the shovel as part of the Whitehead steam train rides, which operate on Sunday afternoons in the summer.

RPSI members are also trained to prepare and service engines and carriages on the mainline outings, and an RPSI representative travels on the footplate to liaise with the professional railway company crew who actually drive the train on the open road.

The Society has also developed considerable expertise in its specialist workshop at Whitehead. Major overhauls, which at one stage had to be sub-contracted, are now carried out in-house with most of the work done by Society volunteers. The RPSI has developed an iron-casting foundry at Whitehead, which is now the last such example in Northern Ireland. These facilities have allowed us to assist other societies with their locomotive and boiler work.

Over the years, Society activities have attracted grant aid from bodies such as the Northern Ireland Tourist Board, Bord Failte,

On 13 September 1986 No 85 *Merlin* was back on the GNR main line, in Society hands, for the first time and is here raising the echoes around Cloghogue Chapel as she tackles the last part of the climb above Bessbrook. Note the GNR Directors' Saloon next the locomotive.

the Ulster Tourist Development Association, the Ireland Fund, The European Regional Development Fund and FAS, the Republic's training and employment authority. Previously, the Society headquarters at Whitehead also received major assistance from Enterprise Ulster and the Northern Ireland Association for the Care and Resettlement of Offenders, both of whom set up training schemes on site.

Among the challenges which the Society has had to face over the years has been the modernisation of the railway system. The installation of overhead electric wires in Dublin for the DART in 1984 was just one problem that had to be overcome. In that case deflectors were fitted to the locomotive safety valves and a cage placed over the open cab of the steam engine.

Speedometers have also been installed on the footplate, to ensure that line limits are observed. The locomotive and carriages undergo a rigorous safety audit each time, before they are allowed to turn a wheel on company metals.

The latest hurdle has been the introduction in 2004 of new railway operating legislation in Northern Ireland. This has forced the Society to adopt a £200,000 programme to withdraw its historic vintage train and to replace it with more modern steel-bodied carriages that are permitted to run at higher speeds.

The Society can reflect with pride on the past forty years. Not only has it achieved its original purpose of keeping steam alive, but it has proved to be an award-winning organisation, widely recognised for its professionalism.

Few of those who established the Society forty years ago truly believed it would still be flourishing – and operating mainline steam – into the 21st century. However, thanks to the unstinting efforts of its members and volunteer workforce, the RPSI is going from strength to strength and is now a firmly established part of the railway scene.

Now for the next forty years and beyond . . . !

Robin Morton

How it all started

How appropriate it is that the RPSI should have chosen the Irish Railway Collection of the Ulster Folk and Transport Museum at Cultra as the venue for its Grand Gala 40th anniversary dinner. The links between the UFTM and the RPSI go back forty years and beyond. It was at Belfast Transport Museum in Witham Street – a former factory building deep in the heart of east Belfast where the railway collection was then housed – that the foundations of the RPSI were laid.

It was through the good offices of Bob Beggs, the curator of the Transport Museum, that a meeting took place at Witham Street in May 1964 to consider the best course of action to form a society to preserve locomotives for live steam operation, together with some of the best examples of railway vehicles and artefacts from the fast changing Irish railway system.

Represented at the meeting were the Belfast branch of the Irish Railway Record Society, the Royal Belfast Academical Institution Railway Society, the Model Engineers Society (NI) and the Northern Ireland Rail and Road Development Association, a ginger group which actively campaigned against the closure of railways by producing consultative documents, organising public meeting and arranging deputations to government ministers and transport companies.

It was unanimously agreed to invite The Lord O'Neill to act as patron, and an ad hoc committee was appointed to make arrangements for an inaugural meeting of the society, to be known as the Railway Preservation Society of Ireland.

That meeting took place in the Presbyterian Hostel in Howard Street, Belfast, on 30 September 1964, and attracted a large attendance. Lord O'Neill presided and among those present were Lord Dunleath, Bob Beggs, George Thompson (Director of the newly opened Ulster Folk Museum) and John Lewis Crosby (local Secretary of the National Trust). Leading officials of the UTA, including Campbell Bailie, (Railways Manager), Bertie Ryan (Public Relations), Harold Houston, Norman and Joyce Topley, Cecil Ogle and Noel Craig, were also present.

In addition to members of the local transport societies, there was a strong contingent from the IRRS in Dublin, led by the renowned Bob Clements, a walking encyclopaedia of the history of Irish railway locomotives.

The Lord O'Neill extended a warm welcome to everyone who had come to give their support to the formation of the RPSI. He said steam power was part of our industrial heritage and should be preserved for the benefit of future generations. The meeting unanimously endorsed both the name and objectives of the Society. Messages of support were received from the Association of Railway Preservation Societies in Britain, the Bluebell line and the Talyllyn Railway.

A discussion about which locomotives should be preserved produced a strong desire for one of the S class to be picked, primarily because of its versatility to operate over most lines. Naturally, there were divisions between the supporters of the GNR, the NCC and the GSR but it was generally agreed that the best locomotives from all three companies should be considered for preservation.

The meeting considered two possible sites for the Society. These were the goods yard adjoining Moira station and the old excursion station at Whitehead. Tentative approval was given to the

Mid afternoon at Portrush on Saturday 2 May 1964, the day of the North West 200. It was also the day of the annual Sunday School excursion from Windsor Gospel Hall (near Adelaide) to Portrush. Fred Graham, a leading light at the Hall, and later a founder member of the Society, liked to get unusual motive power from Adelaide shed and foreman Sam Mahaffey did him proud this day with a GNR 4-4-0 on each train. No 171 *Slieve Gullion* is to left and No 174 *Carrantuohill* the right; both engines have been turned ready for the run home. In the foreground are the two firemen (sadly unidentified). In the distance are (left to right) Derek Henderson, Stephen Rottger and driver Ned O'Hara, whilst driver Jimmy McAllister is on 174.

Drew Donaldson

latter, as it was self-contained and located at a seaside resort.

A committee was approved to follow up the suggestions made. It comprised: Councillor John Harcourt (Chairman), Laurence Liddle, Denis Grimshaw, Craig Robb, Sullivan Boomer, Graham Nevin, Derek Young, Billy McCormick, Derek Henderson, Drew Donaldson, John McGuigan, Harry Frazer, John White and Eamonn Jordan.

The meeting was rounded off with light refreshments and an inspirational film shown by Billy McCormick, a well-known local travel agent and a pioneer in preservation. He had rescued and restored narrow gauge locomotive No 1 from the Larne Aluminium Railway, with which he operated train rides in his back garden. The engine subsequently saw service on the Shane's Castle Railway and is now on the Giant's Causeway Railway.

The mood of the meeting was one of enthusiasm and a determination that the curtain should not be allowed to fall. The rest, as they say, is history. From those humble beginnings, the Society has made tremendous strides, and all those associated with the RPSI over the years have every reason to feel a sense of satisfaction. The fire has been kept alight and how delighted I am to see the Society going from strength to strength. May I take this opportunity of wishing all those involved in the Society now, and in the years to come, every success.

John Harcourt

First Chairman of the RPSI

How the Society acquired its locomotives

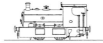

The Guinness engine makes its way along Dufferin Road towards Pollock Basin in Belfast Harbour with the second part of the 'Olderfleet' tour on a very wet 23 March 1968. In the background is HMS *Penelope*, a Leander class frigate. It left that night and took part in the search for an Aer Lingus flight which had gone down off the Tuskar Rock.

Our first loco came about as the result of letters which Committee member Graham Nevin wrote to several local firms, in April 1965, inviting them to donate private owner wagons to the Society. Apart from wagons, the letter brought the Society to the attention of the Guinness Brewery in Dublin. Their broad-gauge link to the yard at Kingsbridge station was due to close on 15 May 1965 so they kindly offered us one of their broad-gauge Hudswell Clarke 0-4-0ST locos. We chose No 3 as the Society's first loco and Guinness organised a handing-over ceremony on 16 June 1965. At some stage during those proceedings, the Guinness Chairman said to the General Manager of CIÉ, "We only had two steam engines and gave these guys one. You must have lots of steam engines. You could give them one too, couldn't you?"

So Lord O'Neill wrote to the CIÉ Board to ask for one of the last J15 0-6-0s that were lying at

Inchicore. By the end of July we were told that we could, indeed, have a J15. Mainly as the result of a sparkling run that he had experienced on a GAA special, Drew Donaldson pushed for the preservation of No 198. Sadly, by the time word reached the scrap line, No 198 was already being cut up. The Society's second choice was No 186, which had put in one of the more reliable performances on the big 1964 tour. Although various engines failed on that tour (including 186), the Committee felt that she had the most manageable list of known defects. On 1 September 1965, No 186 was confirmed for preservation and delivered to Dundalk. She lay there until Saturday 11 December 1965 when she was hauled to Adelaide.

At its very first meeting, the Society had set its eyes on the preservation of a GNR 'S class' locomotive. Now, with two locos acquired, the Committee focused on their primary objective. The UTA still had three running and the Society's first choice seemed to be No 174 *Carrantuohill*. She was the last loco to get a heavy overhaul in Dundalk but her steel firebox was something of a worry. On the advice of

Adelaide foreman Sammy Mahaffey, backed up by advice from York Road staff and some mechanical engineers with extensive steam experience, No 171 *Slieve Gullion* was chosen, since her boiler and copper firebox were in better condition than that of the other survivor, No 170 *Errigal*.

Negotiations were opened with the UTA and in 1966 it was agreed that the RPSI could lease the locomotive for £40 per annum with an option to purchase later. In 2003, with NIR's agreement, the Society exercised its option and the locomotive is now safely ours.

Somewhere about then, too, the last of the 'VS class' three-cylinder simple 4-4-0 locos, No 207 *Boyne*, was going for scrap. While certainly well beyond the Society's funds, there were hopes that it would be bought privately for Society use. However, one problem was the rumoured discovery of cracks in her cylinder block. In those days, such a job was well beyond our imaginings and *Boyne* slipped away.

Four other locos were preservation possibilities about this time. Three were ex-Great Northern 0-6-0 tender locos – UTA Nos 37 (SG3 class), 48 and 49 (UG class). No 37 was lying at Grosvenor Road but thoroughly stripped of all its brasses. No 48 needed its boiler retubed and No 49 had a hot axlebox. The fourth contender was the last of the NCC Moguls, No 97 *Earl of Ulster*, but she was supposed to have damaged frames.

The Society's lack of funds meant that it could not contemplate doing anything about these locos and all went for scrap. We consoled ourselves with the thought that we already had No 186, a lightweight 0-6-0 that could go anywhere. In any event, the problems with each were well beyond our capability and resources to remedy. Nowadays Peter Scott and his team take such things in their stride. How wonderfully things have changed!

Some industrial locos were also vying for our attention about then too. Courtaulds at Carrickfergus had two redundant Peckett 0-4-0ST locos, *Wilfrid* and *Patricia*, and Comlucht Suicre Éireann had various Orenstein and Koppel

(O&K) engines lying out of use. Apart from having no funds whatever to play with, many felt that the Society could have little use for another 'pug'. Our sights were on main line running and, anyway, the 'Guinness' was enough to be getting on with. Courtaulds did, though, donate a lot of trackwork which we recovered for reuse at Whitehead. The O&K saga had another trick up its sleeve and one was later overhauled at Whitehead for our friends in Downpatrick.

Having had to pass up on so many locos, and with the Magheramorne spoil contract drawing to a close, in 1969 the Society began the painfully slow job of raising the funds to buy a 'Jeep'. The last two Class WT 2-6-4Ts, Nos 4 and 53, went into store in Carrickfergus goods yard in early 1971. No 4 was the better of the two and was eventually bought on 11 July 1971; we considered ourselves very fortunate to get her for £1275.

While we were struggling to fund the Jeep appeal, No 27 *Lough Erne* was bought privately by Society chairman Roy Grayson in June 1970. The loco was used at Whitehead on several occasions but Roy discovered just how expensive it was to restore an engine. When Roy emigrated to Wales, he offered the locomotive to the Society. Even in the later 1970s, it was a struggle to raise funds until the Northern Ireland Tourist Board made good the shortfall. There was a ceremony at Whitehead on 3 July 1980 when the NITB cheque was handed over by Rogers Whittaker, the well-known American train and travel writer.

Londonderry Port and Harbour Commissioners No 3 *R.H.Smyth* had been privately purchased by the Reverend Laurence Campbell, a naval chaplain originally from Portstewart. He had hopes of establishing a small train ride operation near Garvagh but, again, found it very expensive to get anything done to the loco. He sold the engine to the Society for £1 on the condition that, if the Society ever wanted to dispose of it, he could buy it for £1. The deal was struck on 1 May 1972 and the engine arrived at Whitehead on 10 June 1972. It was first steamed on 7 June

1977 and soon replaced the 'Guinness' at Whitehead. 'Harvey', as the loco is known, really earned his/her keep on the contract to haul ballast wagons during the relaying of the Bleach Green to Antrim line in 2000.

In the early 1970s, CIÉ set aside three locos for preservation and eventual display. J15 (or '101 class') 0-6-0 No 184, a saturated sister of the Society's No 186, was to go on display at Inchicore, ex-Dublin and South Eastern K2 class 2-6-0 No 461 was to be plinthed at Wexford and ex-Great Northern Q class 4-4-0 No 131 was to be stuffed and mounted at Dundalk. This last was the only part of the plan that came into being.

Nos 184 and 461 were put into store in Cork but came into Society hands in September 1977 when they were moved to the Society's base at Mullingar.

Just about then, Starling Films proposed making the cinema film *The First Great Train Robbery*. In order to provide a dedicated loco for several months, the Society proposed overhauling No 184 and work was agreed that would leave her looking like a loco from 1855, when the story was set.

As part of the deal, we sought long-term custody of the restored No 184 for use on future railtours. This brought the ownership of all the steam engines still in CIÉ hands to a head. A general agreement was reached whereby the RPSI took possession of Nos 184 and 461 for restoration and operation.

At the same time, No 90 (ex-GSWR J30 class 0-6-0T) went to Westrail at Tuam and ex-GNR Q class 4-4-0 No 131 was moved from its plinth at Dundalk for an unsuccessful restoration attempt. Suffice it to say here that No 131 has now arrived in Whitehead for an evaluation of what needs to be done. It should be stressed, however, that No 131 is not a Society engine.

Back in 1965, the Belfast Transport Museum bought the last of the GNR Compounds, No 85 *Merlin*, from CIÉ. The loco eventually made it to Witham Street in late 1969. There things rested until 1977, when an energetic Lord Dunleath offered to fund her restoration. The loco is now the property of the Ulster Folk and Transport Museum and is leased to the Society.

Some Society members had independently preserved a VS class tender in 1965 and No 85 initially used this. Later, 85 temporarily borrowed 171's tender but Whitehead provided a permanent solution by profiling GNR tender No 73 (acquired from CIÉ) to resemble those used by the Compounds.

Another loco that will, hopefully, come into the care of the Society is Ulster Folk and Transport Museum loco No 74 *Dunluce Castle*. She was set aside for preservation by the late Harold Houston and is in NCC maroon livery. The Society is negotiating for No 74 to come out of the Museum and go to Whitehead for eventual overhaul, on a similar basis to *Merlin*.

In addition to its steam engines, the Society has some diesel-powered items. First to arrive was NCC Railcar No 1 which was owned by the Ulster Folk and Transport Museum. It arrived, unannounced, in late 1970 from storage in Ballymena and was later given to the Society.

Our first diesel loco was Hibberd Planet No 23, originally owned by Irish Shell and used to shunt their North Wall terminal at Alexandra Road in Dublin. She was initially given to the Irish Steam Preservation Society at Stradbally. They then donated her to the Society and she arrived at Whitehead by road on 13 October 1973.

The other diesel loco is ex-Comhlucht Suicre Éireann (CSÉ). She was built by Ruston Hornsby in 1951 and was last used by CSÉ at Carlow – hence her nickname 'the Carlow diesel'. After protracted research, she now carries the number '1'. She arrived at Whitehead on 31 August 1981 and returned to traffic in 2001.

The other internal combustion vehicle to be mentioned here is the Unilok 'shunter'. This can work on either road or rail. It was used by the UTA at the railcar shed at Great Victoria Street and, latterly, at the NIR rail welding plant at Lislea Drive. It came to the Society in 1985 and is fully operational.

Charles Friel

Flying high, 30 years on

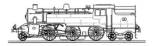

Running steam excursion trains to Portrush is not exactly a new idea. The Belfast and Northern Counties Railway pioneered the idea in the 19th century and regular steam-hauled specials to the popular seaside resort were still running in 1969, in the swansong of steam on Northern Ireland Railways.

But for the RPSI, the 'Portrush Flyer' was still something of a step into the unknown in 1973. Until then, the Society's focus had been on the enthusiast market, with a mix of two-day and one-day trips to various parts of Ireland. But it became clear to the committee in the early 1970s that the market had to be broadened.

Several of ideas were tossed around, the main question being whether a public market existed. Given that steam trains had only just been phased out by NIR, would there be any novelty value? But in the end, the 'Flyer' was an idea whose time had arrived.

The sequence of events can be traced back to the Whitehead Open Day in July 1972. The guest of honour at the event was Hugh Waring, the Managing Director of Northern Ireland Railways. He was clearly impressed by the attractions, which included steam train rides up and down the siding and model railway displays.

However, clearly his day out set him thinking. Mr Waring set up a meeting between RPSI representatives and NIR's newly appointed marketing executive, Danny Young, to explore various possibilities. It was at this meeting that the idea of running a steam train to Portrush during the summer emerged.

Events moved apace and, with the encouragement of NIR, an ambitious plan was drawn up to run four 'Flyers' in the summer of 1973.

Against the backdrop of continuing civil unrest in Northern Ireland, it was a particularly bold proposal, but Mr Young was adamant that it would work.

The plan was to run 'Flyer' trains on two consecutive Saturdays, take a break on the next weekend, and then run on a further two consecutive Saturdays. The train would run from Belfast to Portrush and would be timed to allow passengers around six hours to enjoy the delights of the resort. Although the 'Kingston Flyer' was operating in New Zealand, the 'Portrush Flyer' was the first preserved steam train aimed at the general public to run in the northern hemisphere. An added attraction was that it was launched at a time when there was a virtual ban on mainline steam on British Railways, following their elimination of steam in 1968.

The train would be hauled by 1947-built WT class 2-6-4T No 4, which the Society had purchased from NIR two years earlier, and crewed by NIR footplate staff. The engine was one thing, but the coaches another. At that stage the RPSI owned just a handful of coaches – certainly not enough to make up an eight-coach train. NIR could hire out rolling stock for the day, but the additional costs would have put the finances of the operation into jeopardy.

But help was at hand, and it could not have been better timed. As a result of the McKinsey report on CIÉ in the Republic, the company was disposing of a number of coaches in early 1973. Four coaches were purchased – Nos 1327, 1328, 1333 and 1335 – and, although they dated from Great Southern Railway days, they were almost in ready-to-run condition.

The coaches were available, but could the cash-strapped Society afford to buy them.

With a typically full exhaust bouncing off the sides of the cutting, No 4 blasts her way through Monkstown and on to the single line with the outward bound 'Portrush Flyer' on 4 July 1987.

An application was made to the Northern Ireland Tourist Board for a grant. A meeting was convened, but the complexities of railway coaches proved beyond the grasp of the NITB executives.

Various RPSI committee members were trying to explain why the Society needed to buy the coaches and why modern coaches could not be hauled by a steam locomotive. As they got deeper into their descriptions of the old and new types of coach braking systems, the Tourist Board people were looking more and more confused.

Eventually, RPSI chairman Bob Edwards brought the session to a sudden end by saying: "Look, one system works with a suck and the other one works with a blow". Case proven, and the grant aid was provided!

Naturally, Society members tried everything to

make the first 'Flyer' season a success.

To generate publicity, we organised a photo call for the press at Whitehead with 'Miss Portrush', who posed in front of locomotive No 4, itself adorned with the 'Portrush Flyer' headboard.

The name 'Portrush Flyer' came from a train of the same name which the London, Midland and Scottish Railway, Northern Counties Committee operated from Belfast to Portrush in the 1930s.

Saturday 28 July 1973 was a proud day for the RPSI. At precisely 9.15am (five minutes later than the 1930s time), No 4 pulled out of Belfast (York Road) Station with the inaugural 'Portrush Flyer'.

The NIR driver was Alan Robinson. Also on the footplate was NIR Locomotive Inspector and valued friend of the Society, Frank Dunlop.

Frank was key to ensuring that each 'Flyer' train ran smoothly and, thanks to his influence, many problems were overcome down the years. Despite the other calls on his time, he accompanied almost every 'Portrush Flyer' from 1973 until his retirement in 1990.

For that first 'Flyer' season, the fares for the 130 mile round trip were: adult – £1.40, under 16 – £0.90. Remarkably, a carriage seating 64 people could be booked for £60!

Thankfully, the publicity paid off and the public booked in sufficient numbers to make the venture a success. The 'Flyer' was a steep learning curve for the Society, but it was instrumental in helping the RPSI to see the need for operating trains aimed purely at the public.

From an uncertain start, the 'Flyer' quickly became established as a regular fixture in the Society's calendar. In August 2003, it celebrated its 30th anniversary, as the train, once more with No 4 in charge, and with NIR's Noel Playfair at the regulator, steamed out of Belfast Central, bound for Portrush.

Over the years, only one season has been missed (1990). The problem was that no steam locomotive was available due to maintenance schedules. Down the years, as the NIR network has been modernised, the route has varied. During the years when the Bleach Green to Antrim line was mothballed, the 'Flyer' ran from Central via Lisburn and Antrim to reach Portrush.

A major bonus for the Society and for the 'Flyer' came in 1994 when the Dargan Bridge opened in Belfast, creating a mainline link between Yorkgate (replacing York Road) and Central Station for the first time. This greatly simplified the operation of the 'Flyer', which started its journey from the RPSI's base at Whitehead.

The re-opening of the Bleach Green to Antrim link in 2001 meant that the original route was restored. But although the 'Flyer' is now well established, the operation still requires a considerable effort on the part of the Society in terms of preparing the locomotive and train, and making arrangements with NIR, not to mention marketing the 'Flyer' itself and the add-on afternoon excursion from Portrush to Castlerock (Ballymoney in recent years).

For each 'Portrush Flyer', NIR provide two drivers (one acting as fireman), a locomotive inspector and a guard.

The 'Flyer' would not run without the huge effort put in on the day by a range of Society members, all acting in a voluntary capacity. Someone has to be up at midnight to light the fire in the locomotive and raise steam in the early hours. Another crew has to oil the loco and prepare the train. Meanwhile a team of members is busy stocking the buffet car which, with its coffee bar and drinks bar, is the social hub of every 'Flyer'. The sales staff are opening up the souvenir shop. The train manager and carriage stewards prepare to welcome passengers on board and suddenly, the guard's whistle is blowing.

Another 'Flyer' is under way!

John Friel

Now for the next 40 years . . .

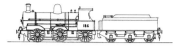

A glimpse of the future? During a shunt at the Ulster Folk and Transport Museum – aka Cultra 'Junction' – to exchange coaches on 26 September 1993, No 171 and NCC No 74 *Dunluce Castle* are seen on the Bangor line. The figure on No 74's tender is a mannequin!

Walt Disney built his Disney empire on creating 'magic moments'. The RPSI does it every time it runs a train! Imagine you are waiting for a steam train. In the distance, you hear the beat of the exhaust grow louder. You can see the smoke and steam curling high into the sky. As the locomotive approaches and passes, you catch a glimpse of the crew hard at work and then hear the carriages sweep past as you savour that unmistakable aroma of smoke, steam and oil. The rhythm dies into the distance, the smoke fades away, but that is a magic moment that won't be forgotten. No surprise that even today, when rockets can land on Mars, many children still dream of being a train driver.

The 40th anniversary of the RPSI is a time to look back, but also a time to look forward. Much has been accomplished over the past forty years but new challenges undoubtedly lie ahead. The RPSI is already widely recognised as a professional provider of quality mainline steam trains. We have done the 'impossible' so many times that most of us can't remember every record we've set and then broken! We've brought steam back to every corner of Ireland – again and again. RPSI-style runpasts and false starts are now commonplace features of many steam specials as far away as South Africa and China.

Whitehead is now firmly established as the Society's nerve centre and ownership of the site means we can move forward with certainty. Our confidence in the future has already been underlined by the investment we have made at Whitehead. In 1992 we officially opened our carriage shed there and in 1997 we opened our new engineering workshop. With a foundry on site, we have the best facilities in the business.

But the key element now, and even more so in the future, will be the commitment of the members. Keeping our steam trains running is a complex business and although we have the tools, we need people to learn the skills and do the job. That sounds daunting but in reality it is fun. After a week in the office there is nothing like pulling on the overalls and enjoying the freedom of a day on the footplate of a steam locomotive. Although railway company personnel are at the controls, our members are playing an increasingly important role in maintaining and preparing our trains, and in overseeing the operation of our locomotives and carriages on the open road. You may need a shower or bath at the end of the day, but it is definitely fun.

Oiling up the steam locomotive or going on the footplate may be the glamourous side of the operation, but there are lots of other ways in which RPSI members keep the wheels turning. Marketing the train and selling the tickets are roles that rely on members. From shunting the carriages at Whitehead to stocking the souvenir shop and crewing the dining car, numerous volunteers are required every time we operate a train.

The longer it is since the steam era, the more difficult it is to keep mainline steam on the go but, although we seem to be swamped by red tape at times, the future is bright. New members are coming forward all the time. Even though they are too young to remember steam in the glory days, they are captivated by the appeal of preserved steam. A new generation is discovering what we are all about and it is vital that we encourage them.

The founding fathers of the Society dared to believe that steam could have a future, even after the railway companies had switched to diesel trains. Now a new generation is gradually taking responsibility, and we need to display that same vision if the Society's future is to be secured. New rolling stock has now been introduced which should guarantee that we meet the operating requirements of the modern railway. The RPSI enjoys cordial relations with both Northern Ireland Railways and Iarnród Éireann. The market for steam is growing all the time, but the Society will have to be innovative in order to meet the ever changing demands of our customers.

Imagine what that future might hold. In 2013, our flagship locomotive *Slieve Gullion* will celebrate her 100th Birthday. How are we to mark this notable anniversary? By coincidence, 2013 will also mark the 50th anniversary of the retirement of our latest Whitehead arrival, Q class No 131. Will she be in steam by then? A tantalising thought and we've got the facilities to do it!

Let's look forward to the golden anniversary of the 'Portrush Flyer' come 2023. No 4 will likely be in action to plough the NCC route, as she was designed to do some 75 years earlier. In fact, No 4 will by that stage have worked for us for over twice as long as she did for the railway companies. Will we see *Dunluce Castle* follow in the same tracks as *Merlin* and leave the museum for a new future on the main line? It does not need to be a dream . . . .

Dreams are usually just that – never-to-be-realised fantasies. But the RPSI isn't really in the business of dreams – the RPSI does aspirations. A fitting thought for the future – we have amassed a vast and varied collection of rolling stock over the last forty years. A branch line operation would be able to do credit to the foresight of our founders. *Lough Erne* heading a mixed goods through our stunning countryside would be a fine sight. Dream or aspiration . . . the future lies in **your** hands!

Phil Lockett and Gerry Mooney

Down memory lane – highlights in RPSI history

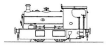

1964   The Society is formed at a meeting in Belfast on 30 September.

1965   The first steam railtour operates: Belfast (York Road)–Portrush–Portadown–Belfast (Great Victoria Street).

1966   The Society sets up home at Whitehead Excursion Station on the Belfast–Larne line.

1967   The 'Dalriada' railtour is the first to use a locomotive (No 186) owned by the Society. The 'Cuchulainn' railtour is the first venture onto CIÉ metals.

1968   The 'St Ciaran' railtour is the first two-day railtour, with an overnight stop in Athlone.

1969   The first open day is held at Whitehead, with three locomotives in steam.

1970   NIR phases out steam operation. The Society launches an appeal to buy No 4.

1971   No 4 is acquired. Work starts on the locomotive shed extension at Whitehead.

1972   No 186 hauls the 'North Kerry' railtour, Limerick–Tralee and return. The first carriage is acquired (No 861).

1973   The 'Portrush Flyer' is launched, with the first season featuring four trains.

1974   The first Schools' Day is held at Whitehead.

1975   The 'Burma Road' railtour is the last steam train on the Claremorris–Sligo line. The Society secures charitable status.

1976   No 4 becomes the first steam locomotive to pass through the new Belfast Central Station. Enterprise Ulster commences a huge work programme at Whitehead, including excavations for new sidings and rebuilding the platform.

1977   Mullingar is established as a base for the restoration of locomotive No 184.

1978   Nos 184 and 186 star in the film *The First Great Train Robbery*. Sean Connery, Donald Sutherland and Lesley-Anne Down also appear!

1979   Whitehead shed extension finally gets a roof. The RPSI sales van takes to the road.

1980   No 171 hauls the first 'Steam Enterprise' train, Belfast–Dublin and return, one week late due to a bomb on the line.

1981   The 'Ben Bulben' railtour traverses the Mullingar–Sligo line, which means that the Society completes its coverage of every railway line still open in Ireland.

1982   The locomotive wheel lathe from Belfast (York Road) is installed at Whitehead.

1983   The Society receives the Association of Railway Preservation Societies annual award for "Operation during 1983 – and for many years past – of steam excursions". No 184 stars in the television series *The Irish RM*, which also features Peter Bowles and Bryan Murray.

1984   No 4 hauls ballast trains for NIR during running-in after an overhaul.

1985   No 85 *Merlin*, on loan from the Ulster Folk and Transport Museum, enters service after an overhaul sponsored by the late Lord Dunleath. The Whitehead Railway Project (a youth training scheme run by the Northern Ireland Association for the Care and Resettlement of Offenders) completes the restoration of former LMS(NCC) coach No 68.

1986 The Society purchases nine coaches from CIÉ to establish a train based in the Republic. Enterprise Ulster installs the former Ballymena turntable in Coleraine, for use by the 'Portrush Flyer'.

1987 NIR charters a Society train, hauled by No 85, for the 40th anniversary run of the 'Enterprise' express.

1988 An RPSI steam train is used for a series of Dublin-based public one-day steam trips to mark the Dublin Millennium.

1989 An RPSI steam train operates scheduled commuter services into Belfast as part of a week of celebrations to mark the 150th anniversary of the Ulster Railway.

1990 RPSI carriages are used in the filming of a television commercial for Satzenbrau beer.

1991 Irish President Mary Robinson officially launches No 461 after its restoration from scrap yard condition.

1992 Belfast's new Yorkgate Station becomes the starting point for the first series of northern Santa steam trains.

1993 No 171 assists in the movement of vehicles from the Belfast Transport Museum to the Irish Railway Collection of the UFTM at Cultra. Work progresses on a new carriage shed at Whitehead, financed in part by grant aid from the Ireland Fund and the European Regional Development Fund.

1994 No 85 becomes the first steam engine to cross the new Dargan Bridge over the River Lagan in Belfast. Nos 171 and 461 feature in the BBC's *Derry to Kerry* 'Great Railway Journey' with Michael Palin.

1995 Nos 171 and 461 star in the film *Michael Collins*. Liam Neeson and Julia Roberts also appear! No 85 becomes the first

steam loco to enter the newly re-opened Great Victoria Street station in Belfast.

1996 Nos 85, 171, 186 and 461 are big attractions at Irish Rail's Inchicore Works 150th anniversary celebrations.

1997 A new locomotive workshop, incorporating a 100 year old overhead crane, is built at Whitehead.

1998 An iron foundry is established at Whitehead to cast replacement parts for overhaul work. No 461 features in celebrations to mark the 150th anniversary of the arrival of the MGWR into Mullingar.

1999 Irish Rail hires No 85 for special trains to celebrate the 150th anniversaries of the arrival of the railway in Dundalk and Cork.

2000 Irish President Mary McAleese officially launches recently restored Irish State Coach No 351. No 3 *R.H.Smyth* is hired by Henry Boot to assist with relaying the Bleach Green–Antrim line.

2001 For the first time, the two-day railtour operates solely in Northern Ireland. It is called the 'Northern Counties' tour.

2002 Dr Joan Smyth, Chairperson of the Northern Ireland Transport Holding Company, carries out a ceremony to mark the re-launch of No 4 after a ten year overhaul.

2003 30th anniversary of the Portrush Flyer – with No 4 at the head of the train. New steel-bodied coaches are acquired and renovated in order to replace the Whitehead-based wooden bodied rolling stock.

2004 A year of celebrations. 50th edition of the Society's magazine *Five Foot Three*, 40th anniversary of the RPSI and 30th anniversary of indoor meetings in Belfast.

RPSI Film contracts

Start date	End date	Name of production	Period portrayed	Locos used	Filming location	Additional comments
10/6/73	10/6/73	Power to Move	1970s	171	Lisburn–Moira	BBC TV programme.
12/6/76	13/6/76	A Portrait of the Artist as a Young Man	1910s	171, 186	Dublin–Cork–Cobh	Filmed on the Society's 'Seandun' railtour.
12/4/78	17/6/78	The First Great Train Robbery	1890s	184, 186	Cork, Dublin (Heuston), Athlone–Mullingar	Not continuously.
23/9/78	23/9/78	Lady Gregory		171	Whitehead	RTE TV production.
22/3/79	22/3/79	The Flame is Love	1890s	184	Bray–Greystones	Set between Paris and Le Havre using coaches from *The First Great Train Robbery*.
16/7/80	16/7/80	My Dear Palestrina	1950s	171	Poyntzpass	BBC TV play.
26/8/80	26/8/80	Canada Dry TV commercial	1930s	171	Malahide	Night filming.
25/9/82	25/9/82	The Life of Richard Wagner	1890s	171	Dublin	Loco transfer date – not necessarily filming date.
20/3/83	20/3/83	Aunt Suzanne	1910s	171	Carrickfergus	BBC TV play.
14/5/83	15/5/83	Country Girls	1960s	171	Waterford area	Lineside shots from the 'Port Lairge' railtour
14/10/83	14/10/83	The Irish RM	1890s	184	Mullingar–Moate	Station scenes at Moate.
20/12/83	20/12/83	A Painful Case		184	Mullingar–Moate	
21/11/86	23/11/86	Remington Steele	1980s	85	Dublin (Connolly)	Static station (supposedly Paddington) with platform fight scene. BR logo on tender.
13/9/87	14/9/87	Troubles	1920s	184	Greystones–Wicklow	TV film.
17/9/87	18/9/87	Echoes	1950s	184	Carrick-on-Suir–Fiddown	
14/10/87	14/10/87	The Old Jest		184	Moate	

Start date	End date	Name of production	Period portrayed	Loco used	Filming location	Additional comments
5/4/89	5/5/89	The Real Charlotte	1890s	184	Moate, Dublin (Heuston)	Loco not in steam.
7/1/90	7/1/90	Satzenbrau TV commercial	1990s	Coaches	Dublin (Heuston)	
9/6/92	9/6/92	NITB TV advert	1990s	171	Downhill	Filmed at tunnels and strand.
25/4/93	25/4/93	Derry to Kerry	1993	171	Derry–Belfast	BBC TV 'Great Railway Journeys'.
2/5/93	2/5/93	Derry to Kerry	1993	461	Dublin–Rosslare	BBC TV 'Great Railway Journeys'.
16/7/95	1/10/95	Michael Collins	1920	171, 461	Dublin, Rush, Laytown, Wicklow	Not continuously.
31/7/95	31/7/95	The Corrs music video	1995	Diner 88	Dublin (Pearse)	Coach 1335 also made an appearance.
28/9/95	28/9/95	Visa TV commercial	1995	Coaches	Killarney	
18/10/95	18/10/95	Bookworm	1995	Coaches	Dublin (Heuston)	BBC/RTE Arts programme.
4/4/96	4/4/96	Karet Coffee commercial	1990s	85	Whitehead–Larne Harbour–Whitehead	Advert for an Israeli coffee company
16/10/97	17/10/97	Amongst Women	1950s	Coaches	Castlerea	BBC/RTE series. Set hauled by ITG's A39 diesel locomotive.
17/8/98	17/8/98	Her Own Rules		461	Malahide	TV production.
19/8/98	20/8/98	Durango		461	Rathdrum	Film production.
29/11/98	20/12/98	Angela's Ashes	1930s	461	Dublin (Pearse)	Film production – two days.
23/5/99	23/5/99	Norah Barnacle	1910s	Coaches	Dublin (Pearse)	Film production.
26/3/00	27/3/00	Rebel Heart	1916	461	Dublin (Pearse)	BBC/RTE production.
1/7/01	2/7/01	Cake	2001	Coach 1463	Inchicore	TV production for TG4.

Locomotives owned by the RPSI

No	Name	Class	Wheels	Builder	Works No	Date built	Wdn	Original operator
1			4W	Ruston & Hornsby	382827	1955	1960s	Comhluct Suicre Éireann
2			4W	Hugo Aeckerle	A/17885	1965	1985	UTA
3	R.H.Smyth		0-6-0ST	Avonside	2021	1928	1959	LP&HC
4		WT	2-6-4T	LMS Derby		1947	1970	LMS(NCC)
23			4W	FC Hibberd	FH3509	1951	1971	Irish Shell
27	Lough Erne	Z	0-6-4T	Beyer, Peacock	7242	1949	1970	SLNCR
171	Slieve Gullion	S	4-4-0	Beyer, Peacock/GNR	5629	1913/38	1965	GNR
184		J15	0-6-0	Inchicore		1880	1963	GSWR
186		J15	0-6-0	Sharp Stewart	2838	1879	1963	GSWR
3BG	Guinness		0-4-0ST	Hudswell Clarke	1152	1919	1965	Guinness Brewery
461		K2	2-6-0	Beyer, Peacock	6112	1922	1962	DSER

Other locomotives linked to the RPSI

No	Name	Class	Wheel layout	Builder	Works No	Built	Wdn	Owner (original)	Comments
49*		UG	0-6-0	Beyer, Peacock	7253	1948	1967	UTA (GNR)	Ex-GNR No 149.
50*		WT	2-6-4T	LMS Derby		1949	1970	NIR (UTA)	
53*		WT	2-6-4T	LMS Derby		1949	1971	NIR (UTA)	
54*		WT	2-6-4T	LMS Derby		1950	1970	NIR (UTA)	
55*		WT	2-6-4T	LMS Derby		1950	1970	NIR (UTA)	
56*		WT	2-6-4T	LMS Derby		1950	1970	NIR (UTA)	
85	Merlin	V	4-4-0	Beyer, Peacock	6733	1932	1963	UFTM (GNR)	On loan from UFTM.
101	Eagle	101	Bo-Bo	Hunslet		1970	1994	NIR	Stored for NIR.
102	Falcon	101	Bo-Bo	Hunslet		1970	2003	NIR	Stored for NIR.
131		Q	4-4-0	Neilson Reid	5727	1901/20	1963	CIÉ (GNR)	
207*	Boyne	VS	4-4-0	Beyer, Peacock	6962	1948	1965	UTA (GNR)	

These locomotives hauled some early RPSI tours. All are now scrapped.

No 131 is at Whitehead for assessment and may be restored in the future.

Steel-bodied coaches

RPSI No	Other Nos	Original Co	Class name	Type	Seats	Built	Acquired
170	5180 (BR)	BR (LMR)	BR Mk 2Z	TSO	64	1967	2003
180*	13475 (BR)	BR (ER)	BR Mk 2A	FK	42	1968	2003
181*	13487 (BR)	BR (WR)	BR Mk 2B	FK	42	1969	2002
300*	822, 934 (NIR)	NIR	BR Mk 2B	SO	62	1970	2002
301	5207 (BR)	BR (LMR)	BR Mk 2Z	TSO	64	1967	2003
302*	5135 (BR)	BR (LMR)	BR Mk 2Z	TSO	64	1967	2003
303	13509 (BR) 902, 920 (NIR)	BR (WR)	BR Mk 2B	SO (FK until 1991)	56	1969	2002
304	13496 (BR), 923 (NIR)	BR (WR)	BR Mk 2B	SO (FK until 1989)	56	1969	•
305	823, 935 (NIR)	NIR	BR Mk 2B	SO	62	1970	2002
460*	9382 (BR)	BR (LMR)	BR Mk 2Z	BSO	31	1966	2002
462	812, 916 (NIR)	NIR	BR Mk 2B	DBSO	31	1970	2002
463	14091, 17091 (BR)	BR (ER)	BR Mk 2Z	BFK	24	1966	2003
547		NIR	BR Mk 2B	Diner	23 + bar seats	1970	2002
+	10651 (BR)	BR Intercity	BR Mk 3A	Sleeping Car (SLE)	26 berth	1980	2004 +

Total: 14

Notes: Only the five vehicles marked * are operational at the time of writing. Nos 301 and 303 are well in hand. No 303 will have wheelchair facilities and No 463 will be fitted with a generator. No 10651 has not yet arrived at Whitehead.

• Purchase not finalised at the time of writing.
+ In store at Heysham at the time of writing.

Wooden-bodied coaches in running order

RPSI No	Other numbers	Original operator	Class code	Type	Seats	Built	Acquired
9	586 (UTA)	GNR	K31	Open brake 3rd (Ex-AEC mule)	72	1954	1975
68	3421 (MR), 4914 (LMS), 274 (UTA)	NCC	F3	Corridor 1st/2nd	56	1922	1978
87	550 (UTA)	UTA	B5	Diner	20	1950	1976
88	552 (UTA)	GNR	B6	Tea car	24	1938	1973
91	472 (UTA)	NCC	K3	'North Atlantic' corridor Brake/3rd	56	1934	1975
238	2993 (MR), 3235 (LMS), 340 (UTA)	NCC	J12	Corridor 3rd	64	1922	1975
241	3300 (MR), 3236 (LMS), 342 (UTA)	NCC	J12	Corridor 3rd	64	1922	1975
351		GSWR		Irish State Coach (owned by IÉ)	25	1902	1995
1097	AM12 (CIÉ)	GSWR		Composite corridor open (wheelchair)	24	1925	1985
1142	1285, 4012 (CIÉ)	GSWR		Corridor 1st	56	1921	1973
1335		GSR		Bredin corridor 3rd	56	1936	1973
1383		CIÉ		Park Royal suburban open 3rd	72	1955	1986
1416		CIÉ		Park Royal suburban open 3rd	72	1955	1985
1463		CIÉ		Laminate open 3rd	64	1958	1985
1916	2168, 1603 (CIÉ)	CIÉ		Laminate open brake/3rd generator van	24	1957	1985
2421		CIÉ		Converted to Bar Car 1996	39	1956	1985
2423	1419 (CIÉ)	CIÉ		Park Royal suburban Snack Car	58	1956	1994

Total: 17

Note: In the earlier days of the Society there were several other preserved wooden bodied coaches but these were unfortunately destroyed as a result of malicious fires.

Stored wooden-bodied coaches

RPSI No	Other numbers	Original operator	Class	Type	Seats	Built	Acquired
1		NCC		Diesel railcar	64	1933	1991
50	150 (UTA)	GNR	A3	Directors' saloon	24	1911	1973
114	114N (CIÉ)	GNR	L13	Brake 3rd	21	1940	1977
243	358 (UTA)	NCC	J6	Corridor 3rd	64	1924	1975
404	613 (UTA)	NCC	V14	Full brake		1936	1984
411	616 (UTA)	NCC	V14	Full brake		1937	1984
788	618 (UTA)	GNR	P2	P van		1934	1979
813	HC7, 529A (CIÉ)	GS&WR		3rd	60	1901	1990
837	HC8, 530A (CIÉ)	GS&WR		3rd	72	1902	2002
861	484A (CIÉ)	GS&WR		12w Brake 1st/3rd	52	1906	1972
1287	1287S (CIÉ)	GS&WR		Camping coach		1915	1978
2422		CIÉ		Diner	39	1956	1985
2979		CIÉ		TPO			Not
62M	486A (CIÉ)	MGWR		6w Compartment 3rd	60	1892	1980

Total: 14

Notes on individual coaches

1	Stalled restoration. Under tarpaulin at Whitehead.
50	Was in traffic until 1996. The wooden underframe means it is no longer allowed to run on trains.
114	Was in traffic until around 1993. Interior vandalised.
243	Stalled restoration. In carriage shed. Was stored at Magheramorne.
404	Grounded as body only. In use as a store.
411	Was in traffic until 1996. No longer required on train. In use as a store.
788	Derelict at Whitehead.
813	Mullingar Tarry.
837	Stored at Mullingar.
861	Externally restored in 1988. In carriage shed but very badly internally vandalised.
1287	Badly damaged by accidental fire in 2003.
2422	Was in traffic until 1994 until put in UFTM. Used for corporate entertainment.
2979	Still owned by An Post.
62M	Was in use as a CIÉ breakdown coach. Under tarpaulin at Whitehead.

Current wagon list

No & former No	Original Co	Type	Wheels	Capacity	Built	Acquired	Livery
23574	CIÉ	20 ton brake van	4 wheel			1983	Grey
R2, 1469(CIÉ)	CIÉ	Flat wagon	bogie	30 ton	1998	1985	Black
R3, 1483(CIÉ)	CIÉ	Flat wagon	bogie	30 ton	1998	1985	Black
R4, 1915(CIÉ)	CIÉ	Flat wagon	bogie	30 ton	1998	c1990	Black
682	CIÉ	Irish Shell oil tanker	4 wheel			1965	None
	CIÉ	Flat wagon		20 ton			
8112N	GNR	Ballast wagon	4 wheel	20 ton		1983	Red
R5, 231(GNR)	GNR	Flat wagon	None	30 ton	1998	1975	Black
R6, 227(GNR)	GNR	Flat wagon	bogie	30 ton	1998	1975	Black
504	GNR	Guinness grain van	bogie	20 ton		1965	Grey
2518	GNR	Guinness grain van	bogie	20 ton		1965	Grey
3169	GNR	Self-propelled steam crane	bogie	15 ton	1912		Red
	GNR	Jib-carrying 4-plank wagon	4 wheel				Red
618, 788(GNR)	GNR	Parcel van	bogie			1980	Brown
81	GNR	Steel-framed brake van	4 wheel			1985	None
R1, 1328(GSR)	GSR	Flat wagon	bogie	15 ton	1998	1973	Black
8309	GSWR	Ballast wagon	4 wheel	20 ton		1983	Red
C69	NCC	4-plank wagon	4 wheel			1969	Red
	NCC	4-plank wagon	4 wheel		1942	1969	Grey
697	NCC	Brown van	4 wheel	10 ton		1980	Brown
C355 / 2355	NCC	Cut down 4-plank wagon	4 wheel		1942	1979	None
5	NCC	Flat wagon	bogie	20 ton		1995	Black
3076	NCC	Hand crane	4 wheel	6.5 ton	1943	1979	Black
	RPSI	Workshop trolley	4 wheel				Black
		Workshop trolley	4 wheel				Black

Total 20

Irish railways in 1964

N

PORTRUSH
COLERAINE
BALLYMONEY
LONDONDERRY
STRABANE
BALLYMENA
LARNE
WHITEHEAD
BANGOR
ANTRIM
OMAGH
COALISLAND
DUNGANNON
BELFAST
LISBURN
LURGAN
PORTADOWN
GORAGHWOOD
NEWRY
WARRENPOINT
DUNDALK
SLIGO
COLLOONEY
BALLINA
BALLYMOTE
FOXFORD
CARRICK
ON SHANNON
CASTLEBAR
BOYLE
KINGSCOURT
WESTPORT
DROMOD
ARDEE
MANULLA
JUNCTION
BALLYHAUNIS
DROGHEDA
LONGFORD
CLAREMORRIS
MOSTRIM
LAYTOWN
CASTLEREA
NAVAN
BALBRIGGAN
ROSCOMMON
MULLINGAR
MOSNEY
SKERRIES
TUAM
RUSH & LUSK
ATHENRY
WOODLAWN
ATHLONE
ENFIELD
HOWTH
GALWAY
CLARA
MAYNOOTH
DUBLIN
ATTYMON
JUNCTION
BALLINASLOE
DUN LAOGHAIRE
LOUGHREA
TULLAMORE
BRAY
PORTARLINGTON
NEWBRIDGE
GREYSTONES
PORT LAOIS
KILDARE
CLOUGHJORDAN
ROSCREA
WICKLOW
ENNIS
ATHY
RATHDRUM
BIRDHILL
BALLYBROPHY
NENAGH
CARLOW
ARKLOW
TEMPLEMORE
LIMERICK
THURLES
MUINE BHEAG
FOYNES
LIMERICK
JUNCTION
KILKENNY
LISTOWEL
TIPPERARY
THOMASTOWN
GOREY
NEWCASTLE
WEST
CAHIR
NEW ROSS
FENIT
RATHLUIRC
ENNISCORTHY
TRALEE
CLONMEL
CASTLEISLAND
CARRICK-ON-SUIR
WEXFORD
FARRANFORE
ROSSLARE STRAND
FERMOY
WATERFORD
ROSSLARE
KILLARNEY
LISMORE
BALLYCULLANE
HARBOUR PIER
RATHMORE
WELLINGTON BRIDGE
MILLSTREET
BANTEER
MALLOW
BRIDGETOWN
COBH
JUNCTION
ROSSLARE HARBOUR
CORK
YOUGHAL
COBH

UTA
CIÉ

31

Forty years of the RPSI in pictures

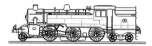

We start with two pictures to represent the popularity of our trains and the extent to which the Society has kept the sights, sounds and smells of Irish steam alive for successive generations of both the enthusiasts and the general public.

Selecting these pictures is by far the most difficult thing that I have ever tried to do with slides. At first sift, I only managed to boil my own slides down to a mere 1300 pictures! Other photographers also contributed some of their best work, particularly from the early days of the Society, taken before I got going properly. I am very grateful to all whose work appears in this book and to one or two others who, in the end, are not represented pictorially. A lot of very fine pictures have not made the final cut and that has been mainly down to the limited number of spaces available; there is easily enough to fill another book!

The photographs are arranged in several themes and in groups of three which I hope you find interesting. The theme idea is probably due to the influence of the late Mac Arnold, though my own photography owes more to Drew Donaldson, variously Mac's ally and sparring partner.

Mac and Drew, and the other Society founding fathers, could not have envisaged how our own trains have covered all of the island of Ireland – several times and in such style.

I very much hope that these pictures convey something of what the Society has achieved – keeping steam alive on the railways of Ireland; without razzmatazz or gimmicks, just honest recreations of the scenes of over 40 years ago. And the great thing is that it is all still there, coming to a station near you!

Opposite top: NCC tank engine No 4 leaves Belfast (York Road), with the ever-popular *Portrush Flyer* on 14 August 1976.

Opposite bottom: J15 No 184 rushes through Ballinasloe with a *Claddagh* excursion from Mullingar to Galway on 27 June 1981.

Early tours

Opposite top: The Society's first railtour was on 11 September 1965 and used three UTA locomotives. Here the final leg of the tour, from Portadown to Belfast (Great Victoria Street), pauses at Lurgan which retained many of its GNR features at that time. No 171 *Slieve Gullion* (not yet a Society engine) is piloting ex-GNR VS class three-cylinder 4-4-0 No 207 *Boyne.*

Richard Whitford

Opposite bottom: The 'Province of Leinster' tour on 14 May 1966 again used non-Society locomotives. Here ex-GNR UG class 0-6-0 No 49 (GNR 149), charges past the photographers and tape recordists during a runpast at Nobber while working south from Kingscourt to Navan on the former MGWR Kingscourt branch.

Des FitzGerald

Above: This was a landmark day for the Society. On 9 September 1967 we brought one of our own engines onto CIÉ metals for the first time. Here J15 0-6-0 No 186 pauses for water at the former Goraghwood station while working south to Dundalk. Reactivating the water supply here was a major challenge for a group of Society members based in Portadown. Note the former quarry in the left background. The formation of the branch to Warrenpoint is to the right of the island platform.

Norman Johnston

Whitehead

Opposite top: On 18 September 1967, UTA loco No 27 *Lough Erne* is delivering our first loco, Guinness Brewery 0-4-0ST No 3BG, from its previous store in Carrickfergus. By this time, the Society had reroofed the original loco shed, bricked up the windows and fitted new doors. Note the absence of track at the platform though some tracklaying was being done behind the photographer. The open wagons contained ash from York Road shed which we used as a rudimentary ballast – and the UTA got some of the wagons back!

Derek Young

Opposite bottom: Twelve years later, there was quite a transformation. This was the view from the King's Road overbridge at the Belfast end of the site, on 2 June 1979. No 186 is about to shunt a 'Steam Gala' special which has just arrived from Belfast (York Road). By now, the platform has been rebuilt and the trackwork was being developed. In the right background, the engine shed extension awaits its roof, while to the left of the water tower, the back field has been fenced for carriage sidings.

Above: Twenty four years later, a more recent picture, taken on 7 December 2003, shows the extensive buildings to the left of the water tower. Curving to the left is the NIR line to Larne Harbour. Next to it is the two-road carriage shed and, behind the water tower, is the locomotive workshop. The 'new' loco shed now has a roof and the platform has acquired a shop. The track layout was designed to allow us to assemble and shunt eight-carriage trains without fouling the NIR main line. The train that has just arrived is the 11.20 Santa special from Belfast Central, hauled by No 85 *Merlin*.

Whitehead – working on locomotives

Opposite top: In the spring of 1974, one of the first big engine boiler jobs that we tackled was the retubing of No 186, then something of a journey into the unknown! Here Irwin Pryce uses a borrowed air tool to expand one of the small tubes at the smokebox end.

Opposite bottom: In the early days, removing an engine's axleboxes was a real challenge. In this November 1976 view, we see that No 171 has had to be jacked vertically by about 20 inches – note the packing on the right between the bogie and the frame. This was to allow the axlebox to drop out of the frames and be removed for repair.

Above: The building of the wheeldrop came as a great relief, as it reduced the sheer human effort needed and made the work much safer. On 21 October 1978, No 4 has had its trailing driving wheels lowered into the pit, then moved to the side and raised for removal and attention.

Whitehead – working on carriages

Opposite top: For some years the Society's carriages were stored, and worked on, in the open in the sidings immediately in front of and beside the loco shed. In this June 1977 view of 16 carriage roofs, there are representatives of GSWR, CIÉ, GNR and NCC-built vehicles. At the platform, on the left, ex-GNR Diner No 88 is having a new roof covering stretched into position.

Opposite bottom: The interior of UTA Diner No 87 is stripped out for repair and refitting in this August 1982 view. To the right is Lavens Steele, one of the Wednesday gang of retired folk who put in a huge amount of work. Note the recycled – but empty! – Guinness kegs, a reminder that our GNR Diner was the first in the world to have draught Guinness and Harp.

Above: The end result of all the hard work. Here NCC North Atlantic brake/third No 91 displays some of Whitehead's finest work. The occasion was the filming of the BBC TV play *Aunt Suzanne* on 20 March 1983. This is Carrickfergus (looking towards Belfast) which masqueraded as Belfast (Great Victoria Street) and is here dressed with enamel signs and loads of mail. Several Society members had supporting roles. The train was worked by No 171 *Slieve Gullion* and the carriage to the right is GSWR First No 1142.

Whitehead – miscellany

Opposite top: Coaling engines at Whitehead depends on the trusty loading shovel which, because the arms are pivoted at the top of the cab, can reach even No 4's extended bunker. Here, on 6 August 1977, an out-of-steam No 4 has been positioned by the Planet diesel loco and Ken Pullin is directing the shovel with its ¾ ton load of coal. In the background, on No 1 shed road, *R.H.Smyth* is being steamed for 'train rides' duty. Beyond the loading shovel is Guinness bogie grain van No 504 and a Great Northern K15 third class coach still in NIR livery.

Opposite bottom: In this summer of 1980 shot, *R.H.Smyth* has been fully lined out and fitted with maker's plates and nameplates. Here she is working a Sunday afternoon 'train rides' with the Rosslare brake/first/third No 861. In the foreground, volunteers are installing a new turnout to give access to the carriage sidings. In the foreground are Johnny Glendinning, Thomas Charters and Paul Newell. Behind them are Ken Pullin and Dermot Mackie with, to their right, Robin Morton. Despite the passage of time, all are still actively involved in Society activities.

Above: To help raise much-needed funds, the Society acquired this travelling shop; the repainting was sponsored by the Northern Bank. Operating under the banner 'Irish Steam Scene', it was kept busy attending traction engine events, ploughing matches, sports days, etc – indeed anywhere that John Richardson could park it! Here Lawrence Morrison and John Beaumont proffer our wares at Whitehead one summer afternoon in 1979.

Celebrations – One

Opposite top: On 28 January 1984, the Society was awarded the Association of Railway Preservation Societies' annual award for outstanding achievement. The citation mentioned our continuing steam railtour programme over both NIR and CIÉ metals, the restoration of loco No 4 and carriages UTA 87, NCC 91 and GSWR 1142. The trophy is a cast coat of arms which once adorned royal trains on the London, Brighton and South Coast Railway; the Society held it for a year.

Opposite bottom: The start of the 1987 'Portrush Flyer' season, on 20 June, saw the running of the fiftieth train. The occasion was marked with a birthday cake and a special headboard on No 171. Here at Belfast (York Road), from the left, are RPSI Chairman Sullivan Boomer, RPSI Vice-President Lord Dunleath, NIR Chairman Sir Myles Humphreys and Lady Humphreys. That year's 'Flyer' season started earlier than usual to accommodate the running of a special in August to mark the 40th anniversary of the first 'Enterprise' express from Belfast to Dublin.

Above: On 16 April 1991, a fully restored No 461 was officially launched at Dublin (Pearse) station (aka Westland Row). No 461 worked a special train to Dun Laoghaire where there was a reception and speeches. That trip was much enlivened by folk along the line who had been alerted by a Radio Éireann broadcast – live from the footplate! Here, a suitably attired President Mary Robinson visits the footplate at Pearse with, from the left, Drivers Nicky Moore and Dan Renehan, Inspector Jack Ahern and a glimpse of RPSI Vice-president Dr Garret FitzGerald.

Celebrations – Two

Opposite top: On 2 July 1993, the Society celebrated No 171's return to traffic and launched its new carriage shed. The latter was partly funded by the International Fund for Ireland. It was declared open by IFI board member Mrs Joan McCrum, seen here between Councillor Janet Crampsie of Carrickfergus Borough Council and Jane Morrice, Head of the European Commission Office for Northern Ireland. Behind are Alan Phair, Recreation Officer, Carrickfergus Council; Ian Henderson, Director, NI Tourist Board; the Society's Ernie Gilmore; Chris Bendsen, USA Vice Consul for Northern Ireland; and RPSI Chairman Sullivan Boomer. The European Regional Development Fund had contributed to the restoration of *Slieve Gullion*, so, after hauling a special train from York Road station, Ms Morrice drove *Slieve Gullion* over twelve detonators, one for each EU country. (The police had been notified!)

Opposite bottom: On 18 October 2000, the Society launched the Irish State Coach, No 351, with a Presidential unveiling at Pearse and a special trip to Dun Laoghaire for a reception. At the reception, President Mary McAleese chats with RPSI Vice-Chairman David Dillon and the Society's David Humphries.

Above: 2003 saw the thirtieth birthday of the 'Portrush Flyer', now surely the longest-established main line steam excursion in the world. Here dining car manager Rita Henderson and RPSI Chairman Norman Foster pose for the press at Belfast Central on 2 August 2003.

Crossing water

Opposite top: No 171 has a small but appreciative audience as she crosses the mighty Shannon at Athlone with the 'Burma Road' railtour on 31 May 1975. *Slieve Gullion* worked the train from Dublin to Claremorris. The leading coach, ex-GNR brake/first 562, is still in NIR livery.

Opposite bottom: A dazzling sunset over Dublin's River Liffey is enhanced by this spectacular shot of No 461 and a returning 'Sea Breeze' train as it makes its way along the Loop Line between Dublin's Pearse and Connolly stations.

Barry Pickup

Above: The tranquility of a Sunday afternoon – and the fishermen – is hardly disturbed by the passage of No 461 as she crosses the River Bann at Portadown. No 461 had been to Dundalk on 24 February 1991 on one of its final trials before working public trains. The loco is running tender first since there is no longer a turntable at Dundalk. Note the large CIÉ 'flying snail' on the tender and painted cabside numerals.

Crossing the River Boyne

Opposite top: No 4 approaches Navan from Drogheda, bunker first, with 'The Boyne' excursion from Dublin to Drogheda and Navan on 27 August 1988. This was one a series of day trips from Dublin in connection with that city's millennium celebrations.

Opposite bottom: No 461 and a private charter train cross the river, this time between Moyvalley and Hill of Down, while working to Mullingar on 3 May 1992. The train marked the wedding of Clare Guinness and Hugo Jacob. The bridge beyond the railway is the Leinster Aqueduct which carries the Royal Canal across the river.

Above: No 171 heads an eight-coach train, resplendent in fresh maroon paint, over the Boyne viaduct at Drogheda. The train is a southbound 'Steam Enterprise' (from Bangor to Dublin) on 19 September 1981.

Departures

Opposite top: *Merlin* strides away from Ballymena at 9.15 am on Monday 23 May 1995 with a 'Big Breakfast' special chartered by the Cancer Research Campaign. The fourth and seventh coaches are in GNR blue and cream livery; the all-important Diner is fifth. The right-hand arm of the still-operational water tank once served the long-gone narrow gauge trains to Larne Harbour and Retreat.

Opposite bottom: No 461 and the Dublin-based set of mostly laminate carriages are seen to good effect as they leave Mullingar for Killucan with the 11.30 Santa train to Killucan on Sunday 8 December 1991, the first of three runs that day, in addition to the three run the day before. The carriage on the extreme left is one of the Park Royal coaches, designed by Bulleid to take full advantage of the Irish loading gauge. Nowadays, these trains operate out of Dublin and are so successful that they have been booked out by late summer!

Above: Between June and November 2000, *R.H.Smyth* was hired to the contractors relaying the main line between Bleach Green Junction and Antrim. The company, Henry Boot, also bought three bogie ballast wagons from NIR. The procedure was to load the wagons at one of several access points and then drop the ballast as required on the new single line track. This is Auld's Bridge, about half a mile below Mossley, known to the contractors as Access 17. On 21 October 2000, RPSI fireman Jeff Spencer leans from the cab as RPSI driver Bob Edwards gets *R.H.Smyth* on the move with three loaded wagons, propelling an estimated load of 180 tons up the 1 in 76½ gradient – no mean feat!

Double heading

Opposite top: The 'Croagh Patrick' railtour in May 1979 brought the Society's two J15s to the Mayo branches. On the Sunday, No 184 pilots 186 as they climb away from Ballinasloe, en route from Claremorris to Athlone. The first coach is No 861, with white upper panels, then comes GSR open third No 1333 and GNR Diner No 88.

Opposite bottom: In a cutting near Rathpeacon, County Cork, Nos 171 and 184 make a fine sight as they head north towards Mallow with the 'Cork 800' tour early on Sunday 12 May 1985.

Above: The Society's two J15 (or '101 class') 0-6-0s approach Islandbridge Junction on Sunday 16 April 1978. They are taking part in the film *The First Great Train Robbery* (see pages 58–59) when Heuston became (London's) London Bridge station. The leading engine, No 184, has had her cab sides and a canvas roof refitted for the trip from Mullingar via Fairview shed. This was a rehearsal day and No 186 had to shunt the film train as it arrived the wrong way round from Mullingar.

Enterprise

Opposite top: No 4 heads for Dublin on 15 September 1984. The train is south of Dundalk, approaching Dromiskin bridge at MP 45¾. The ex-Great Northern Directors' Saloon is next the engine. The mountain in the right background is Slieve Gullion.

Opposite bottom: No 85 *Merlin*, with full headboards, makes a fine sight recovering from a permanent way slack as she approaches Moira en route to Dublin on 15 April 2000. Following the banning of wooden-bodied carriages from double-track main lines, the train is made up of IÉ Cravens with a generator van next the engine.

Above: No 85 again, this time working a Dublin-based 'Enterprise' to Belfast on 23 August 2003. The train is at Plaster Bridge, just north of Mountpleasant, about half way up the climb north from Dundalk and going well. Again the carriages are IÉ Cravens.

Filming – The First Great Train Robbery

Opposite top: This cinema film was shot in Ireland in 1978 and the Society provided 186 and a specially-restored loco No 184 to represent 1855-vintage locos from the South Eastern Railway (between London Bridge and Folkestone). Here, No 184 rushes through the Westmeath countryside with the film train – replica carriages built on the chassis of old luggage vans and one old heating van, whose generator powered the lights. Visible on the roof of the third coach is Sean Connery (who did almost all of his own stunts) after making his way along the carriage roofs from the van at the rear of the train.

Opposite bottom: At Moate, a deathly-looking Donald Sutherland (left) and a roped Sean Connery rehearse the moment when the stolen bullion is thrown from the van at the rear of the moving train to be picked up by an accomplice. On the left, some of the film crew are rigging up a platform for a camera.

Above: The CIÉ crew between takes at Castletown. Left to right are Loco Inspector Eamonn Lacken and Traffic Inspector Ollie Meehan (both from Athlone), Driver Joe Byrne from Mullingar and the fireman, Driver Morgan Darcy from Inchicore. Both Morgan and Joe appeared in several scenes while Ollie's one big moment, as a signalman, came in a shot inside Castletown signal cabin as the train sped past.

Filming

Opposite top: A scene from the television version of *The Irish RM* when Moate became Skebawn. Here a coffin, wrongly carried head first, makes its way to the van in coach No 861 on 14 October 1983. Two of the principals, Peter Bowles and Bryan Murray, are between the coffin and the coach.

Opposite bottom: For filming the BBC TV play *Aunt Suzanne* on 20 March 1983, driver Davy McDonald, Inspector Frank Dunlop and driver Harry Ramsey have been to the make-up department (in the shop at Whitehead). In the event, none appeared in the finished film – much to their relief!

Above: No 461 was used in the cinema film *Michael Collins* in 1995, along with No 171 and several of the Society's coaches. Here No 461 and several carriages are at the south end of Pearse station – note the GSWR crests on the carriage doors and the Society's Chas Meredith emerging from No 461's inside motion.

Barry Carse

Footplatemen – 1

Opposite top: During the photo stop at Cloghjordan on the 'Shannon' tour on 14 May 1985, the Society's Bob Edwards (left) poses with the CIÉ driver Joe Murphy and Inspector Ned Dunphy.

Opposite bottom: Later the same day, No 4 worked empty coaches from Limerick to Galway, via Nenagh and Portarlington. While waiting for an up Cork to overtake, the CIÉ crew of Mick McGuinness, Gerry Kenaghan and Tony Renehan pose on No 4's front apron plate.

Above: No 85 *Merlin* was far from home on the 'Mount Brandon' tour on 15 May 1989. From the left, Inchicore driver Dan Renehan, driver T O'Connor of Cork, Inspector Aidan Ridgeway and driver John Collins of Cork pose at Banteer while working from Tralee to Mallow.

Footplatemen – 2

Opposite top: NIR driver Willie McCaughley was in charge for No 85's first GNR main line trial to Drogheda on 13 September 1986. On the far side of the cab, with the knitted hat, is the fireman, Driver Jackie Kitchen and Inspector Frank Dunlop. The Society's Locomotive Officer Peter Scott is on our side of the cab, standing on the tender. The train is reversing out of Belfast's Central Services Depot to the headshunt, giving us a glimpse of the cab.

Opposite bottom: NIR driver Geordie Gaw, draws on his pipe while contemplating firing No 85 on another Santa run from Belfast Central to Whitehead on 18 December 1994.

Above: The crew for the start of the 30th year of 'Portrush Flyers' pose at Belfast Central before the 'off', on 2 August 2003 – left to right, the Society's Jeff Spencer, NIR Inspector Neville Foster, the fireman, Driver Gary Moore, Driver Noel Playfair and the Society's Locomotive Officer Peter Scott.

Junctions

Opposite top: Mullingar, as seen from the signal cabin, looking east, during the 'Clew Bay' tour on 11 May 1986, with No 4 about to back onto the train in the up Galway platform. The Galway line is to our right and the Sligo line to the left. On the left is a Bredin brake coach which was later destroyed by a vandals' fire. This junction was much simplified in early 2004.

Opposite bottom: This is Limerick Junction on 9 May 1993. No 461 has just collected the single line staff for Tipperary and is crossing the main line en route to Waterford during the 'Sean Ri' tour. Dublin is away to our right; Limerick Junction station, and Cork, to our left.

Above: Dublin (Connolly) (formerly Amiens Street) is seen from the footplate of No 85 *Merlin*, which ran light engine from Limerick Junction to here during the 'American Mail' tour on 14 May 2000. Seen from the fireman's side of the footplate, a '201 class' loco in Enterprise livery waits to leave for Belfast. The other main line platforms and the DART platforms away to the right are empty on this Sunday afternoon.

Landscapes

Opposite top: During the 'Burma Road' tour, on 1 June 1975, No 186 works south past Esker gates, just over a mile south of Swinford, while en route from Sligo to Claremorris.

Opposite bottom: In a scene reminiscent of the late-lamented 'Derry Road', *Slieve Gullion* sweeps around the curves near the River Flesk, about half way between Headford Junction and Killarney, with the 'South Kerry' tour on 17 May 1980. The Mangerton mountains dominate the background.

Above: "Bare Ben Bulben's head" (WB Yeats) broods in the morning mists, as Nos 461 and 171 work hard on the approaches to the closed station of Ballysodare as they head away from Sligo early on 12 May 1996 with the 'Knocknarea' tour.

Larne Lough

Opposite top: No 171 works the last leg of the 'Galway Bay' tour on 14 May 1984, the first time that this short extra train was run to Larne Harbour for the benefit of some participants heading for the Stranraer boat. Here the train crosses the lagoon on the Larne side of Glynn station, framed by a pair of typically hefty Ulster Planter gate pillars.

Opposite bottom: No 85 spins along as it crosses a lagoon near Magheramorne on 11 October 1987. The train is the 'Larne Lough' tour which brought the stock back to Whitehead after the 'Enterprise' season. The trip included a nonstop run from Larne Harbour to Belfast, a recreation of the erstwhile 'Boat Trains'. The Great Northern Directors' Saloon is next the engine, which is running with the large VS class tender.

Above: The view from the Bla Hole, overlooking Whitehead and looking east, as No 4 works another 'Larne Lough' Boat Train run on 5 October 1986. Here No 4 gathers speed on the double track and heads along the coast for the city. Black Head lighthouse is on the farthest headland.

Level Crossings

Opposite top: This is Patrick's Well gates, between Clonmel and Cahir. Here No 186 charges up the 1 in 132 as she heads for Limerick Junction with the 'Silvermines' tour on 18 September 1974.

Opposite bottom: The typical NCC-style gates at Jordanstown have long since been replaced with automatic half-barriers and the station buildings have also been modernised. Here No 171 passes with the final leg of the 'South Kerry' tour on Monday 19 May 1980.

Above: This is the north end of Wexford Quays with No 4 slowly negotiating the crossing with a return 'Sea Breeze' from Rosslare Harbour on 24 June 1989. Despite flashing lights and much engine whistling, the blue car in the middle of the picture has just shot across the bows of No 4.

Mixing with the diesels

Opposite top: A scene from the steps of the signal cabin which used to stand at the north end of the former DSER platforms at Dublin Amiens Street. In this early morning shot, on 10 April 1976, No 186 is making her way from the GNR loco shed to the DSER platforms to pick up her train – the 'Slaney' tour to Wexford. In the left middle distance is the former GNR signal cabin and, further away, is West Road signal cabin. Both were swept away in remodelling for the DART trains.

Opposite bottom: The third trial run for the newly-restored No 184 was on 19 March 1978. The return from Athlone involved the loco's first haulage of passenger carriages for many years. Here a still-to-be-repainted No 184, complete with vice bolted to the running plate, is inspected by CIÉ's Charlie Pemberton while waiting for CIÉ 082 to depart with a train for Galway.

Above: Not all of the big tours take place in good weather! Here a damp No 461 waits at Banteer for IÉ 218, with the 14.10 from Tralee, to clear the section from Millstreet and give up the single line staff. This was the 'Slieve Mish' tour, en route to Tralee, on 10 May 1997.

Morning

Opposite top: Just after 6.00 am on 22 May 1978, No 184 sets off from Mullingar for *The First Great Train Robbery* film set at Moate. Sadly, the goods traffic has gone and the track here has been much simplified.

Opposite bottom: The opening of the 1980 'South Kerry' tour was a boat train from Dun Laoghaire Pier to Connolly. Here, after gathering up participants at Booterstown, from the hotel behind, No 184 bowls along the coast towards Merrion gates early on a shining 17 May 1980.

Above: A black No 171 leaves Whitehead as it works the stock for that day's 'North Atlantic Express' towards Belfast on 16 September 1995. The train is working 'wrong road' through the tunnel since the up line, nearer the sea, was closed for repairs. No 171 was in a black livery of sorts for the film *Michael Collins* but is here in freshly-applied proper GNR black livery and, correctly, without the nameplates.

Multiple locomotives

Opposite top: This is Portarlington on 15 September 1968, the Sunday of the 'Naomh Ciaran', the first-ever two-day tour. No 186 has just worked the train from Athlone and handed over to NIR No 4 (still in UTA livery) which here waits to work forward to Dublin and on to Belfast. On the left, No 186 is now sitting on a train of dining cars and tabled open carriages which were used to provide lunch and refreshments.

Derek Young

Opposite bottom: This was another red letter day in Society history – 14 February 1993. As part of moving the exhibits from the Belfast Transport Museum to their new home at Cultra, on the Bangor line, *Slieve Gullion* was used to haul GSR B1a class 4-6-0 No 800 *Maedhbh* and NCC U2 class 4-4-0 No 74 *Dunluce Castle*. At Cultra 'Junction', the shunting was done by a waiting NIR Hunslet diesel electric. Here, the Hunslet has already lifted No 74, leaving a GM diesel to act as a buffer stop behind No 800. *Slieve Gullion* ran forward to the Rockport emergency crossover and here, running light engine and tender first to Belfast, she has been stopped to pose alongside a towering *Maedhbh*. Will we ever see the like again?

Above: Whitehead Excursion Platform, as seen from the King's Road overbridge during the 'Belfast and Northern Counties' tour on 12 May 2001. No 4 has just arrived with the train, which had been to Bangor, Ballymena and Larne Harbour. No 85 is about to take over for a run to Yorkgate and Ballymena. In the background, No 171 is in 'light steam' (sic) in preparation for the next day's run to Londonderry.

Overhead cranes

Opposite top: On 23 January 1982, No 85 *Merlin* is being craned the length of the Engine Works at Harland and Wolff's shipyard. The loco is about to be loaded onto the road lorry which will bring her to York Road next day. No 85 was hauled to Whitehead on the following Saturday where the overhaul work was completed.

Opposite bottom: On 9 October 1993, No 461 is lifted clear of the main driving axle by two overhead cranes in 'Diesel One' shop, at IÉ's main works at Inchicore in Dublin. This allowed the driving axle boxes to be removed, remetalled and refitted.

Above: The Society's own overhead crane came from the BCDR works at Queen's Quay, Belfast. It dates from 1897 and is now installed, compete with its original columns, in the Loco Workshop at Whitehead, where it has earned its keep with all sorts of heavy lifts. Here, in April 2002, loco No 186 sits dismantled at ground level and, to the right of No 186's firebox, you can see the ex-York Road wheel lathe and resident Locomotive Officer Peter Scott. The wheel drop, seen earlier on page 39, is outside the workshop to the right of the wheel lathe.

Portrush Flyer

Opposite top: At the start of its second season, No 4 flies through Kellswater and past an NCC somersault signal on 20 July 1974. Note the varied liveries of the carriages – only the third has been repainted maroon. The last vehicle is the North Atlantic brake which, in those days, was hired from NIR for the day as we had only one brake coach!

Opposite bottom: As seen earlier in 'Celebrations One' (pages 44–45), the first 'Flyer' of the 1987 season, on 20 June, was marketed as the fiftieth run of the train. Here No 171 gets away from York Road, adorned with a second headboard which included NCC-style '7's.

Above: The long series of 'Portrush Flyers' with wooden-bodied coaches came to an end on 30 August 2003. Here No 4 brings the homeward-bound train over the top of Ballyboyland bank, between Ballymoney and Dunloy.

Reflections

Opposite top: Not an engine to enjoy much of the limelight, the Guinness loco is seen here, shortly after a repaint, at the 1973 'Steam Gala'. The nameplates are from the brewery's diesel loco and arrived with No 3BG in 1965. Strictly speaking 3BG was just known as 'No 3' in the Guinness fleet, but as Guinness also had a narrow gauge fleet with, at one time, another 'No 3', our engine was usually referred to as '3BG', though this was not carried. Note the National Coal Board-style sleeper across the fireman's door to increase coal capacity.

Opposite bottom: No 4 and her eight coach train catch the setting sun as they ease away from the Newry stop and cross the 19-arch Craigmore Viaduct with a return 'Steam Enterprise' on 15 September 1984.

Above: *Merlin* and her train reflect the winter light as they cross the Dargan bridge over the River Lagan with the 14.10 Santa train for Whitehead Excursion on 7 December 2003. This was one of the last times that the Society's vintage wooden-bodied carriages were allowed to carry passengers on NIR's network.

Santa trains

Opposite top: No 186 heads the first of the day's Santa trains, the 11.00 from Mullingar to Multyfarnham, on a seasonal 12 December 1981. The temperature had fallen to minus 13 Celsius the night before! The shaded side of the train hardly thawed at all during the day.

Opposite bottom: Santa poses on the front of No 171 at Whitehead – because he was so busy, Santa asked John Richardson to stand in for him and avoid disappointing the children who came to see him.

Above: No 85 and her train catch the low sun as they come off the main line and pull slowly into Whitehead Excursion with the first train of the day from Belfast Central on 7 December 2003.

Seaside

Opposite top: No 4 rounds Bray Head as she heads south with one of the Greystones shuttle trains on 7 July 1990. The train is about to enter the fifth and longest of the tunnels. In the background, one of the disused tunnels marks where the line was moved away from the encroaching sea. The Irish Sea is in a calm mood on this dull morning.

Opposite bottom: It's all danger and excitement at Downhill. Here No 171 is working a special from Londonderry to Belfast Yorkgate on 25 April 1993 as part of Michael Palin's BBC TV programme *From Derry to Kerry*. The train is approaching the first, and longer, of the tunnels. To the right is the helicopter used for the impressive aerial footage; its pilot is about to swerve sharply out to sea to avoid a stack of rock.

Above: No 4 forges north with 'The Tara' excursion on 13 August 1988. Here, at ebb tide, the train is crossing the long viaduct (just north of Malahide station) that separates the Irish Sea (on our left) from the aptly-named Broadwater estuary.

Barry Pickup

Sea Breeze

Opposite top: This is Rathdrum Viaduct and No 4 is slowing for the water stop here with a southbound 'Sea Breeze' on 24 June 1989.

Opposite bottom: No 461 is on home ground as she works north on a return 'Sea Breeze' train at Clough, just south of Gorey, on 22 August 1992.

Above: No 461 picks her way slowly along Wexford Quays with the southbound 'Sea Breeze' working towards Rosslare Harbour on 20 August 1994.

Sheds

Opposite top: In this timeless scene, No 461 brews up for the busy day ahead at Westport shed, early on 10 May 1992, while taking part in the 'Grainne Uaile' tour.

Opposite bottom: The RPSI takes over at Inchicore! Three Society engines, all built by Beyer Peacock, line up sometime before 6.00am on the morning of 20 May 1995. Later, No 461 worked empty stock to Ballybrophy while No 85 followed with the 'William Dargan' tour train. Sadly No 171 is 'hors de combat' but still . . . .

Above: Another early morning shot, this time at the Society's base at Whitehead. Both Nos 85 and 4 had been in use the day before on the 'Belfast and Northern Counties' railtour, but on the Sunday, 13 May 2001, it was No 171's turn to run to Londonderry (Waterside) and back with the tour train.

Ships

Opposite top: This is the old Larne Harbour, before the building of the new terminal. Here No 171 has a two-coach running-in train, the 'King Fergus', on 28 April 1973. After arrival and running round, No 171 propelled the short train past the moveable part of the platform (on the right). In the background, the *Ailsa Princess* displays the seafaring version of the BR double arrows symbol on her funnel.

Opposite bottom: At Dun Laoghaire Pier early on the first day of the 'South Kerry' tour, 17 May 1980, No 184 gets the connecting boat train to Dublin (Connolly) under way. The branch onto the pier closed when the DART came in 1984.

Above: No 184 features again, but this time she is leaving Cobh with the 'Cork 800' tour on 11 May 1985. In the background, two ships lie alongside, where once weeping exiles boarded tenders to bring them out to the transatlantic liners at anchor, in deeper water off Roche's Point. *Titanic* called here in 1912 before making her fateful appointment with destiny on the other side of the Atlantic. The overgrown trackbed to the right of the train once led to a turntable.

Signal Cabins

Opposite top: Harry Mulholland accepts the single line token, from Antrim at Knockmore Junction, on 29 May 1975. The train is the empty carriages to Dublin, ahead of the 'Burma Road' tour worked by No 171. The cabin, junction, et al were swept away two years later, on 28 May 1977. This photograph is a reminder that, before the cross-harbour link was opened in November 1994, any train from Whitehead to anywhere south of Lisburn faced a 61 mile trip (and three reversals) to get beyond Lisburn; now it is a straight run of a mere 25 miles.

Opposite bottom: This is Dundalk Central cabin on 13 September 1986 with *Merlin* recreating something of our past with this trial train from Belfast to Drogheda, complete with the Directors' Saloon in pole position. The cabin is now preserved on the passenger platform here, thanks to the dedication of the Station Master, Brendan McQuaide. Is Navan the last operational GNR cabin?

Barry Pickup

Above: Ballymoney sported a typical NCC cabin at the south end of the station but by this time its canopies were much truncated. Here, on 4 August 1988, No 171 has a homeward bound 'Portrush Flyer' and waits in the loop for a Derry railcar to cross. The bay, just out of sight on the right, was once used by Ballycastle narrow gauge trains.

Staff Exchanging

Opposite top: No 461 and the 'Sean Ri' tour train take the Foynes branch at Limerick Check cabin on 8 May 1993 and collects the single line staff from the signalman just visible to the left of the engine.

Opposite bottom: No 461 on home ground again – she was built for Wexford to Dublin goods trains. This is Arklow and the train is heading south with a 'Sea Breeze' to Wexford and Rosslare Harbour on 20 August 1994. The fireman is about to surrender the Rathdrum–Arklow staff and collect the Arklow–Gorey staff, each in a helpful wire hoop, from the signalman on the down platform.

Above: Claremorris used to be a busy spot and the cabin here once had five separate single line token machines. This is the Sunday of the 'Corrib' tour on 11 May 2003. The Athlone pilot driver is about to give up the Manulla Junction–Claremorris staff at the cabin. The signalman is anxious to tell him just how far away the service train from Dublin is.

Stour

Opposite top: Drew Donaldson, one of the founders of the Society, used this term to describe the clouds of black smoke that resulted from a freshly made-up fire – the term is an Ulster-Scots word used to describe smoke or dust, such as the cloud of dust that surrounds a working threshing machine. Here No 184 blackens the sky west of the Shannon as it leaves the Athlone Midland station with a returning 'Claddagh' excursion to Mullingar on 17 April 1982.

Opposite bottom: No 461 renews her acquaintance with the 1 in 90 of Glenealy bank, north of Rathdrum. The train is the southbound 'Decies' tour on 11 May 1991.

Above: No 85 gets to grips with a heavy Santa train on the testing 1 in 65 climb from Belfast Central station on the Dargan bridge. This was the heavily loaded 14.30 to Whitehead Excursion on 18 December 1995.

Terminals

Opposite top: As part of the 'Shannon' tour, No 4 worked a couple of local excursions from Galway to Athenry on the Sunday morning, 15 May 1988. Here No 4 gets the first departure under way, past the signal cabin and the remarkable double slip giving access to the goods yard. There is a GM diesel in the shed yard. The former branch to Clifden hugged the grass bank on the right and passed under the bridge beyond the white oil tank.

Opposite bottom: This is Fenit, on the southern shores of the Shannon estuary and once the European terminus for the transatlantic flying boats. No 461 is approaching the train shed with the 'Sean Ri' tour on 8 May 1993.

Above: This is Bangor, County Down, which we visited on Monday 16 May 1989 towards the end of the 'Mount Brandon' tour. Due to water problems earlier, the loco did not get cleaned before leaving Belfast. But during the Bangor stop, the RPSI crew set to and made things right. Here, a splendid No 85 thumps her way out of the terminus and past the closed signal cabin.

Richard Whitford

Turntables

Opposite top: These are vital for operating steam locos, because of the difficulties associated with running tender or bunker first, and we are fortunate that so many survive all over the island. This is Galway with No 184 about to make use of the facility. To the right, the Society's Paddy O'Brien chats to Inspector Eamonn Lacken (with the cap). This was after bringing in a 'Claddagh' working from Mullingar on 17 April 1982.

Opposite bottom: On 24 June 1989, during a 'Sea Breeze', No 4 is swung on the turntable at Rosslare shed, though, strictly speaking, this is Ballygeary.

Above: No 186, still in *First Great Train Robbery* film livery is turned at Bray during the Bray Shuttle trains on 23 September 1978. This turntable has now gone, though the Society's Peter Rigney and Paddy O'Brien, to the left of the engine, are still very active members. Two of the coaches from the film can be seen below and beyond the water tank.

Barry Pickup

Ulster Railway 150

Opposite top: To commemorate the 150th anniversary of the opening of the Ireland's second railway – the Ulster Railway (from Belfast to Lisburn) – NIR hired No 85 and train to work a series of morning commuter trains into Belfast from Larne Harbour, Antrim, Bangor and Portadown. This is the first train, 8.07 am from Larne Harbour on Monday 7 August 1989, seen leaving Larne Town.

Opposite bottom: This is Portadown (Craigavon West) on the morning of Thursday 10 August 1989, with No 85 waiting to leave with the 8.14 am to Belfast. Note that No 85 carries one headlamp at the chimney, denoting a stopping passenger train. Little did anybody think then that the driving trailer on the left, forming the front of the 8.00 am to Belfast, would eventually be in Society hands as part of the new Mark 2 train; it will be No 462.

Above: Saturday 12 August saw a series of eight round trips between Belfast Central and Lisburn. Here No 85 approaches Lisburn with the 11.02 from Belfast Central and is about to enter the back of the island platform. Note the '150th Anniversary' shield on the loco.

Viaducts

Opposite top: Bleach Green Junction boasts one of Ireland's largest structures made of reinforced concrete. The viaduct helped trim a couple of miles off the Belfast to Londonderry route but, more importantly, obviated reversing trains at Greenisland. Here No 461 and train catch the morning light as they set out with a trial train bound for Coleraine on 18 November 1990.

Opposite bottom: This was the spectacular view from the top of Liberty Hall, on the north bank of the Liffey on 12 April 1980. No 184 is seen working south from Connolly station, on the 'Loop Line', with one of that day's 'Bray Shuttle' trains. The train is crossing Beresford Place and is about to cross the River Liffey. Liberty Hall is the headquarters of the Irish Transport and General Workers Union, now known as SIPTU.

Above: This is the ill-fated Suir viaduct, just west of Cahir station. In 1955 a westbound beet train ran away and crashed through the end of a siding and onto the unrailed deck of the bridge. The loco and several wagons fell through the decking, killing the driver and fireman. More recently, in October 2003, an eastbound cement train derailed and the result was a massive collapse of the platework in the bridge floor. On a much happier occasion, a black-liveried No 171 crosses the viaduct and approaches Cahir station with the Limerick Junction to Waterford portion of the 'Gall Tir' tour on 9 May 1998.

Working for a living

Opposite top: After some repairs at York Road works in 1967, No 186 spent some time as passenger station pilot at Belfast (York Road). Driver Alfie Crawley and his fireman, Brian Nicholl, made the engine their own and did much to put small things right. Here No 186 is shunting two of the newly-arrived spoil wagons on 17 August that year.

Derek Young

Opposite bottom: In early 1984, after an extensive overhaul, No 4 spent a week running-in while working on NIR. Here she passes Old Mill Bay, between Ballycarry and Whitehead, on 10 February, with a Magheramorne to Belfast ballast train. The leading wagon is an ex-Southern Railway (England) 'Walrus'; the others are former spoil wagons.

Above: *R.H.Smyth*, as seen earlier in 'Departures', was hired to help rebuild the Bleach Green Junction to Antrim line. During the contract something like 50,000 tons of ballast was moved in around 400 movements. The loco was in steam for 90 days and worked about 1000 miles with no recorded failures. Twenty two RPSI people crewed at different times – some handling!

Richard Whitford

The future

Finding skilled, professional enginemen is a growing problem. Irish Rail has taken a lot of trouble to train up new blood, even sending inspectors to the Severn Valley Railway (England) to become proficient on steam. Here a crew training train, with No 4 in charge, passes the site of Hill of Down station en route to Enfield on 15 April 2003.

J A Cassells

As the result of wooden-bodied coaches being banned on several lines, the Society has had to invest in a fleet of Mark 2 coaches, some from NIR and some from Britain. Here No 85 and the first five 'new' coaches have just arrived at Whitehead on 1 May 2004, after an NIR acceptance trial to Ballymena.

Forty years of RPSI trains

29 March 1965 85 Engine movement
No 85 hauled from Inchicore to Dublin Amiens Street (and on to Dundalk on 13 May).

15 May 1965 2BG Closure of Guinness Brewery railway
Closure of the Guinness brewery railway system. BG2 worked the last train out of the brewery witnessed by an RPSI party, and 3BG was earmarked for the Society.

16 June 1965 3BG Official handover
Dinner to officially mark the hand over of 3BG to the Society. In conversation at this function, the Chairman of Guinness suggested to Frank Lemass, the Chairman of CIÉ, that they should give us an engine too, as they had plenty of them! Mr Lemass suggested that we write to his Board, requesting the gift of a J15 locomotive. Thus we gained our first main-line engine.

28 July 1965 49 Bangor–Lisburn
Not really a Society special, but this was the last steam passenger working from Bangor to Lisburn before the severing of the Belfast Central Railway, and the Society had three reserved coaches on this extra advertised excursion. The fare was 7 shillings (35 pence!) for a round trip using an MED service train Queens Quay–Bangor, special Bangor–Lisburn and regular service back to Belfast (Great Victoria Street). The driver was Ned O'Hara of Adelaide, who later drove the first ever RPSI 'Steam Enterprise' in 1980.

31 August 1965 3BG Engine movement
Our first engine – minus wheels – was hauled in a well wagon on the 3.55pm goods from Dublin, en route to York Road works. Her wheels followed on 6 September on the 8.35pm goods from Dublin! In January 1966 her wheels were machined from tramway profile to railway profile, and her right hand crosshead made good, in York Road works.

11 September 1965 49, 171, 207 Inaugural outing.
No 49 Belfast (York Road)–Portrush–Lisburn. Nos 171 and 207 Lisburn–Portadown–Belfast (Great Victoria Street). All were company engines – Class UG 0-6-0 No 49 (ex-GNR 149) and ex-GNR Class VS 4-4-0 207 *Boyne*. This was the only occasion when a UG class locomotive worked to Portrush, and the last time VS No 207 worked.

11 December 1965 186 Engine movement
CIÉ loco B163 hauled 186, out of steam, from Dublin to Adelaide. The charge for this movement was £27-1-4d!

14 May 1966 49, 54 'Province of Leinster' railtour.
WT 2-6-4T No 54 Great Victoria St–Dromin Junction then light engine to Drogheda. UG 0-6-0 No 49 light engine Adelaide–Dromin Junction then Dromin Junction–Ardee–Drogheda–Kingscourt–Drogheda. No 54 Drogheda–Great Victoria St, followed by No 49 light engine Drogheda–Adelaide.

14 May 1966 171 Engine movement
Hauled BCDR horsebox, open wagon, Inglis bread container

on flat wagon and 186 out of steam from Adelaide to Ballymena, via Lisburn and Antrim, for storage.

29 September 1966 171 Light engine
Light engine Ballymena–Belfast (York Road). Her first working as an RPSI engine.

7 October 1966 171 Light engine
Test run Belfast (York Road)–Carrickfergus–York Road.

8 October 1966 171 railtour
Belfast (York Road)–Larne Harbour–York Road. First railtour worked by an RPSI-owned engine.

December 1966 186
Some work was done on 186 in connection with a film contract *Journey to the Moon*. The steam scenes were cancelled, but not before some work was done and paid for by the film company!

10 May 1967 186 NIR work
Used by NIR as Belfast (York Road) station pilot

11 May 1967 186 NIR work
Light to Magheramorne and then two NIR ballast workings to Carrickfergus and Ballycarry.

13 May 1967 53, 55, 186 'Dalriada' railtour
No 186 light engine Belfast (York Road)–Ballymena. No 55 York Road–Ballymena. Nos 55 and 186 Ballymena–Coleraine. No 55 was the last-minute substitution for No 4, which blew a fusible plug the day before the outing. The engines then worked a steam shuttle service of 17 round trips on the Portrush branch (including service trains). Nos 55 and 186 Coleraine–Ballymena. Nos 53 and 55 fast run to York Road. No 186 light engine Ballymena–York Road. (No 53 was working back light to Belfast after working forward the overnight railcar-hauled Dublin–Derry goods, which had failed at Dunloy the previous night. No 53 arrived in Ballymena, running light back to Belfast, just in time to double head – very briskly – back to York Road.)

2 June 1967 186 NIR work
Used by NIR as Belfast (York Road) station pilot

9 August 1967 186 NIR work
NIR Ballast working York Road–Carrickfergus–York Road.

3 August 1967–16 September 1967 186 NIR work
Used by NIR as Belfast (York Road) station pilot for a long period. Denis Grimshaw has provided the following dates, which may not be exhaustive: August 3–6/8–12/17–19/21–25, September 5–7/11–16. On some of these days 186 was observed shunting the Harbour Commissioners' sidings in the Port of Belfast.

9 September 1967 186 'Cuchulain' railtour
Belfast (York Road)–Antrim–Lisburn–Dundalk (Barrack Street) and back, piloted by WT No 5 from York Road to Kingsbog. From Dundalk Junction to Barrack Street CIÉ

provided ex-GSWR gas-lit rolling stock. No 186 was the first RPSI-owned engine to steam on CIÉ metals, and the tour advertising proved prophetic: "This railtour may herald the beginning of a new era of long-distance steam railtours in Ireland – please give it your support".

18 September 1967 27, 3BG Engine movement
By this time 3BG was stored at Carrickfergus goods shed. No 27 worked light to Carrickfergus and hauled 3BG to Whitehead. No 27 returned light engine to York Road.

28 October 1967 27, 186 'Killultagh' railtour
Nos 27 and 186 Belfast (York Road)–Kingsbog Junction. No 186 light engine Kingsbog–Antrim. No 27 Kingsbog Junction–Antrim. No 186 Antrim–Great Victoria Street– Antrim. Nos 186 and 27 Antrim–Kingsbog. No 186 alone Kingsbog–York Road, with 27 following light. (No 27 *Lough Erne* was an ex-SLNCR 0-6-4T, still in Company service.)

7 February 1968 186 Light engine
Worked light Belfast (York Road)–Whitehead to take up residence for the first time. In March 1968 186 was paired with a 3345 gallon ex-GSWR tender, purchased for £210. (Another source quotes 24 February for this working.)

23 March 1968 3BG, 27 'Olderfleet' railtour
No 27 Belfast (York Road)–Larne Harbour–York Road, including a lunch stop at Whitehead Excursion station. No 3BG tour of Belfast Harbour Commissioners' tramway system. The Guinness engine's only Society tour to date, though she has of course hauled passenger trains on the Downpatrick Railway.

2 April 1968 3BG Engine movement
Hauled out of steam Belfast (York Road)–Whitehead by WT class No 6.

12 April 1968 171 Engine movement
Delivered to Harland and Wolff for heavy overhaul.

24 April 1968 186 Light engine
Light engine Whitehead to Belfast (York Road).

3 May 1968 186 Engine movement
Positioning run for 'Slieve Cualann' railtour. Belfast (York Road)–Antrim–Lisburn–Dublin with NIR (former GNR Directors' saloon No 50 and ex LMS(NCC) brake first 198.

4 May 1968 56, 186 'Slieve Cualann' railtour
No 56 Great Victoria St–Dublin (Connolly). At Dublin, official hand over by CIÉ of 186 to the Society. No 186 Dublin (Connolly)–Wicklow Goods–Wicklow Passenger– Dublin (Connolly). No 186 was piloted by B147 from Wicklow to Bray, as tender-first running was not permitted around Bray Head. No 56 Dublin–Great Victoria St (No 56 was an ex-LMS(NCC) 2-6-4T). While 186 was working to Wicklow, 56 went light to Enfield to check clearances for the following two-day tour.

5 May 1968 186 Empty carriages
Empty carriages after 'Slieve Cualann' railtour. Dublin– Lisburn–Antrim–York Road. No 186 light engine York Road–Whitehead. The same two coaches as 3 May 1968

26 July 1968 171 Engine movement
No 171 left Harland and Wolff after overhaul.

14 September 1968 4, 186 'Naomh Ciaran' railtour
The first RPSI two-day tour. No 4 Belfast (Great Victoria Street)–Dublin (Connolly). Nos 4 and 186 double-headed Dublin (Connolly)–Enfield and 186 ran alone Enfield– Athlone–Ballinasloe–Athlone. No 4 light engine Enfield– Dublin.

15 September 1968 4, 186 'Naomh Ciaran' railtour
No 186 Athlone–Roscommon–Athlone–Clara (stub of Streamstown branch)–Portarlington. No 4 with empty dining cars Dublin–Portarlington, where lunch was served in the dining cars whilst engines were serviced. No 4 worked the tour train forward Portarlington–Dublin (Connolly). No 186 followed Portarlington–Dublin with the empty dining cars and worked special boat connection Dublin (Connolly)–Dun Laoghaire Pier–Dublin (Connolly). No 4 finished the day Dublin (Connolly)–Belfast (Great Victoria Street).

29 September 1968 186 Charter
Charter by Irish Railway Record Society. Dublin (Heuston)– Kilkenny–Dublin (Heuston). The first tour involving diesel drivers Dan and Tony Renehan, who were booked as a 'support crew' by Inspector Ned Comerford after expressing some interest in working on steam engines! This was the start of an association with the RPSI which has lasted to the present day.

2 November 1968 50, 186 'Colmcille' railtour
No 50 Belfast (York Road)–Antrim. Nos 50 and 186 Antrim– Portadown. Train splitting Portadown–Poyntzpass. Nos 50 and 186 Poyntzpass–Dundalk. No 50 Dundalk–Portadown. Nos 50 and 186 Portadown–Belfast (York Road) via Antrim. This tour had been planned to run to Londonderry Waterside, but was altered (at 5.30am on the morning of the tour!) after flooding washed away Glarryford bridge the previous evening. Craig Robb, then the Society's railtour Officer, negotiated with NIR to allow a tour of some sort, as some thirty participants were enduring a rough overnight sea crossing from Britain, especially for the tour.

27 January 1969 171 Light engine
York Road–Antrim–Lisburn goods store for painting. No 85 was in store here since the closure of Adelaide shed in November 1966. Painting was done by RPSI members.

March 1969 171 Light engine
Light engine Lisburn–Antrim–Belfast (York Road) after repainting, precise date unknown.

April 1969 171 NIR work
In use as York Road station pilot for part of this month.

3 April 1969 171 NIR work
Used by NIR on steam crane special Belfast (York Road)– Antrim–Knockmore Junction–Antrim–Belfast (York Road) after derailment of goods train.

??April 1969 171 NIR work
Used on Permanent Way Department sleeper train Belfast (York Road)–Cullybackey and return.

8 April 1969 171 NIR work
Worked timetabled 10.25 Belfast (York Road)–Portrush holiday extra. NIR crew, driver Joe Cairns and fireman Johnny Magill with Inspector Frank Dunlop. Ran hot and unable to take up the return working. Held at Coleraine.

9 April 1969 171 Engine movement
No 171 returned from Coleraine to Belfast (York Road) with train of bad-order rolling stock.

17 April 1969 171 Unadvertised test train
Empty carriages Belfast (York Road)–Coleraine–York Road.

25 April 1969 4 Light engine
York Road–Antrim–Lisburn–Dublin (Connolly) for 'Brian Boru' railtour. No 4 was still a company engine at this time.

27 April 1969 171 'Brian Boru' railtour
No 171 light engine Belfast (York Road)–Antrim–Lisburn–Great Victoria Street to work special train of CIÉ stock Belfast (Great Victoria Street)–Dublin (Connolly). No 4 Dublin (Connolly)–Cork. No 171 light engine Dublin (Connolly)–Cork and worked tour train Cork–Cobh–Cork. A day of misfortunes for the engines. No 171 blew a piston gland at Castlebellingham en route to Dublin, and No 4's pony truck became derailed in the shed yard at Cork on arrival.

28 April 1969 171, 4 'Brian Boru' railtour
Nos 171 and 4 false start for photographers Cork–Rathduff–Cork. Nos 171 and 4 double headed Cork–Rathduff, and 171 alone Rathduff–Limerick Junction–Limerick, followed by No 4 light engine. At Limerick No 4 derailed a second time and the decision was taken to run the train with 171 to Dublin via the direct loop at Limerick Junction (the first steam train to use what was then a new piece of track) rather than via Nenagh as planned. No 4 followed light engine and bunker first, and both engines double-headed Ballybrophy–Dublin (Connolly). No 171 Dublin–Belfast (Great Victoria Street). Final arrival in Belfast was at 3.00am on the morning of the 29th, which made this into the Society's first three day tour!

29 April 1969 4 Light engine
Dublin (Connolly)–Antrim–Lisburn–Belfast (York Road)

31 May 1969 171 'Sorley Boy' railtour
Belfast (York Road)–Coleraine–Antrim–Belfast (Great Victoria Street)–Antrim–Belfast (York Road).

5–6 September 1969 Cancelled tour
A two-day railtour to Kilkenny. The 'Saint Canice', was to have been run on the weekend of 5-6 September 1969, but was cancelled due to lack of support, particularly from Great Britain.

21 March 1970 171, 186 'Inver nOllarbha' railtour
No 186 Empty carriages Belfast (York Road)–Antrim–Great Victoria Street, then Great Victoria Street–Portadown–Lisburn–Antrim. (Last steam passenger train to use the 1862 station at Portadown). No 171 LE Belfast (York Road)–Antrim to work tour train Antrim–Ballymena–Belfast (York Road). No 186 LE to York Road, then worked train York Road–Larne Harbour–Carrickfergus. No 171 LE York Road–Carrickfergus, then double-headed train with 186 to Greenisland. No 171 finished alone with a sprightly run to York Road.

23 May 1970 186 'Royal Meath' railtour
Dundalk–Drogheda–Kingscourt–Dublin. Tour began at Dundalk, 186 running light from Belfast (York Road) due to operating difficulties. (In those more relaxed days, problems of crewing were more simply solved. Jimmy Houston, the depot foreman at Great Victoria Street, informed the organisers that driver Charlie Mulgrave was on a rest day. He told them that if they could persuade Charlie to turn out, he would be booked on the job. Bill Scott, Drew Donaldson and the author duly visited the Mulgrave household on the Friday evening, and the job was done!).

?? May 1970 186 Light engine
Dublin–Lisburn–Antrim–Belfast (York Road)–Whitehead after railtour.

?? June 1970 27 Light engine
Belfast (York Road)–Whitehead for preservation. Steamed for the first time in RPSI ownership on 13 June 1970.

26 June 1970 53, 171 Engine movement
No 171 and WT class 53 (both out of steam) hauled from store at Carrickfergus to Whitehead for Open Day on 27 June 1970. No 53 was returned to Carrickfergus on 28 June 1970.

17 October 1970 171 'Colmcille' railtour.
Belfast (York Road)–Londonderry–Coleraine–Portrush–Coleraine–Belfast (York Road). This tour replaced a similar one, with the same name, due to be run on 18 October 1969 but cancelled due to lack of support.

5 March 1971 186 Engine movement
No 186 hauled dead from storage at Carrickfergus to Whitehead

6 March 1971 171, 186 Engine movement
No 186, in steam, hauled 171 (dead) to storage at Carrickfergus. No 186 light engine to Whitehead.

16 April 1971 186 Engine movement
No 186, in light steam, was hauled from Whitehead to Belfast (York Road) by Hunslet diesel loco 101, and then worked light York Road–Antrim–Great Victoria Street. At this time 186 was the only loco in the British Isles permitted, and able, to work on a main line! GWR No 6000 *King George V* did not re-enter mainline service until October 1971.

17 April 1971 186 'Slieve Gullion' railtour
Belfast (Great Victoria Street)–Dunleer–Dromin Junction–Ardee–Drogheda–Cement factory–Dublin (Connolly).

18 April 1971 186 'Coolnamona' railtour
Dublin (Heuston)–Curragh Main Line–Curragh racecourse siding–Port Laois–Coolnamona siding–Port Laois–Dublin (Heuston). Engine later worked light to the RPSI's base at Sallins.

July 1971 4 Engine movement
No 4 moved from Carrickfergus to Whitehead. No 4

officially became the RPSI's property on 11 July 1971 for the sum of £1275.

11 September 1971 186 'St Manntan' railtour
Dublin (Connolly)–Arklow–Dublin (Connolly), followed by a tour of the Dublin dock lines, including North Wall. No 186 ran light engine Sallins–Dublin (Connolly) before, and Dublin (Connolly)–Sallins after, this tour.

9 October 1971 4 Whitehead
First steaming at Whitehead under Society ownership.

29 April 1972 27 Whitehead
The Governor of Northern Ireland, Lord Grey of Naunton, visited Whitehead and had a footplate ride on site on 27. No 27's last steaming was on or about 8 July 1972.

1 May 1972 LPHC 3 Engine movement
The date of purchase of ex Londonderry Port & Harbour Commissioners' No 3 *R.H.Smyth* from the Rev LH Campbell. She was moved to Whitehead by low loader on 10 June 1972.

4 June 1972 186 'North Kerry' railtour
The only two-day tour to start and finish in Limerick. No 186 worked Limerick–Castlemungret cement factory–Limerick–Barnagh–Tralee–Fenit–Tralee. A small party travelled from the North by minibus, the passenger complement including both Lord O'Neill and one of the great characters of the early days of the RPSI, Drew Donaldson.

5 June 1972 186 'North Kerry' railtour
No 186 Tralee–Gortatlea–Castleisland–Gortatlea–Tralee–Ballingrane–Foynes–Limerick.

7 October 1972 186 'Eblana' railtour
Dublin goods lines tour including North Strand Junction–Church Road–North Wall and the stub of the Broadstone line at Liffey Junction, then Dublin (Connolly)–Howth –Dublin (Connolly)–Dundalk. Train extended to Whitehead with newly acquired coach 861 – the first complete RPSI train! This tour was run to transfer 186 from its temporary base at Sallins to Whitehead. It arrived at Whitehead in the early hours of 8 October 1972. No 861 had no lights whatever.

25 November 1972 4 Inaugural tour
Whitehead–Belfast (York Road)–Whitehead with coach 861. Operated in conjunction with the 1972 AGM as No 4's inaugural tour as an RPSI locomotive. This train unique in that 'standing only' seats were sold and over 70 squeezed into 861 on her journey!

28 April 1973 171 'King Fergus' railtour
Whitehead–Larne Harbour–Belfast (York Road)–Whitehead. The train comprised coaches 861 and 50.

12 May 1973 171 'Massereene' railtour
Whitehead–Belfast (York Road)–Antrim–Great Victoria Street (but not Adelaide yard as had been originally intended)–Lisburn–Antrim–York Road–Whitehead.

10 June 1973 171 Film contract for *Power to Move*
Whitehead–Belfast (York Road)–Antrim–Lisburn–Moira–Portadown–Moira and back by the same route. This was

a BBC TV series introduced by Dr Alan McCutcheon of the Ulster Museum. The train involved the first use of four Bredin coaches purchased from CIÉ on 19 May 1973 and delivered by diesel from Dundalk to Lisburn. It was also the first run in Society ownership for ex-GNR diner 88, withdrawn from Great Victoria Street and delivered to Lisburn. No 88 and the fourth Bredin coach were actually added to the train at Lisburn for the run back to Whitehead.

28 July 1973 4 Inaugural 'Portrush Flyer'
Whitehead–York Road–Portrush–York Road–Whitehead. The crew on this historic occasion was driver Alan Robinson and fireman Aubrey Ryans. (It's an interesting comment on inflation to note that the first season's fares were £1.40 adult return, or a whole coach bookable for £60!)

4 August 1973 4 'Portrush Flyer'
Whitehead–York Road–Portrush–York Road–Whitehead.

18 August 1973 4 'Portrush Flyer'
Whitehead–York Road–Portrush–York Road–Whitehead. This was to have been 171 with a 'Colmcille' special from York Road–Londonderry–Portrush–York Road, but 171 failed about 3.00am and No 4 had to be hurriedly lit up in her place. In the shunt to clear the way for No 4, the large GNR tender came off the track near the road bridge over the site. The train did not leave Whitehead until 11.00am and ran only to Portrush, rather than to Londonderry.

25 August 1973 4 'Portrush Flyer'
Whitehead–Belfast (York Road)–Portrush–York Road. No 4 blew tubes on the return trip. Whole train, including engine, was hauled from York Road to Whitehead by a 70 class diesel set.

12 September 1973 171, 186 Engine movement
No 171 hauled 186 in light steam Whitehead–York Road–Antrim–Lisburn–Dublin (Connolly) with coaches 88 and 861. No 186 had a hot big end remetalled in Dublin, and began the 'Three Rivers' tour without any running-in at all!

15 September 1973 171, 186 'Three Rivers' railtour
No 186 Dublin (Connolly)–Arklow with train consisting of two CIÉ and two RPSI-owned coaches. A fifth coach was added at Arklow for the run to Ballygeary. No 171 ran light engine Dublin (Connolly)–Kildare–Kilkenny–Waterford–Ballygeary (she was at this time banned from the DSER) and backed on to the end of the train. No 186+train+171 Ballygeary–Rosslare Harbour. No 171 Rosslare Harbour–Waterford, followed by 186 light engine. No 186 Waterford–New Ross–Waterford.

16 September 1973 171, 186 'Three Rivers' railtour
No 171 suffered a major failure at Waterford, and 186 had to undertake a marathon day's operation. No 186 worked Waterford–Ballinacourty–Waterford–Kilkenny–Dublin (Connolly)–Belfast (Great Victoria Street). No 171 was towed by an A class diesel locomotive Waterford–Kilkenny–Sallins.

17 September 1973 186 Empty carriages
Belfast (Great Victoria Street)–Lisburn–Antrim–Whitehead. Empty stock after the two-day tour, which at this time was

not an official part of a two-day tour weekend.

13 October 1973 23 Whitehead
Planet diesel loco No 23 arrived at Whitehead.

27 October 1973 171 Light engine
Sallins–Dublin (Connolly), then empty stock to Whitehead with coaches 1142 and 91.

20 April 1974 171, 186 'King Fergus II' railtour
No 186 Whitehead–Belfast (York Road)–Whitehead. No 171 Whitehead–Lame Harbour–Whitehead. This was the last steam train to use the original route through the old Larne Town station. From 23 June 1974 a new route, closer to the sea was used. This train included a photo call involving Miss Portrush to advertise the new season of 'Portrush Flyers'!

22 May 1974 171 Light engine
Whitehead–York Road–Antrim–Lisburn–Dublin (Connolly).

23 May 1974 186 Empty carriages
Whitehead–Belfast (York Road)–Antrim–Lisburn–Great Victoria Street.

25 May 1974 'St Laurence' railtour–cancelled
This was to have featured 186 Belfast–Dublin via Buckies Siding, Drogheda and 171 Dublin–Belfast via the Irish North stub Dundalk. No 186 worked light engine to Sallins and No 171 light engine and Empty carriages to Whitehead on 27 May 1974.

?? June 1974 4 Light engine
Running-in trip Whitehead–Larne Harbour–Whitehead.

20 July 1974 4 'Portrush Flyer'
Whitehead–Belfast (York Road)–Portrush–Belfast (York Road)–Whitehead.

3 August 1974 4 'Portrush Flyer'
Whitehead–Belfast (York Road)–Portrush–Belfast (York Road)–Whitehead.

17 August 1974 171, 4 'Portrush Flyer'
No 171 Whitehead–Belfast (York Road)–Portrush. No 4 light engine Whitehead–Bleach Green emergency crossover–Portrush–Belfast (York Road)–Whitehead. No 171 worked the outward trip of a 'Flyer' that was to have been extended to Londonderry, but failed at Portrush after a weary trip with the engine suffering from very bad coal. While No 4 was lit up at Whitehead, the engine crew were taken to Whitehead by car to bring No 4 light to Portrush. No 171 was eventually towed dead back to Belfast.

31 August 1974 4 'Portrush Flyer'
Whitehead–Belfast (York Road)–Portrush–Belfast (York Road)–Whitehead.

23 September 1974 186 Light engine
Whitehead–Belfast (York Road)–Antrim–Lisburn–Dublin–Sallins.

25 September 1974 4 Empty carriages
Whitehead –Belfast (York Road)–Antrim–Lisburn–Dublin (Connolly) for 'Silvermines' tour.

28 September 1974   4, 186 'Silvermines' tour.
No 4 Dublin (Connolly)–Limerick Junction. No 186 Limerick Junction–Clonmel–Limerick Junction. No 4 Limerick Junction–Limerick, followed by 186 light engine.

29 September 1974 4, 186 'Silvermines' tour
Nos 4 and 186 Limerick–Shalee, where all passengers had to leave the train after CIÉ rescinded permission for passengers to travel to Silvermines. The train ran empty Shalee–Silvermines. No 186 having run a hot tender axlebox, No 4 worked the train forward to Ballybrophy, then on to Dublin (Connolly) and forward to Belfast (Great Victoria Street). No 186 ran light Shalee–Ballybrophy–Sallins.

30 September 1974 4 Empty carriages
Belfast (Great Victoria Street)– Lisburn–Antrim–Belfast (York Road) –Whitehead.

26 October 1974 171 RPSI 10th anniversary railtour
Whitehead–Belfast (York Road)–Antrim–Londonderry–Antrim–Belfast (York Road)–Whitehead.

24 January 1975 186 Light engine
Light engine from Sallins to Mullingar. The destination was to have been the old carriage shed at Dundalk North, but a steam engine living beside a substantial oil tank was deemed too much of a fire risk. The decision to divert the engine was taken at Dublin (Connolly) and the Dundalk crew worked through, delivered home by road at 2.30 next morning by Charles and John Friel!

5 April 1975 171 'Ballymena and Larne' railtour
Whitehead–Belfast (York Road)–Ballymena–York Road–Larne Harbour–Belfast (York Road) –Whitehead.

?? May 1975 171 Light engine
Running-in trip Whitehead–Larne Harbour–Whitehead.

17 May 1975 186 Light engine
Trial run for CIÉ Mullingar–Athlone–Mullingar.

28 May 1975 171 Empty carriages
Empty carriages for the 'Burma Road' railtour. Whitehead–Belfast (York Road)–Antrim–Lisburn–Dublin (Pearse).

31 May 1975   171, 186 'Burma Road' railtour
No 171 Dublin (Connolly)–Castlerea, followed by 186. Train splitting Castlerea to Claremorris, using both engines. No 186 Claremorris–Sligo, and the empty train taken to Sligo Quay for servicing. Due to a fortunate misunderstanding on the crew's part, the entire train worked out on to the Sligo Harbour Commissioners' tramway.

1 June 1975 171, 186 'Burma Road' railtour
No 186 Sligo–Claremorris. No 171 Claremorris–Dublin (Connolly)–Belfast (Great Victoria Street). This was the last two-day tour to terminate at the old Great Victoria Street terminus.

19 July 1975 4 'Portrush Flyer'
Whitehead–Belfast (York Road)–Portrush–York Road–Whitehead. (From October 1974–August 1975, Whitehead to Carrickfergus operated as two single lines, with up line used only by the Cloghan Point spoil trains. Hence the 1975

'Portrush Flyer' used a slightly unusual route at the start of its journey.)

2 August 1975 171 'Portrush Flyer'
Whitehead–Belfast (York Road)–Portrush–Belfast (York Road)–Whitehead. No 171 ran light engine Portrush–Coleraine–Londonderry–Coleraine–Portrush to turn.

16 August 1975 4 'Portrush Flyer'
Whitehead–Belfast (York Road)–Portrush–Belfast (York Road)–Whitehead. This and the following 'Flyer' were record ten bogie loadings.

30 August 1975 4 'Portrush Flyer'
Whitehead–York Road–Portrush–York Road–Whitehead.

3 October 1975 171 Empty carriages
Whitehead–Belfast (York Road)–Antrim–Lisburn–Belfast (Great Victoria Street).

4 October 1975 171 'Ardee' railtour
Belfast (Great Victoria Street)–Dunleer–Ardee–Dromin Junction–Drogheda–Lisburn–Antrim–Belfast (York Road)–Whitehead. Last steam train from the old Great Victoria Street terminus before its closure on 12 April 1976 and also the last passenger train on the Ardee branch.

19 November 1975 184, 461 Engine movement
Towed dead from Inchicore to Thurles, and onwards to Cork for storage the following day, by loco B154.

10 April 1976 186 'Slaney' railtour
Dublin (Connolly)–Wexford–Dublin (Connolly). No 186 worked light to Dublin and back from its new base at Mullingar.

22 May 1976 4 'Belfast Central' railtour
Whitehead–York Road–Antrim–Lisburn–Bangor–Central Service Depot–Belfast Central–Lisburn–Antrim–York Road–Whitehead. The first steam train to use Belfast Central Station, which had opened on 12 April. The route also included the stub of the BCDR line into Queens Quay, which became part of the Central Service Depot complex in the years before the opening of the Cross Harbour Link.

31 May 1976 171 Light engine
Running-in trip Whitehead–York Road–Whitehead.

10 June 1976 171 Empty carriages
Whitehead–York Road–Antrim–Lisburn–Dublin (Pearse) for two-day tour. The engine stabled at Fairview diesel depot, as Connolly shed was at that time out of use.

11 June 1976 186 Engine movement
Mullingar–Dublin (Pearse) with coach 583, then light engine Dublin–Cork.

12 June 1976 171, 186 'Seandun' railtour
No 171 Dublin (Heuston)–Cork. No 186 Cork–Youghal–Cobh Junction. No 171 light engine Cork–Cobh Junction, then took the train Cobh Junction–Cobh–North Esk Yard–Cork. No 186 light engine Cobh Junction–Cork. The first steam working into the new goods yard at North Esk.

13 June 1976 171, 186 'Seandun' railtour
No 186 Cork–Cobh–Cork (in place of a planned goods transfer from Cork Kent over the city railways to Albert Quay, for which CIÉ rescinded permission previously given.) Nos 186 and 171 Cork–Rathpeacon–Cork–Mallow, then 171 alone Mallow–Dublin (Heuston)–Belfast Central. No 186 light engine Mallow–Mullingar. This was the first two-day tour to terminate at Belfast Central.

14 June 1976 171 Empty carriages
Empty carriages after two-day tour. Central Service Depot–Lisburn–Antrim–Belfast (York Road)–Whitehead. Engine turned on the new turntable at Central Service Depot.

17 July 1976 4 'Portrush Flyer'
Whitehead–York Road–Portrush–York Road–Whitehead.

31 July 1976 4 'Portrush Flyer'
Whitehead–York Road–Portrush–York Road–Whitehead.

14 August 1976 4 'Portrush Flyer'
Whitehead–York Road–Portrush–York Road–Whitehead.

28 August 1976 4 'Portrush Flyer'
Whitehead–York Road–Portrush–York Road–Whitehead.

24 September 1976 4 Empty carriages
Empty carriages for the 'Festival' railtour Whitehead–Belfast (York Road)–Antrim–Lisburn–Belfast Central–Bangor. The engine ran Bangor–Central Service Depot to stable.

25 September 1976 4 'Festival' railtour
Bangor–Belfast Central–Antrim–Londonderry–Antrim–Belfast (York Road)–Whitehead. First through steam train from Belfast Central to the NCC main line. The engine ran light from Central Service Depot to Bangor.

19 March 1977 184, 461 Engine movement
Nos 184 and 461 towed dead from Cork to Mallow. No 461 ran hot leading axleboxes during this movement.

30 April 1977 186 'Claddagh'
Mullingar–Galway–Mullingar. Connection by service train ex-Dublin at Mullingar. Due to late running the return Dublin connection was missed and the nominally empty carriages were used to convey passengers Mullingar–Dublin (Connolly) – the first RPSI diesel-hauled train!

9 June 1977 4 Empty carriages
Empty carriages for 'Cu na Mara' railtour. Whitehead–Belfast (York Road)–Antrim–Lisburn–Dublin (Connolly). As Knockmore Junction had closed on 28 May, this was the first steam train to use the newly laid third line between Knockmore and Lisburn.

11 June 1977 4, 186 'Cu na Mara' railtour
No 4 Dublin (Heuston)–Limerick Junction direct curve–Limerick. No 186 light engine Mullingar–Athlone–Athenry–Limerick and worked tour train forward Limerick–Athenry–Galway. No 4 light engine Limerick–Limerick Junction direct curve–Portarlington–Athlone–Galway.

12 June 1977 4, 186 'Cu na Mara' railtour
No 186 Galway–Athenry–Claremorris–Athenry. No 4 light engine Galway–Athenry and doubled headed with 186

Athenry–Woodlawn. No 4 worked the train Woodlawn–Athlone–Mullingar–Dublin (Connolly)–Belfast Central. At Connolly No 4 was, unusually, turned on the small turntable on the DSER side of the station. No 186 ran light engine Woodlawn–Athlone–Mullingar. (1977 was the year that the Society established a base here.)

13 June 1977 4 Empty carriages
Empty carriages after 'Cu na Mara' railtour. Belfast Central–Lisburn–Antrim–Belfast (York Road)–Whitehead.

19 June 1977 3 *R.H.Smyth* First RPSI steaming
This loco was steamed for the first time in RPSI ownership. It worked brake van trips at Whitehead site for Cystic Fibrosis on 25 June and was boiler tested on 7 July. Its first use on Whitehead site train rides was on 24 July 1977.

28 June 1977 171 Light engine
Test run Whitehead–Larne Harbour–Whitehead.

2 July 1977 171 Running-in trip
Whitehead–Greenisland–Belfast (York Road)–Antrim–York Road–Whitehead. Last train to use the stub of the 'back line' (the former main line before the building of the direct route over the Bleach Green flying junction) at Greenisland.

23 July 1977 4 'Portrush Flyer'
Whitehead–York Road–Portrush–York Road–Whitehead.

6 August 1977 4 'Portrush Flyer'
Whitehead–York Road–Portrush–York Road–Whitehead.

20 August 1977 4 'Portrush Flyer'
Whitehead–York Road–Portrush–York Road–Whitehead.

3 September 1977 171 Running-in trip
Whitehead–Belfast (York Road)–Londonderry–Belfast (York Road)–Whitehead.

21 September 1977 85 Engine movement
No 85 taken by road from Belfast Transport Museum, Witham Street, to Harland & Wolff for overhaul.

23 September 1977 171 Empty carriages
Empty carriages for Boyne Valley railtour. Whitehead–Belfast (York Road)–Antrim–Lisburn–Bangor.

23 September 1977 184, 461 Engine movement
Nos 184 and 461 towed dead from Mallow to Thurles.

24 September 1977 171, 186 'Boyne Valley' railtour
First outing to start from two centres. No 171 Bangor–Belfast Central–Drogheda. No 186 Dublin (Pearse)–Drogheda. No 171 Drogheda–Navan, then topped and tailed with 186 Navan–Tara Mines, Nevinstown and back (First steam train to use this section). No 171 and two support coaches Navan–Drogheda and back to service loco. No 186 Navan–Kingscourt and back. Nos 171 and 186 double headed Navan–Drogheda. No 171 Drogheda–Belfast Central. No 186 Drogheda–Dublin and then light engine to Mullingar.

24 September 1977 184 Engine movement
No 184 towed dead from Thurles to Mullingar, followed at a later date by 461. (RPSI Council decided at this time that, following restoration, 461 should be known as such, rather

than as DSER No 15.)

26 September 1977 171 Empty carriages
Central Service Depot–Lisburn–Antrim–Belfast (York Road)–Whitehead.

5 March 1978 184 First steaming for film
First steaming at Mullingar.

12 March 1978 184 Test train
No 184 Mullingar–Castletown–Mullingar with brake van, following restoration in record time for filming *The First Great Train Robbery*. The run was to have been to Athlone, but was terminated here due to a hot tender bearing.

15 March 1978 184 Test run
No 184 Mullingar–Athlone–Mullingar with van.

20 March 1978 184 Test run
Further unadvertised test run Mullingar–Athlone–Mullingar. Outward hauling van, returning with three bogies. John Bellwood, chief engineer of the National Railway Museum at York, represented Starling Films and praised the restoration effort.

5 April 1978 184 Test run
Mullingar–Castletown–Mullingar – partly a test run, and partly a rehearsal day before filming began in earnest.

12–14 April 1978 184 Film contract
Film contract *The First Great Train Robbery*. Filming took place each day between Mullingar and Castletown.

15 April 1978 184, 186 Engine movement
Mullingar–Dublin (Fairview) with stores van and goods brake van.

16 April 1978 184, 186 Film contract
Film contract *The First Great Train Robbery*. Both engines, with van and brake, Fairview–Connolly–Heuston for filming.

23/27–30 April 1978 184, 186 Film contract
Film contract *The First Great Train Robbery*. Filming daily at Dublin (Heuston). No 186 alone in steam on 23 and 27 April. No 184 alone in steam on 30 April.

2–5 May 1978 184, 186 Film contract
Film contract *The First Great Train Robbery*. Night filming at Heuston, 8.00pm–6.00am. Locomotives out of steam.

5 May 1978 186 Light engine
Dublin (Heuston)–Islandbridge Junction–Church Road Junction–Mullingar.

6 May 1978 186 'Claddagh'
Mullingar–Athlone–Galway–Athlone–Mullingar. No 186 continued light engine Mullingar–Dublin.

8–10 May 1978 184, 186 Film contract
Film contract *The First Great Train Robbery*. Filming in Dublin area. No 184 only in steam on 9 May, neither engine in steam on 10 May.

12 May 1978 184, 186 Engine movement
Dublin–Mullingar with stores van and goods brake van.

13 May 1978 184+186 Engine movement
Dublin (Fairview)–Connolly–Islandbridge Junction–Heuston with stores van and goods brake van.

16–23 May 1978 184, 186 Film contract
Film contract *The First Great Train Robbery*. Filming between Mullingar and Athlone, based mainly around Moate.

27 May 1978 171 Running-in trip.
Light engine Whitehead–Ballycarry–Whitehead –Larne Harbour–Whitehead, then with four coaches Whitehead–Belfast (York Road)–Larne Harbour–Whitehead.

8 June 1978 4 Empty carriages
Empty carriages for 'South Wexford' railtour Whitehead–Belfast (York Road)–Antrim–Lisburn–Dublin (Pearse).

8 June 1978 184, 186 Engine movements
Ran light engine Mullingar–Dublin, then with coach 114 Dublin–Thurles, where 184 stabled. No 186 and coach alone, Thurles–Limerick Junction–Waterford.

10 June 1978 4, 186 'South Wexford' railtour.
No 4 worked Empty carriages Pearse–Heuston then, with tour train Dublin (Heuston)–Limerick Junction–Carrick-on-Suir. No 186 worked light engine Waterford–Carrick-on-Suir, after No 4's crew expressed concern about whether No 4 had enough water to take them on to Waterford. The heavy use of water was due to running some distance with the steam brake inadvertently on. Nos 4 and 186 double-headed Carrick-on-Suir–Waterford. No 186, with four bogies, Waterford–New Ross–Waterford. No 186 light engine Waterford–Rosslare Strand–Wexford South. No 4 and six bogies Waterford–Rosslare Strand–Wexford South. No 4 light engine Wexford South–Rosslare Harbour. No 186 and six bogies Wexford South–Wexford North. No 186 with support coach Wexford North–Rosslare Harbour.

11 June 1978 4, 186 'South Wexford' railtour
No 186 with support coach Rosslare Harbour–Wexford and worked the tour train Wexford–Rosslare Pier. Nos 4 and 186 double headed Rosslare–Waterford–Limerick Junction. (At Cahir No 4 was detached and ran light across the viaduct, where double-heading was not permitted.) No 186 detached at Limerick Junction and ran to Cork with 184, which was at the Junction in steam, for further filming. No 4 worked the tour train Limerick Junction–Dublin (Pearse) for a connection to Belfast worked by an NIR two-car 80 class DEMU set.

11 June 1978 184, 186 Engine movements
No 184 light engine Thurles–Limerick Junction. Nos 184 and 186 Limerick Junction–Cork with coach 114 for more filming.

12 June 1978 4 'South Wexford' railtour
Dublin (Pearse)–Lisburn–Antrim–Belfast (York Road)–Whitehead. Until this year, the run back to Belfast after the two-day tour was nominally Empty carriages, with Northern participants as passengers! This year it was decided to offer main tour participants an extra day's steam on the Monday.

15–16 June 1978 184, 186 Film contract
Film contract *The First Great Train Robbery*. Filming in the Cork area. Cork station represented Folkestone in the film!

17 June 1978 184, 186 Engine movement
Cork–Dublin–Mullingar with coach 114. This ended their career as film stars!

22 July 1978 4 'Portrush Flyer'
Whitehead–York Road–Portrush–York Road–Whitehead.

29 July 1978 171 Running-in trip
Light engine Whitehead–Glynn–Whitehead. Then with four coaches Whitehead–York Road–Larne Harbour–Whitehead.

5 August 1978 4 'Portrush Flyer'
Whitehead–York Road–Portrush–York Road–Whitehead.

19 August 1978 4 'Portrush Flyer'
Whitehead–York Road–Portrush–Coleraine–Castlerock–Coleraine–Portrush–York Road–Whitehead. York Road–Whitehead. The first ever Castlerock extension.

2 September 1978 171 'Belfast Lough' railtour
Whitehead–York Road–Antrim–Lisburn–Central–Bangor–Central–Bangor–Central–Antrim–York Road–Whitehead.

23 September 1978 186 'Dublin Bay' shuttle
Dublin (Connolly)–Bray–Dublin (Connolly)–Bray–Dublin (Connolly)–Bray–Dublin (Connolly).

23 September 1978 171 Film contract for *Lady Gregory*
Booked to work Belfast–Dublin, but stopped by hot boxes and line closure through bomb scares. Instead, 171 was filmed at Whitehead for RTE's *Lady Gregory*, starring Siobhan McKenna.

22 March 1979 184 Film contract for *The Flame is Love*
Light engine Mullingar–Dublin (Connolly)–Bray and filmed with 1978 film train between Bray and Greystones. Since tender-first working was banned around Bray Head, the train was diesel-hauled for its return to Bray.

21 May 1979 171 Running-in trip
Light engine Whitehead–Belfast (York Road) then hauled five ex-GNR BUT trailers to Antrim and return. Light engine Belfast (York Road)–Whitehead.

24 May 1979 171 Empty carriages
Empty carriages for 'Croagh Patrick' railtour Whitehead–Belfast (York Road)–Antrim–Lisburn. No 171 light engine back to Whitehead after developing a hot box. Train diesel-hauled Lisburn–Dublin.

26 May 1979 184, 186 'Croagh Patrick' railtour
Diesel-hauled Dublin (Connolly)–Mullingar, then 184 and 186 Mullingar–Athlone–Athenry–Claremorris–Westport. The first two-day tour to begin diesel-hauled from Dublin, and the only one, so far, to feature both our J15 class engines.

27 May 1979 184, 186 'Croagh Patrick' railtour
Nos 184 and 186 Westport–Balla. No 186 Balla–Manulla Junction–Ballina–Claremorris. No 184 light engine Balla–Claremorris. Nos 184 and 186 Claremorris–Athlone, with diesel haulage Athlone–Mullingar–Dublin (Connolly). Nos

184 and 186 plus support coach Athlone–Mullingar and 186 alone Mullingar–Dublin.

28 May 1979 186 Empty carriages
Empty carriages after 'Croagh Patrick' railtour Dublin (Connolly)–Lisburn–Antrim–York Road–Whitehead.

2 June 1979 171, 186 Steam gala specials
Specials in connection with Whitehead steam gala day. No 171 Whitehead–Belfast (York Road)–Whitehead; 186 Whitehead–Belfast (York Road)–Whitehead.

21 July 1979 171 'Portrush Flyer'
Whitehead–Belfast (York Road)–Portrush. Engine ran hot while running light Portrush–Coleraine–Londonderry–Coleraine to turn. (Coleraine's turntable had been removed during redevelopment of the engine shed site.) Train diesel-hauled Portrush–Belfast (York Road)–Whitehead and 171 followed light engine under easy steam.

1 August 1979 171 Running-in trip
Whitehead–Belfast (York Road)–Ballymena–Belfast (York Road)–Whitehead. An unadvertised running-in trip after a busy weekend by the locomotive department.

4 August 1979 171 'Portrush Flyer'
Whitehead–Belfast (York Road)–Portrush–Belfast (York Road)–Whitehead. Engine ran light Portrush–Coleraine–Londonderry–Coleraine–Portrush to turn.

18 August 1979 171 'Portrush Flyer'
Whitehead–Belfast (York Road)–Portrush–Belfast (York Road)–Whitehead. Engine ran light Portrush–Coleraine–Londonderry–Coleraine–Portrush to turn.

1 September 1979 186 'Lough Foyle' railtour
Whitehead–Belfast (York Road)–Londonderry–York Road–Whitehead. No 186's sole appearance in Derry, to date.

12 September 1979 186 Centenary celebration
Centenary Celebration for 186, organized by NIR. Whitehead–Belfast (York Road)–Antrim–Lisburn–Belfast Central–Bangor–Belfast Central–Central Service Depot.

13 September 1979 186 Empty carriages
Central Service Depot–Belfast Central–Lisburn–Antrim–Belfast (York Road)–Whitehead.

22 September 1979 184 'Dublin Bay' shuttle
Light engine Mullingar–Dublin (Connolly), then Dublin (Connolly)–Bray–Dublin (Connolly)–Bray–Dublin (Connolly)–Bray–Dublin (Connolly). Light engine Dublin (Connolly)–Mullingar.

20 October 1979 'MPD Farewell' railtour
NIR railcars 51-63-64 plus Diner 552 Belfast (York Road)–Antrim–Lisburn–Bangor–Lisburn–Antrim–Belfast (York Road). MPD set ran round the diner at Antrim and Bangor, when travel was reversed. this was one of the Society's few incursions into the modern traction market!

12 April 1980 184 'Dublin Bay' shuttle
Light engine Mullingar–Dublin (Connolly), then Dublin (Connolly)–Bray–Dublin (Connolly)–Bray–Dublin (Connolly)–Bray–Dublin (Connolly).

13 April 1980 184 'Dublin Bay' shuttle
Dublin (Connolly)–Howth–Dublin (Connolly)–Howth–Dublin (Connolly)–Howth–Dublin (Connolly) (diverted from Bray due to engineering work). Light engine Dublin–Mullingar.

19 April 1980 171, 186 Carrickfergus 800 celebrations
No 171 Empty carriages Whitehead–York Road, then York Road–Carrickfergus–York Road–Carrickfergus–York Road. No 186 York Road–Carrickfergus–York Road–Whitehead. The engines swopped at Carrickfergus.

15 May 1980 171 Empty carriages
Empty carriages for 'South Kerry' railtour. Whitehead–Belfast (York Road)–Antrim–Lisburn–Dublin (Connolly).

17 May 1980 171, 184 'South Kerry' railtour
No 184 Dublin (Pearse)–Dun Laoghaire Pier–Dublin (Connolly). No 171 Dublin (Connolly)–Mallow–Tralee.

18 May 1980 171, 184 'South Kerry' railtour
No 171 Tralee–Mallow–Dublin (Connolly). No 184 Dublin (Connolly)–Dun Laoghaire Pier. Due to a misunderstanding, 184 worked light engine Dun Laoghaire Pier–Dublin, leaving the tour train stranded. The train eventually reached Dublin hauled by the engine of the regular boat train. No 171 Dublin (Connolly)–Belfast Central–Central Service Depot.

19 May 1980 171 'South Kerry' railtour
Belfast Central Service Depot–Lisburn–Antrim–Belfast (York Road)–Whitehead.

3 July 1980 27 Official handover
Official handing over of ex-SLNCR *Lough Erne* (UTA No 27) to the Society by her former owner Roy Grayson. A Northern Ireland Tourist Board cheque was presented by American railway author Rogers Whittaker.

5 July 1980 171, 186 Steam gala specials
Steam and Vintage Transport Gala, Whitehead. No 171 Whitehead–Belfast (York Road)–Whitehead. No 186 Whitehead–Belfast (York Road)–Whitehead. No 186's last day in steam before long-term withdrawal.

16 July 1980 171 Television contract *My Dear Palestrina*
Whitehead–York Road–Antrim–Lisburn–Poyntzpass. Poyntzpass–Bridge 200–Poyntzpass wrong line working. Poyntzpass–Lisburn–Antrim–York Road–Whitehead.

26 July 1980 171 'Portrush Flyer'
Whitehead–Belfast (York Road)–Portrush–Coleraine–Londonderry–Coleraine–Portrush–York Road–Whitehead. Afternoon trip from Portrush to Londonderry. First steam train to use the new Waterside station in Londonderry.

9 August 1980 171 'Portrush Flyer'
Whitehead–Belfast (York Road)–Portrush–Coleraine–Castlerock–Coleraine–Portrush–York Road–Whitehead.

23 August 1980 171 'Portrush Flyer'
Whitehead–Belfast (York Road)–Portrush–Coleraine–Castlerock–Coleraine–Portrush–York Road–Whitehead.

25 August 1980 171 Engine movement
No 171 and support coach Whitehead–Belfast (York Road)–

Antrim–Lisburn–Dublin (Connolly).

26–27 August 1980 171 Film contract 'Canada Dry'
Filming for Canada Dry TV commercial. Dublin (Connolly)–Malahide–Dublin (Connolly). The commercial later won a Clio Advertising Award in Amsterdam!

28 August 1980 171 Engine movement
No 171 and coach 114 Dublin–Lisburn–Antrim–Belfast (York Road)–Whitehead.

12 September 1980 171 Empty carriages
Whitehead–Belfast (York Road)–Antrim–Lisburn–Central Service Depot.

20 September 1980 171 'Steam Enterprise'
Belfast Central–Dublin (Connolly). and return. this trip was postponed from 13 September following a bomb scare. Appropriately this inaugural working was handled by an all ex-Great Northern crew of driver Ned O'Hara, fireman Willie McCaughley and guard Andy Lawlor.

22 September 1980 171 Empty carriages
Central Service Depot–Lisburn–Antrim–Belfast (York Road)–Whitehead.

27 April 1981 171 Running-in trip
Whitehead–York Road–Whitehead Empty carriages.

1 May 1981 171 Empty carriages
Whitehead–Belfast (York Road)–Antrim–Lisburn–Bangor. No 171 light engine to Central Service Depot.

2 May 1981 171 'Bangor Belle'
Light engine Central Service Depot–Bangor and empty carriages Bangor–Belfast Central. Central–Bangor–Central–Bangor–Central–Bangor–Central, then empty to Bangor. No 171 and workshop coach Bangor–Central Service Depot. This was the inaugural steam 'Bangor Belle'.

9 May 1981 171 Empty carriages
No 171 and workshop coach Central Service Depot–Bangor. No 171 Bangor–Belfast Central–Lisburn–Antrim–York Road–Whitehead. Train was to have worked to Dublin, but 171 was diverted to Whitehead following engine failure.

27 June 1981 184 'Claddagh'
Mullingar–Galway–Athenry–Galway–Mullingar.

4 July 1981 171 Steam gala
Run in conjunction with Whitehead Community Association. Empty carriages Whitehead–Belfast (York Road). Belfast (York Road)–Whitehead–York Road private charter by NIR, conveying government officials (Michael Allison, one of the Northern Ireland Office Ministers, was an enthusiast!). Empty carriages Belfast (York Road)–Whitehead. First use of ex-GNR Directors' Saloon No 50 following refurbishment at York Road shops by NIR staff.

25 July 1981 171 'Portrush Flyer'
Whitehead–Belfast (York Road)–Portrush–Coleraine–Castlerock. Light engine Castlerock–Londonderry–Castlerock to turn engine. Castlerock–Coleraine–Portrush–Belfast (York Road)–Whitehead. The last year that the Londonderry turntable was in use.

5 August 1981 171 Running-in trip
Empty carriages Whitehead–Belfast (York Road)–Whitehead–Greenisland–Whitehead.

8 August 1981 171 'Portrush Flyer'
Whitehead–Belfast (York Road)–Portrush–Coleraine–Castlerock. Light engine Castlerock–Londonderry–Castlerock to turn engine. Castlerock–Coleraine–Portrush–Belfast (York Road)–Whitehead.

22 August 1981 171 'Portrush Flyer'
Whitehead–Belfast (York Road)–Portrush–Coleraine–Castlerock. Light engine Castlerock–Londonderry–Castlerock to turn engine. Castlerock–Coleraine–Portrush–Belfast (York Road)–Whitehead.

31 August 1981 171 Empty carriages
Positioning run for 'Steam Enterprise'. Whitehead–Belfast (York Road)–Antrim–Lisburn–Belfast Central–Bangor. Coaches stabled at Bangor; engine and support coach ran Bangor–Central Service Depot. On the same day the Carlow diesel arrived in Whitehead.

5 September 1981 171 'Steam Enterprise'
No 171 and workshop coach Central Service Depot–Bangor to collect train, which for this 'Enterprise' season worked Bangor–Belfast Central–Dublin (Connolly)–Central–Bangor. Engine and workshop coach Bangor–Central Service Depot.

19 September 1981 171 'Steam Enterprise'
No 171 and workshop coach Central Service Depot–Bangor to collect train then 171 Bangor–Belfast Central–Dublin (Connolly)–Central–Bangor. Engine and workshop coach Bangor–Central Service Depot.

21 September 1981 171 Empty carriages
Positioning run for 'Ben Bulben' railtour. No 171 and the support coach Central Service Depot–Bangor, then worked the train Bangor–Belfast Central–Dublin (Pearse) for the two-day tour. No 171 and the support coach worked Dublin (Pearse) to Mullingar.

26 September 1981 171, 184 'Ben Bulben' railtour
No 171 and support coach Mullingar–Dublin (Connolly), then with tour train Dublin (Connolly)–Mullingar. Nos 184 and 171 double headed Mullingar–Longford. Here 171 detached with injector trouble and 184 worked all eight bogies Longford–Ballymote (only having to stop for a brief blow-up on Kilfree bank!). No 171 light engine Longford–Ballymote, then 171 and 184 double-headed Ballymote–Sligo. At Collooney a short ceremony was held commemorating the completion of the RPSI's coverage of the entire Irish railway network.

27 September 1981 171, 184 'Ben Bulben' railtour
Nos 171 and 184 Empty carriages Sligo–Sligo Quay–Sligo, then Sligo–Carrick-on-Shannon. No 184 light engine Carrick on Shannon–Mullingar. No 171 alone, Carrick-on-Shannon–Dublin (Connolly) via Newcomen Junction. No 171 slipped to a stand within sight of Connolly and was eventually diesel-hauled into Connolly. No 171 with three bogies Dublin (Connolly)–Belfast Central. Ex-MGWR six wheel coach No 62 was attached at Drogheda. This vehicle was newly-

acquired by the Society, and worked through to Whitehead.

28 September 1981 171 Empty carriages
Central Service Depot– Lisburn–Antrim–Whitehead.

10 October 1981 184 Test run
No 184 light engine Mullingar–Athlone–Mullingar.

12 December 1981 184 Santa specials
Mullingar–Multyfarnham–Mullingar–Killucan–Mullingar
–Castletown–Mullingar–Castletown–Mullingar.

24 January 1982 85 Engine movement
Taken by road from Harland & Wolff to York Road.

6 February 1982 85 Engine movement
Towed to Whitehead by NIR diesel hydraulic loco 3.

? April 1982 184 Test run
Mullingar–Athlone–Mullingar.

10 April 1982 184 Easter Bunny specials
Mullingar–Multyfarnham–Mullingar–Castletown–Mullingar–
Castletown–Mullingar. The RPSI's first 'Easter Bunny'
specials.

17 April 1982 184 'Claddagh'
Mullingar–Galway– Attymon Junction–Galway–Mullingar.

8 May 1982 171 Empty carriages
Positioning run Whitehead–Mullingar for 'Thomond' railtour.

15 May 1982 171, 184 'Thomond' railtour
No 171 Empty carriages Mullingar–Dublin (Connolly),
and main tour Dublin (Connolly)–Portarlington–Athlone.
No 184 Athlone–Athenry–Limerick. No 171 and support
coach Athlone–Portarlington–Limerick Junction–Limerick
(banned from working between Athenry and Limerick). No
184 and two coaches nominally empty Limerick–Limerick
Junction–Limerick to turn the engine, Limerick having lost
its turntable. (This tour produced a possible record of eleven
reversals!)

16 May 1982 171, 184 'Thomond' railtour
No 184 Limerick–Foynes–Limerick (including the stub
of the North Kerry line at Ballingrane). No 171 and 184
Limerick–Roscrea. No 171 alone Roscrea–Ballybrophy–
Dublin (Connolly). Due to hot bogie axlebox, 171 was failed
at Dublin and the tour continued diesel-hauled to Dundalk,
where it terminated due to industrial action on NIR.

17 May 1982 171 Light engine
Dublin–Lisburn–Antrim–Belfast (York Road)–Whitehead

18 May 1982 Diesel loco Empty carriages
RPSI Empty carriages Dundalk–Lisburn–Antrim–Belfast
(York Road) –Whitehead. (See entry for 16 May 1982.)

14 July 1982 4 Running-in trip
Light engine Whitehead–Belfast (York Road)–Antrim–York
Road–Whitehead.

19 July 1982 4, 171 Running-in trips
No 4 light engine Whitehead–Belfast (York Road)–
Carrickfergus–Greenisland–York Road–Whitehead. No 171
light engine Whitehead–Belfast (York Road)–Whitehead.

22 July 1982 4 Empty trial train
Whitehead–Belfast (York Road)–Whitehead. The train was to
have run to Ballymena, but the engine ran hot and the train
returned from Belfast.

24 July 1982 171 'Portrush Flyer'
Whitehead–Belfast (York Road)–Portrush–Belfast (York
Road)–Whitehead. No Castlerock extension

5 August 1982 4 Running-in trip
Empty carriages Whitehead–York Road–Whitehead, then
light engine Whitehead–Greenisland–Whitehead.

7 August 1982 4, 171 'Portrush Flyer'
No 4 Whitehead–Belfast (York Road)–Portrush. No 171
Whitehead–Bleach Green–Portrush–Coleraine–Castlerock–
Coleraine–Portrush–York Road–Whitehead. No 4 light
engine Portrush–York Road. No 4 ran a hot driving axlebox
and big ends while working to Portrush. The crew were
conveyed from Whitehead to Portrush by car. No 171 was
lit up and worked light engine Whitehead–Portrush, via the
Bleach Green emergency crossover, in time to work the
Castlerock extension and bring the train back to Belfast. No 4
followed light to Belfast (York Road), having to stable as the
Larne line had by this time closed for the night.

10 August 1982 4 Engine movement
Towed by diesel loco Belfast (York Road)–Whitehead.

21 August 1982 171 'Portrush Flyer'
Whitehead–Belfast (York Road)–Portrush–Coleraine–
Castlerock–Coleraine–Portrush–York Road–Whitehead.

30 August 1982 171 Empty carriages
Positioning run for 'Steam Enterprise' Whitehead–Belfast
(York Road)–Antrim–Lisburn–Central Service Depot.

4 September 1982 171 'Steam Enterprise'
Empty Central Service Depot–Belfast Central. Tour train
Central–Dublin (Connolly)–Central. Empty to Central
Service Depot.

18 September 1982 171 'Steam Enterprise'
Empty Central Service Depot–Central. Tour train Central–
Dublin (Connolly)–Central. Empty to Central Service Depot.

25 September 1982 171 Dublin shopping special
Empty Central Service Depot–Central. Special Central–
Dublin one way. The train was required in Dublin for film
contract *The Life of Richard Wagner*. No 171 returned
to Whitehead later. the unavailability of 184 meant the
cancellation of the Howth shuttle planned for the same day.

28 September 1982 171 Film contract
Contract for *The Life of Richard Wagner*. Light engine
Dublin (Connolly)–Dublin (Heuston)–Inchicore–Dublin
(Heuston)–Dublin (Connolly) for filming. The coaches were
worked to Sallins by diesel for filming, then returned to
Heuston before dispatch to Mullingar.

29 September 1982 171 Empty carriages
Dublin–Lisburn–Antrim–Belfast (York Road)–Whitehead.
Train composed of coaches 114 and 88.

18 December 1982 184 Santa specials
Mullingar–Athlone–Moate–Athlone–Moate–Athlone–Moate–
Athlone–Mullingar.

19 December 1982 184 Santa specials
Mullingar–Multyfarnham–Mullingar–Killucan–Mullingar–
Castletown–Mullingar–Castletown–Mullingar.

20 March 1983 171 Film contract *Aunt Suzanne*
Whitehead–Carrickfergus (for filming)–Whitehead.

2 April 1983 184 Easter Bunny specials
Mullingar–Multyfarnham–Mullingar–Killucan–Mullingar–
Castletown–Mullingar–Castletown–Mullingar.

23 April 1983 184 'Claddagh'
Mullingar–Athlone–Galway–Attymon Junction–Galway–
Athlone–Mullingar.

6 May 1983 171 Empty carriages
Empty carriages for 'Port Lairge' two-day tour Whitehead–
York Road–Antrim–Lisburn–Dublin (Connolly)–Mullingar.
First year of running 'under the wires' in the Dublin area.

14 May 1983 171, 184 'Port Lairge' railtour
No 171 Empty carriages (at 1.15am ex Mullingar!)
Mullingar–Athlone–Portarlington–Dublin (Heuston), then
with main tour Dublin (Heuston)–Kildare–Kilkenny. No 184
Kilkenny–Waterford–Campile–Waterford, then light engine
Waterford–Rosslare–Waterford to turn. No 171 and support
coach Kilkenny–Kildare–Limerick Junction–Limerick to
stable. A most complex day's operation necessitated by 171
being banned from entering Waterford due to structural
problems with an underbridge at Dunkitt. The very early start
from Mullingar (on which some hardy passengers did travel)
was to get round a major engineering possession due to
resignalling in the Dublin area. At one point on the Saturday
the train was in Waterford, 184 was in Rosslare and 171 was
in Limerick!

15 May 1983 171, 184 'Port Lairge' railtour
No 171 and support coach Limerick–Limerick Junction–
Carrick-on-Suir. No 184 Waterford–Carrick-on-Suir. Nos 171
and 184 double-headed Carrick-on-Suir–Limerick Junction.
At Limerick Junction 171 was detached and reversed into the
Waterford and Limerick bay. No 184 drew the train over the
square crossing clear of the direct curve. No 171 ran via the
direct curve to the other end of the train, which was drawn
forward and reversed into the main platform. No 171 took
the train forward to Dublin (Connolly) and thence to Belfast
Central. No 184 ran light Limerick Junction–Portarlington–
Athlone–Mullingar. Lineside shots on this tour were used in
the television production of *The Country Girls*.

16 May 1983 171 Empty carriages
Central Service Depot–Belfast Central–Lisburn–Antrim–
Belfast (York Road)–Whitehead after two-day tour.

23 July 1983 171 Tenth anniversary 'Portrush Flyer'
Whitehead–Belfast (York Road)–Portrush–Coleraine–
Castlerock–Coleraine–Portrush–York Road–Whitehead.

6 August 1983 4, 171 'Portrush Flyer'
Whitehead–York Road–Portrush–Coleraine–Castlerock–

Coleraine–Portrush–York Road–Whitehead. Nos 4 and 171
double-headed to and from Portrush, and No 4 worked the
Castlerock extension alone. This was a running-in test for
No 4.

18 June 1983 184 Private charter
Private charter by General Council for County Councils.
Mullingar–Athlone–Mullingar. Arranged for Mr Mullins, the
Mullingar Station Master.

27 July 1983 4 Running-in trip
Light engine Whitehead–York Road–Whitehead. Engine was
taken into the works on the traverser and weighed.

4 August 1983 4 Running-in trip
Empty carriages Whitehead–Belfast (York Road)–
Ballymena–Belfast (York Road)–Whitehead.

18 August 1983 4 Running-in trip
Empty carriages Whitehead–Belfast (York Road)–
Ballymena–Belfast (York Road)–Whitehead.

23 August 1983 171 'Portrush Flyer'
Whitehead–Belfast (York Road)–Portrush–Coleraine–
Castlerock–Coleraine–Portrush–York Road–Whitehead.

29 August 1983 4 Empty carriages
Whitehead–Belfast (York Road)–Antrim–Lisburn–
Belfast Central–Central Service Depot. Positioning run for
'Steam Enterprise'.

?? August 1983 184 Running-in trip
Light engine Mullingar–Moate–Mullingar.

3 September 1983 4 'Steam Enterprise'
Empty Central Service Depot–Belfast Central. Special
Central–Dublin (Connolly). No 4 failed at Dublin, and an
NIR GM loco worked light to Dublin to bring the train back.
No 4 returned light engine Dublin–Whitehead, and the same
crew brought 171 light engine Whitehead–Belfast (York
Road)–Antrim–Lisburn–Central Service Depot.

5 September 1983 171 Private charter
Private charter by Belfast Chamber of Commerce. Belfast
Central–Portadown–Belfast Central.

17 September 1983 171 'Steam Enterprise'
Empty Central Service Depot–Belfast Central. Special
Central–Dublin (Connolly)–Central–Central Service Depot.

24 September 1983 184 'Dublin Bay' shuttle
Light engine Mullingar–Dublin (Connolly), then Dublin
(Connolly)–Bray–Dublin (Connolly)–Bray–Dublin
(Connolly)–Bray–Dublin (Connolly). Empty carriages
Dublin–Mullingar.

25 September 1983 171 'Belfast Lough' railtour
Central Service Depot–Belfast Central–Lisburn–Antrim–
Belfast (York Road)–Larne Harbour–York Road–Whitehead.
Until the banning of RPSI wooden-bodied stock on the
'Steam Enterprise', this became a traditional post-Enterprise
Sunday tour to return the coaches to Whitehead.

14 October 1983 184 Film contract
Film contract for television series *The Irish RM* – Mullingar–

Moate–Mullingar.

20 December 1983 184 Film contract
Film contract for *A Painful Case* – Mullingar–Moate–Mullingar.

30 January 1984 4 ARPS Award special
Celebration of the RPSI's winning the Association of Railway Preservation Societies' Annual Award. Empty carriages Whitehead–Belfast (York Road), then York Road–Carrickfergus (for reception)–Belfast (York Road). Empty carriages York Road–Whitehead.

6 February 1984 4 Running-in work on NIR
Beginning a week of running-in on scheduled NIR permanent way trains, with an experienced, economical and highly enthusiastic crew of Harry Ramsey and Davy McDonald. ("If me and Harry had this engine all the time" said Davy, "we'd burn no coal at all.") Light engine Whitehead–Carrickfergus–Magheramorne. Ballast hoppers to York Road and shunted. Ballast hoppers York Road–Magheramorne, then light engine to Whitehead.

7 February 1984 4 Running-in work on NIR
Light engine Whitehead–Magheramorne. Ballast hoppers to Milepost 18 to discharge. Return to Magheramorne and light engine to Whitehead.

8 February 1984 4 Running-in work on NIR
Light engine Whitehead–Belfast (York Road). Bogie flats to Ballymena to load sleepers. Wagons of sleepers and empty hoppers to Belfast (York Road). Empty hoppers York Road–Whitehead.

9 February 1984 4 Running-in work on NIR
Empty hoppers Whitehead–Magheramorne. Loaded hoppers to milepost 18 to discharge. Returned to Magheramorne to shunt. Light engine to Whitehead.

10 February 1984 4 Running-in work on NIR
Light engine Whitehead–Magheramorne. Loaded hoppers to Belfast (York Road). Shunted York Road and diesel shed. Worked bogie heating van York Road to Belfast Central, then light engine Central Service Depot–Lisburn–Antrim–Belfast (York Road)–Whitehead.

23 March 1984 184 Running-in trip
Light engine Mullingar–Killucan–Mullingar

6 April 1984 4 Running-in trip
Empty carriages Whitehead–Belfast (York Road), where fitted vans were added to the train to convey bicycles for a charity cycle marathon. The augmented train worked Belfast (York Road)–Antrim–Lisburn–Bangor, where the vans were detached, then Empty carriages to Central Service Depot. No 4 ran light engine Central Service Depot–Lisburn–Antrim–Belfast (York Road)–Whitehead.

7 April 1984 184 Enfield shuttle
Engine and one coach Mullingar–Dublin (Connolly) then one Dublin–Enfield–Dublin public excursion. A second round trip was cancelled due to a blown gland on the engine. Empty carriages Dublin–Mullingar.

?? April 1984 Empty stock working
An NIR 70 class diesel set worked an RPSI coaching stock transfer Whitehead–Belfast (York Road)–Antrim–Lisburn–Dublin, returning with a different set of vehicles.

21 April 1984 184 'Claddagh'
Mullingar–Galway–Attymon Junction–Galway–Mullingar.

5 May 1984. 171 Empty carriages
Whitehead–Belfast (York Road)–Antrim–Lisburn–Dublin (Connolly)–Mullingar for 'Galway Bay' tour.

12 May 1984 171, 184 'Galway Bay' railtour
No 171 Empty carriages Mullingar–Dublin (Connolly). No 184 light engine Mullingar–Athlone–Claremorris. No 171 and main tour Dublin (Connolly)–Mullingar–Athlone–Claremorris. No 184 Claremorris–Athenry–Galway. No 171 and two coaches Claremorris–Castlerea as a local public excursion, returning by service train, then with empty stock Castlerea–Athlone–Mullingar (for servicing)–Athlone–Galway.

13 May 1984 171, 184 'Galway Bay' railtour
Train split and 'leap frogging' with both engines Galway–Ballinasloe. Both trains could be photographed side by side at Athenry, and 171 was overtaken by 184 at Attymon Junction. Nos 171 and 184 double-headed Ballinasloe–Athlone, then 171 alone worked Athlone–Mullingar–Dublin (Connolly)–Belfast Central–Central Service Depot. No 184 ran light Ballinasloe–Athlone–Mullingar to stable.

14 May 1984 171 Empty carriages
Empty carriages after 'Galway Bay' railtour. Central Service Depot–Belfast Central–Lisburn–Antrim–Belfast (York Road)–Larne Harbour–Whitehead.

30 June 1984 4 Private charter by Lord O'Neill
Whitehead–York Road–Portrush–York Road–Whitehead. A rare occasion when No 4 worked bunker first to Portrush.

11 July 1984 184 Filming for *Remington Steele*
Worked train Mullingar–Blakestown crossing (12.25 miles from Broadstone)–Mullingar for filming.

21 July 1984 4 'Portrush Flyer'
Whitehead–Belfast (York Road)–Portrush–Coleraine–Castlerock–Coleraine–Portrush–York Road–Whitehead.

4 August 1984 4 'Portrush Flyer'
Whitehead–Belfast (York Road)–Portrush–Coleraine–Castlerock–Coleraine–Portrush–York Road–Whitehead.

18 August 1984 4 'Portrush Flyer'
Whitehead–Belfast (York Road)–Portrush–Coleraine–Castlerock–Coleraine–Portrush–York Road–Whitehead.

27 August 1984 4 'Bangor Belle'
Whitehead–Whiteabbey–Antrim–Belfast Central–Bangor. Resignalling at Belfast (York Road) meant that the station was closed. So this train ran to Greenisland normally, then DH1 (the only recorded instance of a passenger train being worked by this class of diesel!) was attached as train engine, with No 4 banking to Whiteabbey. No 4 then worked train over the Bleach Green emergency crossover on to the down

line and so to Antrim. Route thereafter was Antrim–Lisburn–Bangor–Belfast Central–Bangor–Central and empty to Central Service Depot.

1 September 1984 4 'Steam Enterprise'
Empty Central Service Depot–Belfast Central. Special Belfast Central–Dublin (Connolly)–Central. Empty Belfast Central–Central Service Depot.

15 September 1984 4 'Steam Enterprise'
Empty Central Service Depot–Belfast Central. Special Belfast Central–Dublin (Connolly)–Central. Empty Belfast Central–Central Service Depot.

29 September 1984 Cancelled tour
A planned 'Enfield Express' was cancelled as it would have run at a loss following the cancellation of a film contract for *The Irish RM* series. A planned steam connection from Belfast was also cancelled.

30 September 1984 4 'Larne Lough' railtour
Central Service Depot–Belfast Central–Lisburn–Antrim–Belfast (York Road)–Whitehead RPSI for water–Larne Harbour–Belfast (York Road)–Whitehead.

25-26 November 1984 461 Engine movement
Brought by road from Mullingar to Whitehead. 'Stabled' overnight at the Irish Republic Customs Post on the Dundalk–Newry road! (Her tender followed by road, with a similar overnight, on 26–27 January 1985.)

24 December 1984 85 First steaming at Whitehead
No 85 steamed for the first time at Whitehead. Interest (if not total enthusiasm!) was shown in this engine by ex-NCC drivers who at that time regularly worked our trains. Inspector Frank Dunlop speculated on whether to send them on a course to the then Jordanstown Polytechnic to teach them how to drive her!

? May 1985 184 Test run
Light engine Mullingar–Athlone–Mullingar.

4 May 1985 171 Empty carriages
Stock movement Whitehead–Belfast (York Road)–Antrim–Lisburn–Dublin (Connolly)–Mullingar for 'Cork 800' tour.

10 May 1985 184 Light engine
Mullingar–Athlone–Portarlington–Cork for 'Cork 800' tour.

11 May 1985 171, 184 'Cork 800' railtour
No 171 Empty carriages Mullingar–Dublin (Connolly), then the tour train Dublin (Connolly)–Cork. Before the main tour arrived in Cork, 184 had already worked two local trips Cork–Cobh–Cork–Cobh–Cork. No 184 worked the main train Cork–Cobh–Cobh Junction (set back into the Youghal branch)–Cork.

12 May 1985 171, 184 'Cork 800' railtour
Nos 171 and 184 double-headed Cork–Mallow. No 184 and the front portion of the train Mallow–Charleville (overtaken by 171)–Limerick Junction. No 171 and the rear portion of the train Mallow–Limerick Junction. No 171 and the recombined train Limerick Junction–Dublin (Connolly)–Belfast Central–Central Service Depot. No 184 light engine

Limerick Junction–Portarlington–Athlone–Mullingar.

13 May 1985 171 'Cork 800' railtour
Central Service Depot–Belfast Central–Lisburn–Antrim–Larne Harbour–Whitehead, with connection at Larne for cross channel tour passengers. This was the first deliberate attempt to get participants to take part in a third day of the 'Two-day Tour', by transforming the traditional Empty carriages working into a mini-railtour.

17 May 1985 Coach 411 BBC trial
RPSI coach 411 was attached to back of the 11.35 Belfast Central–Londonderry and 14.40 Londonderry–Central. This was an unsuccessful attempt by the BBC to operate the studio coach of what would have been a steam operation to Portrush broadcasting the Radio Ulster programme *Day by Day* live from the train.

29 June 1985 4 Charity 'Portrush Flyer'
Operated for the Rotary Club of Belfast, in aid of the Jack Kyle Medical Fund. Whitehead–Belfast (York Road)–Portrush–Belfast (York Road)–Whitehead.

9 June 1985 4, 171 Private charter
Private charter by the Permanent Way Institute. No 4 Empty carriages Whitehead–Belfast (York Road)–Portrush to collect PWI delegates, then Portrush–Antrim. No 171 light engine Whitehead–York Road–Antrim and took the special forward Antrim–Lisburn–Belfast Central–Cultra. Then Empty carriages to Bangor, before running light engine Bangor–Central Service Depot–Bangor for servicing. No 171 again Empty carriages Bangor–Cultra, then with passengers Cultra–Belfast Central–Lisburn–Antrim. No 4 light engine Antrim–York Road–Whitehead–York Road–Antrim and took the special forward to Portrush, returning Empty carriages Portrush–York Road–Whitehead. No 171 light engine Antrim–York Road–Whitehead. This train was of special importance to the footplatemen involved, as it was very much a special run for railway employees. For the record, the crews involved that day were as follows:

No 4: Driver Tom Crymble and fireman George Gaw, relieved in the afternoon by driver Davy McDonald and fireman Barney McCrory.

No 171: Driver George Houston and fireman Harry Ramsey, with pilot driver Andy Rushe from Lisburn to Bangor.

Inspector Frank Dunlop was in charge of the entire day's operations, beginning with his arrival at Whitehead at 5.00am and ending at the same place around midnight!

20 July 1985 4 'Portrush Flyer'
Whitehead–Belfast (York Road)–Portrush–Coleraine–Castlerock–Coleraine–Portrush–York Road–Whitehead.

3 August 1985 4 'Portrush Flyer'
Whitehead–Belfast (York Road)–Portrush–Coleraine–Castlerock–Coleraine–Portrush–York Road–Whitehead.

15 August 1985 85 Inaugural main line test
Whitehead–Belfast (York Road)–Whitehead. While returning light under test 85 was called to the rescue of the 13.30 York Road–Larne and propelled it from Clipperstown to Whitehead. The diesel set had struck a herd of cattle and

became a failure. No 85 hauled the failed diesel set empty from Whitehead to Belfast (York Road) and returned light engine to Whitehead. This is the only known occasion when a steam locomotive has hauled an 80 class set. Quite a debut after her long overhaul!

17 August 1985 4 'Portrush Flyer'
Whitehead–Belfast (York Road)–Portrush–Coleraine–Castlerock–Coleraine–Portrush–York Road–Whitehead.

26 August 1985 171 'Bangor Belle'
Empty carriages Whitehead–York Road–Antrim–Lisburn–Belfast Central. Special Central–Bangor–Central–Bangor–Central. Empty carriages Central–Central Service Depot.

7 September 1985 171 'Steam Enterprise'
Central Service Depot–Belfast Central–Dundalk. No 171 failed at Dundalk and the rest of the trip was diesel-hauled. No 171 ran light Dundalk–Whitehead. No 4 ran light Whitehead–Central Service Depot that same evening.

21 September 1985 4 'Steam Enterprise'
Central Service Depot–Belfast Central–Dublin (Connolly)–Belfast Central–Central Service Depot.

23 September 1985 184 Test run
Light engine Mullingar–Moate–Mullingar.

29 September 1985 4 'Larne Lough' railtour
Central Service Depot–Belfast Central–Lisburn–Antrim–York Road–Larne Harbour–Belfast (York Road)–Whitehead.

12 October 1985 NIR DEMU '70 class' farewell
Diesel tour – three car DEMU: 77-728-75 Belfast (York Road)–Londonderry–Coleraine–Downhill–Coleraine–Antrim–Lisburn–Belfast Central. A farewell to the 70 class diesels and probably a record time of 84'06" non stop to Derry. A lineside bus was organized for the working to Downhill – possibly a first ever feature on a diesel railtour?

13 October 1985 85 Running-in trip
Whitehead–York Road–Whitehead–York Road–Whitehead.– No 85's inaugural public working in the RPSI's custody.

26 October 1985 184 Maynooth shuttle
Empty carriages Mullingar–Dublin (Connolly). Shuttle Dublin (Connolly)–Maynooth–Dublin (Connolly)–Maynooth–Dublin (Connolly). A third trip was cancelled due to operational problems. Empty carriages Dublin (Connolly)–Mullingar. First operation by Mullingar-based RPSI coach set.

27 October 1985 85 Running-in trip.
Whitehead– Greenisland–Larne Harbour–Greenisland–Larne Harbour–Whitehead.

9 November 1985 85 Running-in trip.
Whitehead–York Road–Antrim–York Road–Whitehead.

23 November 1985 85 Running-in trip
Whitehead–Belfast (York Road)–Antrim–Lisburn–Belfast Central–Lisburn–Antrim–York Road–Whitehead.

14 December 1985 184 Santa specials
Mullingar–Killucan–Mullingar–Killucan–Mullingar–

Killucan–Mullingar.

? April 1986 184 Running-in trip
Light engine Mullingar–Athlone–Mullingar.

3 May 1986 4 Empty carriages
Positioning run for 'Clew Bay' railtour Whitehead–Antrim–Lisburn–Dublin (Connolly)– Mullingar.

10 May 1986 4, 184 'Clew Bay' railtour
No 4 with Whitehead-based RPSI set, nominally Empty carriages (but in fact carrying passengers and providing a full breakfast service!), Mullingar–Dublin (Connolly), then Dublin (Connolly)–Mullingar–Athlone. No 184 and the Mullingar-based RPSI set 'leapfrogged' No 4 and the Whitehead set Athlone–Claremorris, with No 4 overtaking 184 at Knockcroghery and both trains stopping at Roscommon. Nos 4 and 184 double-headed the Whitehead set Claremorris–Westport. This tour ran on the day after the cessation of regular services between Mullingar and Athlone. The Midland routing of the tour was due to a ban by the Irish Department of Transport on wooden-bodied stock on the Cork main line.

11 May 1986 4, 184 'Clew Bay' railtour
No 184 light engine Westport–Claremorris. No 4 with Whitehead set Westport–Claremorris. No 184 with Mullingar set Claremorris–Tuam–Claremorris. No 4 with Whitehead set Claremorris–Athlone–Mullingar–Dublin (Connolly)–Belfast Central–Central Service Depot. No 184 and Mullingar set Claremorris–Roscommon (two local trips)–Athlone–Mullingar.

12 May 1986 4 'Clew Bay' railtour
Central Service Depot–Belfast Central–Antrim–Belfast (York Road)–Larne Harbour–Whitehead.

28 June 1986 85 Official launch at Whitehead
Official launch of 85's career with the RPSI – in steam at Whitehead. Appropriately, Lord Dunleath drove 85 through a ceremonial ribbon.

5 July 1986 4 Charity 'Portrush Flyer'
Organised jointly by the RPSI and the Rotaract Club of East Belfast in aid of the Royal Victoria Hospital Children's Cancer Unit. Whitehead–Belfast (York Road)–Portrush–York Road–Whitehead. No 4 used the newly installed Coleraine turntable for the first time. This had previously seen service at Ballymena and then at Belfast (Great Victoria Street), where it was used by 186 and 171 in 1970s. The turntable had been rebuilt and extended at Whitehead and installed at Coleraine by RPSI volunteers. Its use on this occasion was, strictly speaking, unauthorized as it had not been officially passed for use.

19 July 1986 4, 85 'Portrush Flyer'
Double-headed by Nos 4 and 85 Whitehead–Belfast (York Road)–Portrush. No 4 worked Castlerock extension Portrush–Coleraine–Castlerock–Coleraine. No 85 banked return 'Flyer' Portrush–Coleraine. No 4 worked alone Coleraine–Belfast (York Road)–Whitehead. No 85 followed light engine Coleraine–Belfast (York Road)–Whitehead. This day was the first official use of the new turntable,

appropriately commemorated.

26 July 1986 184 'Claddagh'
Mullingar– Athlone–Galway–Athenry–Galway–Athlone–Mullingar.

2 August 1986 4 'Portrush Flyer'
Whitehead–Belfast (York Road)–Portrush–Coleraine–Castlerock–Coleraine–Portrush–York Road–Whitehead.

9 August 1986 85 Test trip after modifications to tender
Whitehead–York Road–Portrush–York Road–Whitehead.

16 August 1986 85 'Portrush Flyer'
Whitehead–Belfast (York Road)–Portrush–Coleraine–Castlerock–Coleraine–Portrush–York Road–Whitehead

23 August 1986 184 Maynooth shuttle
Empty carriages Mullingar–Dublin (Connolly) then Connolly–Maynooth–Connolly–Maynooth–Connolly–Maynooth–Connolly. Empty carriages Dublin (Connolly)–Mullingar.

25 August 1986 4 'Bangor Belle'
Whitehead–Belfast (York Road)–Antrim–Lisburn–Belfast Central then two return trips Belfast Central–Bangor. Empty to Central Service Depot.

6 September 1986 4 'Steam Enterprise'
Central Service Depot–Belfast Central–Dublin (Connolly)–Belfast Central–Central Service Depot.

9 September 1986 85 Light engine
Whitehead–Belfast (York Road)–Antrim–Lisburn–Central Service Depot.

13 September 1986 85 Proving run
Central Service Depot–Belfast Central–Drogheda–Belfast Central–Central Service Depot. The train ran to Drogheda as there was a working turntable there.

20 September 1986 85 'Steam Enterprise'
Central Service Depot–Belfast Central–Dublin (Connolly)–Central–Central Service Depot. The third RPSI engine to work a 'Steam Enterprise' and the return of a Great Northern Compound to Dublin for the first time in twenty-four years!

27 September 1986 85 Light engine
Central Service Depot–Lisburn–Antrim–Belfast (York Road)–Whitehead.

5 October 1986 4 'Larne Lough' railtour
Central Service Depot–Belfast Central–Lisburn–Antrim–Belfast (York Road)–Larne Harbour–York Road–Whitehead.

21 November 1986 85 Contract for TV detective series *Remington Steele*
Empty carriages Whitehead–Belfast (York Road)–Antrim–Lisburn–Dublin (Connolly) for filming. On this occasion Connolly doubled as London Paddington.

24 November 1986 85 Empty carriages
Dublin (Connolly)–Lisburn–Antrim–Belfast (York Road)–Whitehead after film contract. Planned for 23 November, but delayed due to a film over-run.

10 January 1987 3BG Engine movement
Guinness engine taken by low-loader from Whitehead to Downpatrick for use on the Downpatrick Railway.

? April 1987 Steam Heritage Award
No 85's return to traffic gained the RPSI a certificate of commendation in the annual Steam Heritage Award run by British Coal. Lord Dunleath accepted this award on behalf of the RPSI at a ceremony in Buckinghamshire.

2 May 1987 4 Empty carriages
Positioning run for 'Lough Gill' railtour. Whitehead–York Road–Antrim–Lisburn. No 4 failed at Lisburn and was worked light engine to Central Service Depot. The carriages continued, diesel-hauled, to Dublin (Connolly) on 8 May.

7 May 1987 171 Empty carriages
Whitehead–Belfast (York Road). No 171 continued light engine York Road–Antrim–Lisburn–Central Service Depot. Running-in trip after 171 was hurriedly 'called up' for main line duty – with three new bearings, as yet not fully run in, and a brick arch built only the previous day!

8 May 1987 171 Light engine
Central Service Depot–Dublin (Connolly)

9 May 1987 171 'Lough Gill' railtour
No 171 Dublin (Pearse)–Connolly–Sligo–Ballymote–Sligo–Ballymote–Sligo. The rather fraught story of how this tour nearly did not run at all is detailed in *Five Foot Three* No 34.

10 May 1987 171, 85 'Lough Gill' railtour
No 171 light engine Sligo–Sligo Quay–Sligo for coaling, then worked tour train Sligo–Mullingar–Moate–Mullingar–Dublin (Connolly). No 85 worked forward Connolly–Belfast Belfast Central–Central Service Depot. No 171 followed as recorded below. As well as 85's debut on two-day tours, this was an unofficial test for the following August's 'Enterprise' anniversary, as 85 ran Dublin–Belfast without taking water.

10 May 1987 85, 171 'Steam on Sunday'
No 85 light engine Whitehead–Belfast (York Road), then worked three coaches York Road–Antrim–Lisburn–Dublin to bring 85 south for the final leg of the 'Lough Gill' railtour. some participants returned Dublin (Connolly)–Belfast Central with 171, while 85 headed the main tour train.

11 May 1987 85 'Lough Gill' railtour
Central Service Depot–Belfast Central–Lisburn–Antrim–Coleraine–Belfast (York Road)–Whitehead. After the previous year's successful 'third day', participants were offered a full railtour, which was well supported.

13 May 1987 171 Stock movement
No 171, with support coach, Central Service Depot–Lisburn–Antrim–Belfast (York Road)–Whitehead

5 June 1987 184 Empty carriages
Mullingar–Athlone–Athenry–Ennis. Engine lost left-hand cotter during the run, and Inspector Eamonn Lacken organized temporary repairs using scrap metal. Part of a redundant signal lever, gathered up at Ardrahan, was worked on at Ennis to produce a new cotter for the weekend's activities.

6 June 1987 184 Ennis Festival charter
Ennis–Gort–Ennis–Gort–Ennis–Gort–Ennis.

7 June 1987 184 Ennis Festival charter
Ennis–Gort–Ennis–Gort–Ennis–Gort–Ennis. The RPSI support team had arranged to travel back that night from Ennis to Dublin on the empty stock of a GAA special. Somewhat to their surprise, they found themselves arriving in Cork at 1.00am the following morning!

13 June 1987 184 Empty carriages
Ennis–Athenry–Athlone–Mullingar.

20 June 1987 171 'Portrush Flyer'
Whitehead–Belfast (York Road)–Portrush–Coleraine –Castlerock–Coleraine–Portrush–Belfast (York Road)– Whitehead. Advertised as the 50th Flyer.

26 June 1987 4 Irish Locomotive Appeal special
Whitehead–Belfast (York Road)–Larne Harbour–York Road -Whitehead. An evening supper train to raise funds for locomotive appeal – a forerunner of the midsummer jazz specials which in recent years have filled this slot.

4 July 1987 4 'Portrush Flyer'
Whitehead–Belfast (York Road)–Portrush–Coleraine –Castlerock–Coleraine–Portrush–York Road–Whitehead.

18 July 1987 4 'Portrush Flyer'
Whitehead–Belfast (York Road)–Portrush–Coleraine –Castlerock–Coleraine–Portrush–York Road–Whitehead.

1 August 1987 4 'Portrush Flyer'
Whitehead–Belfast (York Road)–Portrush–Coleraine –Castlerock–Coleraine–Portrush–York Road–Whitehead.

8 August 1987 85 Empty carriages
Whitehead–Belfast (York Road)–Antrim–Lisburn–Belfast Central–Central Service Depot.

11 August 1987 85, 171 40th anniversary of the 'Enterprise'
Charter of locomotive and coaches to NIR, celebrating the 40th anniversary of the 'Enterprise' express. No 85 Central Service Depot–Belfast Central–Dublin (nonstop)–Dundalk. Nos 85 and 171 Dundalk–Central–Central Service Depot. No 171 ran light engine Whitehead–Antrim–Lisburn –Newry (instead of Dundalk – due to diesel failure in preceding section) to stand pilot in case of failure, then followed special to Drogheda, turned at Drogheda and ran to Dundalk. NIR's guests returned to Belfast by modern traction, whilst 85 returned Dublin–Dundalk with the train of preserved coaches. No 171 piloted the special from Dundalk to Central. Empty Central–Central Service Depot. Given that Central–Dublin is a longer distance than Great Victoria Street–Dublin, this was almost certainly the longest nonstop run that any ex-Great Northern engine has ever done!

14 August 1987 184 Empty carriages
Mullingar–Dublin (Pearse). The engine ran light from Pearse to Dublin (Connolly), becoming the first steam engine to be stabled at Connolly shed following its reopening as a diesel shed.

15 August 1987 184 Clonsilla shuttle
Light engine Connolly–Pearse, then Dublin (Pearse)– Clonsilla–Pearse–Clonsilla–Pearse–Clonsilla–Pearse. The loco ran round in Boston Yard. The first trip was via Newcomen Junction, the rest via North Strand Junction. Light engine Pearse–Connolly, and coaches diesel hauled to Heuston.

15 August 1987 4, 171 Empty carriages
No 4 Whitehead–York Road–Antrim–Lisburn–Belfast Central, returning with 171 Belfast Central–Lisburn–Antrim– York Road–Whitehead. Run as an engine exchange working.

22 August 1987 85 'Steam Enterprise'
Central Service Depot–Belfast Central–Dublin (Connolly)– Belfast Central–Central Service Depot.

31 August 1987 4 'Bangor Belle'
Central Service Depot–Belfast Central–Bangor–Central– Bangor–Central–Bangor–Central–Bangor–Central–Central Service Depot. Last year of semaphore signals at Bangor.

12 September 1987 4 'Steam Enterprise'
Central Service Depot–Belfast Central–Dublin (Connolly)– Belfast Central–Central Service Depot.

12 September 1987 184 Clonsilla shuttle
Dublin (Connolly–Clonsilla–Connolly–Clonsilla– Connolly– Clonsilla–Dublin (Connolly).

12 September 1987 NIR GM 111 Empty carriages
Empty carriage working for film contract. No 111 hauled three RPSI coaches Whitehead–Belfast (York Road)–Antrim– Lisburn–Dublin (Connolly). Around lunchtime on this memorable day there were seventeen RPSI coaches and two RPSI locomotives in steam in the vicinity of Connolly station – a situation unlikely ever to be repeated.

13 September 1987 184 Film contract *Troubles*
Dublin (Connolly)–Greystones–Wicklow–Greystones– Wicklow–Greystones–Wicklow–Greystones. Engine stabled at Greystones. Train diesel-hauled Connolly–Bray, followed by 184 light engine, due to delays in completion of watering. Sunbathers on the beach had interesting additions to their suntans when the engine primed rather violently during one of the sequences.

14 September 1987 184 Film contract *Troubles*
Greystones–Wicklow–Greystones–Wicklow–Greystones– Wicklow–Greystones. Engine stabled at Greystones.

15 September 1987 184 Stock movement
Empty carriages Greystones–Rosslare Harbour–Waterford to site of next film contract. The RPSI Mullingar coaches were brought by a diesel locomotive Mullingar–Dublin (Connolly)–Greystones. The diesel engine returned to Mullingar with the Whitehead coaches used for the sequences for *Troubles*. No 184 watered at Gorey, where the local fire brigade had been expecting to water a traction engine rather than a railway engine.

17 September 1987 184 Film contract *Echoes*
Waterford–Carrick-on-Suir (posing as Castlefinn!) then two return workings Carrick–Fiddown propelling the train on

returns between Carrick and Waterford.

18 September 1987 184 Film contract *Echoes*
Waterford–Carrick-on-Suir, then two return workings
Carrick–Fiddown, propelling train on returns between
Carrick and Waterford.

19 September 1987 184 Empty carriages
Empty carriages after film contract work. Waterford–
Limerick Junction (using all junctions and loops at this
complex junction whilst shunting)–Limerick (reversal)–
Athenry–Athlone–Mullingar. This was the first time steam
had been controlled by the new electric signals at Limerick
Junction.

26 September 1987 85 'Steam Enterprise'
Central Service Depot–Belfast Central–Dublin (Connolly)–
Belfast Central–Central Service Depot.

3 October 1987 4 'The Wedding Belle' private charter
Central Service Depot–Central–Bangor empty. Bangor–
Antrim–York Road–Whitehead. First known use in Ireland
of a mainline steam train for a wedding reception, and
possibly the only time a steam train ran under a (temporary)
footbridge at Holywood station, erected in connection with
permanent way work. The train ran to a slow schedule on
the Bangor line to facilitate the reception and speeches, and
the crew (Jack Kitchen, Cecil McAdam and Inspector Frank
Dunlop) wore sprigs of white heather in their caps!

11 October 1987 85 'Larne Lough' railtour
Central Service Depot–Central–Lisburn–Antrim–York Road–
Whitehead–Larne Harbour–York Road–Whitehead.

14 October 1987 184 Film contract *The Old Jest*
Mullingar–Moate–Mullingar.

22 April 1988 4 The 'Curtain Raiser'
Evening supper special Whitehead–Belfast (York Road)–
Antrim–Lisburn–Belfast Central–Central Service Depot.

30 April 1988 4 'Bangor Belle'
Central Service Depot–Belfast Central–Bangor–Central–
Bangor–Central–Bangor–Central–Lisburn (engine only, for
water)–Central–Bangor–Central–Central Service Depot.
First steam working on the Bangor line to be controlled by
the newly installed automatic colour light signalling. Due to
operational problems, the engine was sent light to Lisburn for
water between third and fourth trips.

7 May 1988 4 Empty carriages
Positioning run of Whitehead-based set for 'Shannon'
railtour. Central Service Depot–Dublin (Connolly).

9 May 1988 184 Empty carriage test run
Mullingar–Killucan–Mullingar.

13 May 1988 184 Empty carriages
Positioning run of Mullingar-based set for 'Shannon'
railtour.Mullingar–Athlone–Clonnydonnin–Athlone (local
public excursion)–Athenry–Limerick. No 184 then worked
Limerick–Limerick Junction–Limerick with one coach to
turn on the triangle.

14 May 1988 184 Local trip ahead of 'Shannon' railtour
Limerick–Birdhill–Limerick–Birdhill.

14 May 1988 4, 184 'Shannon' railtour
RPSI Whitehead set diesel-hauled empty Dublin–Ballybrophy. No 4 and Irish Rail Cravens set Dublin (Heuston)–
Ballybrophy, as Irish Rail had now banned wooden
bodied stock from the Cork main line. The Cravens were
immediately taken back empty to Dublin by diesel loco. No
4 and Whitehead set Ballybrophy–Limerick. Uniquely in the
history of two-day tours, two alternatives were now on offer.
(1) No 4 and Whitehead set: Limerick–Roscrea (passengers
transferred to buses as travel on wooden bodied
stock was banned on the Cork main line) then empty
Roscrea–Ballybrophy–Portarlington. Passengers rejoined
at Portarlington and train worked Portarlington–Athlone
–Galway.
(2) No 184 and Mullingar set: Limerick–Tipperary–Limerick.

15 May 1988 4, 184 'Shannon' railtour.
At 10.00am this morning three RPSI engines were
simultaneously on the move: No 184 from Ennis, No 4 from
Galway and 85 from Whitehead. The total mainline steam
passenger mileage of 588 was probably a record for any
preservation society. The two railtour options continued as
follows to Athenry:
(1) No 4 and Whitehead set began with two local excursions
Galway–Athenry–Galway–Athenry–Galway, then with the
tour proper Galway–Athenry.
(2) No 184 and Mullingar set Limerick–Athenry
No 184 and Mullingar set Athenry–Athlone and worked
local trip Athlone–Clara–Athlone before continuing empty
Athlone–Mullingar. No 4 and Whitehead set Athenry–
Athlone–Mullingar–Dublin (Connolly).
No 85 and Whitehead set of no less than nine coaches
Dublin (Connolly)–Belfast Central–Central Service Depot.
No 4 remained in Dublin for the 'Millennium' tours detailed
below.
Due to a rostering mix up, no guard had been provided for
No 4's train from Athenry forward. The unsung hero who
saved the hour was off-duty Guard Greg Rabbitte, who was
contacted on his way to church by the Athenry stationmaster
and worked the train through to Dublin – resplendent in his
Sunday suit!

15 May 1988 85 Engine movement
No 85 with one coach (861) Whitehead–Dublin to work the
'Shannon' railtour forward to Belfast Central.

16 May 1988 85 'Shannon' railtour
Central–Lisburn–Antrim–Portrush–York Road–Whitehead,
once again with the substantial load of nine bogies.

21 May 1988 171 The 'Carnival Coaster'
Public charter in connection with a Carrickfergus medieval
carnival. Whitehead–Belfast (York Road)–Carrickfergus–
Larne Harbour–Carrickfergus–York Road–Whitehead.

29 May 1988 184 Last steaming to date
No 184's last steaming to date, at Mullingar, to shunt stock
for the Dublin summer season specials.

4 June 1988 4 The 'Cooley'
Dublin (Connolly)–Dundalk–Drogheda–Dundalk–Dublin (Connolly). The first in a series of public excursions in connection with the Dublin Millennium celebrations. RPSI stock worked empty from Mullingar to Dublin (Connolly) by CIÉ diesel locomotive. Public participation was disappointing, due to the rival attraction of the European Soccer Championships!

5 June 1988 85 Sunday afternoon tea special
Whitehead–Belfast (York Road)–Antrim- Lisburn–Belfast Central–Central Service Depot.

11 June 1988 85 The 'Mafeking Express'
Public charter by South Belfast District Scout Group. Central Service Depot–Belfast Central–Lisburn–Antrim–Portrush–Antrim–Lisburn–Central–Central Service Depot. Engine ran light from Portrush to Coleraine and back to turn.

18 June 1988 4 Clonsilla shuttle
Further excursion in connection with Dublin Millennium. Dublin (Connolly)–Clonsilla–Dublin (Connolly)–Clonsilla–Dublin (Connolly)–Clonsilla–Dublin (Connolly)–Clonsilla–Dublin (Connolly). Each working was extended Empty carriages from Connolly to Grand Canal Street sidings to run round and service the engine.

9 July 1988 85 'Portrush Flyer'
Central Service Depot–Central–Lisburn–Antrim–Portrush–Coleraine–Castlerock–Coleraine–Portrush–Antrim–Lisburn–Central–Central Service Depot. The train remained at Castlerock station while the engine ran light Castlerock–Coleraine–Castlerock to turn. The 1988 'Flyers' ran from Belfast Central due to carriage shed work at Whitehead.

23 July 1988 85 'Portrush Flyer'
Central Service Depot–Belfast Central–Lisburn–Antrim–Portrush–Coleraine–Castlerock–Coleraine–Portrush–Antrim–Lisburn –Belfast Central–Central Service Depot. The train remained at Castlerock station while the engine ran light Castlerock–Coleraine–Castlerock to turn.

16 July 1988 4 The 'Shannon'
Further excursion in connection with Dublin Millennium. Dublin (Connolly)–Carrick-on-Shannon–Boyle–Carrick-on-Shannon–Dublin (Connolly). Film sequences of this outing appeared on RTE's *The Long Acre* programme.

23 July 1988 85 'Portrush Flyer'
Central Service Depot–Belfast Central–Lisburn–Antrim–Portrush–Coleraine–Castlerock–Coleraine–Castlerock (engine only, to turn)–Coleraine–Portrush–near Kellswater. No 85's tender became derailed between Kellswater and Cookstown Junction on the return trip. The 19.05 ex-Londonderry was strengthened to a six car unit and worked wrong line to pick up 'Flyer' passengers at the site of the derailment. Tender later rerailed by NIR and train worked empty into Belfast Central around 3.00am on 24 July.

30 July 1988 The 'Lough Ree'
Further excursion in connection with Dublin Millennium. Dublin (Connolly)–Mullingar–Athlone–Ballinasloe–Athlone–Mullingar–Dublin (Connolly). The train was hauled from

Athlone MGWR to Athlone GSWR station by a diesel locomotive while the engine was being serviced.

4 August 1988 85, 171 Engine transfer
No 85 light engine Central Service Depot–Lisburn–Antrim–Belfast (York Road), then hauled coach 861 to Whitehead. No 171 with coach 50 Whitehead–Belfast (York Road)–Antrim–Lisburn–Central Service Depot.

6 August 1988 171 'Portrush Flyer'
Central Service Depot–Central–Lisburn–Antrim–Portrush–Coleraine–Castlerock–Coleraine–Portrush–Antrim–Lisburn–Central–Central Service Depot. Engine left train at Castlerock and ran light to Coleraine and back to turn.

13 August 1988 4 The 'Tara'
Further excursion in connection with Dublin Millennium. Dublin–Drogheda–Navan–Mosney–Navan–Drogheda–Dublin. The first known working of this class of engine on the Meath branch.

20 August 1988 171 'Portrush Flyer'
Central Service Depot–Central–Lisburn–Antrim–Portrush–Coleraine–Castlerock–Coleraine–Portrush–Antrim–Lisburn–Central–Central Service Depot. Engine left train at Castlerock and ran light to Coleraine and back to turn.

27 August 1988 4 The 'Boyne'
Final excursion in connection with the Dublin Millennium. Dublin–Drogheda–Navan–Drogheda–Dublin. Unless IÉ policy forbidding passenger trains on goods only branches changes, this may well have been the last steam passenger train from Navan to Drogheda.

3 September 1988 171, 4 'Steam Enterprise'
No 171 Central Service Depot–Belfast Central–Dublin (Connolly)–Dundalk. No 4 worked light engine Dublin (Connolly)–Dundalk and Nos 4 and 171 double-headed Dundalk–Central–Central Service Depot. This returned No 4 to Belfast following her 'Dublin Millennium' season.

17 September 1988 4 'Steam Enterprise'
Central Service Depot–Belfast Central–Dublin (Connolly)–Belfast Central–Central Service Depot.

1 October 1988 4 'Steam Enterprise'
Central Service Depot–Belfast Central–Dublin (Connolly)–Belfast Central–Central Service Depot.

2 October 1988 171, 4 'Larne Lough'
Nos 4 and 171 Central Service Depot–Central–Lisburn–Antrim–Belfast (York Road)–Whitehead RPSI, then worked by No 4 Whitehead–Larne Harbour–York Road–Whitehead.

1989 was the Society's silver jubilee year, and also the year when a new operating agreement was signed with NIR Negatively, by the end of the 1989 the Irish Republic's Ministry for Transport and Tourism had extended the ban on wooden bodied coaches to cover not only Dublin–Cork, but also Cherryville Junction–Waterford, and Portarlington–Athlone–Galway, Westport and Ballina.

20 April 1989 4 Empty carriages
Whitehead–Belfast (York Road)–Antrim–Lisburn–Central

Service Depot for a film contract. they were delayed at Central for two days due to a closure of the Dublin line.

22 April 1989 4 Empty carriages
Belfast Central–Dublin for film contract *The Real Charlotte*.

4 May 1989 184 Film contract *The Real Charlotte*
Film sequences at Moate for *The Real Charlotte*. Diesel worked, with 184 out of steam. As 184's boiler was out of certificate, the film's 'special effects' experts positioned an industrial boiler on a flat wagon behind the engine. A flexible steam pipe delivered steam to the smokebox and solenoids operated by switch gear in the cab produced a reasonable approximation to a steam locomotive start! To avoid damage, the connecting rods were taken down.

5 May 1989 184 Film contract *The Real Charlotte*
Film sequences at Dublin (Heuston). Locomotive not in steam.

10 May 1989 85 Empty carriages
Whitehead–York Road–Lisburn–Antrim–Central Service Depot, followed by test run light engine Central Service Depot–Lisburn–Central Service Depot. As the engine was carrying some heat in the tender axleboxes, the southward working to Dublin was deferred until the following day.

11 May 1989 85 Test run
Light engine Central Service Depot–Lisburn–Central Service Depot, followed by empty carriages Central Service Depot–Dublin for the 'Mount Brandon' tour. Inchicore Inspector Brendan Curtis and driver Mick McGuinness travelled as passengers to Portadown and rode with the NIR crew to gain familiarization with a GNR compound.

13 May 1989 4, 85 'Mount Brandon' railtour
No 4 and RPSI Mullingar set Dublin (Heuston)–Limerick Junction–Mallow (no passengers permitted). No 85 and a Cravens set Dublin (Heuston)–Mallow. No 4 and Mullingar set Mallow–Tralee. No 85 and the Cravens set worked a public excursion, steam one way Mallow–Killarney and ran light engine Killarney–Tralee. The Cravens coaches were diesel-worked Killarney–Mallow.

14 May 1989 4, 85 'Mount Brandon' railtour
No 4 light engine Tralee–Mallow. No 85 and the Mullingar set Tralee–Mallow, then with the empty Mullingar set Mallow–Dublin (Connolly) behind the tour train. No 4 and the Cravens set Mallow–Dublin (Connolly). No 85 and the Whitehead set Dublin (Connolly)–Belfast Central–Central Service Depot. The tour featured three sets of coaches – a total of 22 vehicles!

15 April 1989 85 'Mount Brandon' railtour
Central Service Depot–Belfast Central–Bangor–Antrim–Belfast (York Road)–Larne Harbour–Whitehead.

20 May 1989 4 Empty carriages
Dublin (Connolly)–Lisburn–Antrim–Belfast (York Road)–Whitehead. The engine was going north for attention after the two-day tour and the coaches were being returned after a film contract.

28 May 1989 85 Light engine
Whitehead–Bleach Green emergency crossover–Antrim–Lisburn–Dublin (Connolly), to work the tour on 3 June.

3 June 1989 85 The 'Cooley'
Dundalk anniversary public charter. Dublin (Connolly)–Dundalk–Mosney–Drogheda–Mosney–Dundalk–Dublin (Connolly). Originally scheduled to be worked by No 4.

18 June 1989 4, 85 'Mystery Tour'
No 4 Whitehead–York Road–Antrim–Lisburn–Dundalk, then light engine to Dublin. No 85 light engine Dublin (Connolly)–Dundalk, then worked train back to Whitehead. Advertised as a 'Mystery Tour' (the first time such a train has been run by RPSI) and run to re-position both engines for summer specials. Such is the efficiency of the 'grapevine' among Irish enthusiasts that very few – if any – passengers on the train had any doubt as to where they were going!

24 June 1989 4 'Sea Breeze'
Dublin (Connolly)–Wexford–Rosslare Harbour–Wexford–Dublin (Connolly). First visit of No 4 to the ex DSER main line and her first use of the turntable at Rosslare Harbour, which gained a narrow reprieve from the scrapman's torch. The RPSI's new Vice President, former Taoiseach Dr Garret FitzGerald, travelled from Dun Laoghaire to Greystones.

8 July 1989 85 'Portrush Flyer'
Whitehead–Belfast (York Road) –Portrush–Coleraine–Portrush–Belfast (York Road)–Whitehead. For 1989, the 'Flyer' reverted to operation from York Road. The train ran empty (but not publicly advertised) from Whitehead, since it had originally been intended to base the stock in Belfast for the season and work only diner and brake from and to Whitehead each working day The short working was to Coleraine only, rather than Castlerock.

15 July 1989 4 The 'Shannon'
Public excursion Dublin (Connolly)–Carrick-on-Shannon–Dublin (Connolly) with local working Carrick-on-Shannon–Sligo–Carrick-on-Shannon. Engine ran light to Sligo Quay to take coal. First working to Sligo by an engine of this class and the last steam run before retirement of driver John Clynes, who was a familiar footplate figure on many of our earlier railtours.

22 July 1989 85 'Portrush Flyer'
Whitehead–Belfast (York Road)–Portrush–Coleraine–Portrush–Belfast (York Road)–Whitehead. Again the train ran empty (but not publicly advertised) from Whitehead, since it had originally been intended to base the stock in Belfast for the season and work only diner and brake from and to Whitehead each working day. The short working was to Coleraine only, rather than Castlerock.

5 August 1989 85 'Portrush Flyer'
Whitehead–Belfast (York Road)–Portrush–Coleraine–Portrush–York Road–Whitehead.The final leg from York Road–Whitehead was composed only of 85+diner+coach 114. The rest of the stock was retained at York Road for cleaning and dispatched to Whitehead on 6 August by NIR diesel locomotive. This was the last steam train to be controlled by the NCC electric signals at Coleraine.

7 August 1989 85 Ulster Railway 150
6.20am special Whitehead–Lame Harbour. 8.07 relief passenger Lame Harbour–Belfast (York Road). 9.05 special York Road–Whitehead. The original intention had been a kind of 'plandampf' with regular trains being steam-substituted, but in the event relief trains were run on four commuter routes. The trains were exceptionally well patronized, many season ticket holders opting for the steam train – and making use of the luxury of the dining car! Normal tickets were valid on these trains hence, for the only time in the Society's history, NIR conductor guards sold tickets through the train. A small band of members bought NIR Seven Day Rover tickets and travelled on all the trains.

8 August 1989 85 Ulster Railway 150
5.28am special Whitehead–York Road–Antrim. 8.09 relief passenger Antrim–Central. Empty to Central Service Depot.

9 August 1989 85 Ulster Railway 150
Empty train Central Service Depot–Belfast Central. 6.58am special Belfast Central–Bangor. 8.23 relief passenger Bangor–Lisburn. 10.10 special Lisburn–Belfast Central. Empty to Central Service Depot.

10 August 1989 85 Ulster Railway 150
Empty train Central Service Depot–Belfast Central. 6.25am special Belfast Central–Portadown. 8.14 relief passenger Portadown–Central. Empty to Central Service Depot.

12 August 1989 85 Ulster Railway 150
Eight return workings Belfast Central–Lisburn to mark the 150th anniversary of the Ulster Railway (the second railway in Ireland). Timings of the specials reproduced the timetable followed on 12 August 1839. Train ran empty from and to Central Service Depot.

12 August 1989 4 'Sea Breeze'
Dublin (Connolly)–Wexford–Rosslare Harbour–Wexford–Dublin (Connolly).

19 August 1989 85 'Steam Enterprise'
Central Service Depot–Central–Dublin (Connolly)–Central–Central Service Depot. The 'Steam Enterprise' covered some new track, running via the loop at Mosney to set down a party which had missed the 9.00am Belfast–Dublin service train. Train stopped at Malahide to allow passengers to travel to Malahide Castle to see the Fry Model Railway.

2 September 1989 85 'Steam Enterprise' (diverted)
Central Service Depot–Belfast Central–Lisburn–Antrim–Coleraine–Antrim–Lisburn–Belfast Central–Central Service Depot. The GNR main line was closed by a bomb alert on the day of the tour. Tour organiser Ernie Gilmore gathered passengers together at Central Station and asked for a show of hands of those in favour of going to Coleraine as an alternative to cancelling the train! With the willing co-operation of NIR, the train therefore ran as shown above. Pathing difficulties prevented the train from going further, but tickets were valid by service train to Portrush. The most disappointed person on the train was probably veteran ex-GNR fireman Jimmy Donnelly who had really been savouring one last chance to work a compound to Dublin!

9 September 1989 4 Maynooth shuttle
Dublin (Connolly)–Maynooth–Dublin (Connolly)–Maynooth–Dublin (Connolly)–Maynooth–Dublin (Connolly). Each working ran empty between Connolly and Boston Yard, Grand Canal Street, to run the engine round the train.

16 September 1989 85 'Steam Enterprise'
Central Service Depot–Belfast Central–Dublin (Connolly)–Belfast Central–Central Service Depot. Train stopped at Malahide in each direction to allow passengers to visit the Fry Model Railway at Malahide Castle.

23 September 1989 85 'Steam Enterprise'
Central Service Depot–Belfast Central–Dublin (Connolly)–Belfast Central–Central Service Depot. Train stopped at Malahide in each direction to allow passengers to visit the Fry Model Railway at Malahide Castle. This train was booked to be double-headed by Nos 85 and 4 between Dundalk and Belfast (to bring No 4 north for the winter). While running light Dublin (Connolly)–Dundalk, No 4 sustained a hot crankpin and it was decided to continue light engine direct to Central Service Depot Belfast.

8 October 1989 4, 85 'Atlantic Coast Express'
Nos 85 and 4 double-headed Belfast Central–Lisburn–Antrim. Driving No 4 was Tommy Crymble, another York Road 'sixties steam specialist, driving his last steam engine before retirement. It was only right that it should be No 4, of a class on which he had excelled. The train was divided at Antrim and No 4 plus two coaches ran empty to York Road, then light engine to Whitehead. No 85 and seven coaches ran Antrim–Londonderry–Belfast (York Road), then York Road–Whitehead with two coaches. Remaining stock stored at York Road pending trackwork at Whitehead.

23 November 1989 85 Private charter by WA Gilbey Ltd
Empty carriages Whitehead–Belfast (York Road)–Antrim–Lisburn–Belfast Central, then charter train Belfast Central–Cultra to launch a drink called 'Sullivan'! Empty carriages Cultra–Bangor–Cultra then charter train Cultra–Belfast Central. Finally, Empty carriages Belfast Central–Lisburn–Antrim–York Road–Whitehead.

A word of explanation of a rather thin year's record for 1990! 1989 had finished with the ban on the general use of wooden-bodied coaches on much of the Irish railway system, effectively finishing (for some years anyway) the popular 'Steam Enterprise' workings. 1990 was the year Nos 85 and 171 were both stopped, 85 with worn firebox sides and 171 for major boiler work. To make matters worse, the single available main line engine, No 4, suffered a failure on the first day of the two-day tour. On the credit side, 1990 was the year No 461 re-entered traffic.

29 April 1990 4 Running-in trip
No 4 worked diner 88 and brake/third 91 Whitehead–Belfast (York Road)–Whitehead to run in diner 88 after a brake and axlebox overhaul. 461 was in steam for a boiler inspection on the same day.

5 May 1990 4 Light engine
Whitehead–Belfast (York Road)–Antrim–Lisburn–Dublin.
Reports that No 4 hauled a dead MV locomotive during this
run have not been corroborated.

11 May 1990 4 'Comeragh' international railtour
No 4 and IR Cravens worked Dublin (Heuston)–Limerick
Junction–Carrick-on-Suir–Bansha. The loco became a total
failure near MP 29 after bursting a boiler tube. Irish Rail No
055 hauled the whole train into Limerick Junction. No 4 was
removed and 055 continued to Limerick. No 055's rescue
movement was greatly expedited by the presence on the train
of Mr Michael Murphy, Irish Rail's District Manager (Main
Line Operations) and an early use of mobile phones.

12 May 1990 'Comeragh' international railtour
The tour continued with diesel haulage. Irish Rail loco 161
Limerick–Athenry–Galway–Athlone–Portarlington–Dublin
(Connolly). Changed to loco 038 Dublin (Connolly)–
Dundalk. Changed at Dundalk to NIR MV No 108 plus six
RPSI coaches, which worked through to Belfast Central.
No 4 was hauled by Irish Rail loco 055 to Inchicore for
repairs – which in the end amounted to replacement of all the
small tubes in the boiler! The work was done on the exact
road in the works where Bulleid's Turf Burner had her static
trials.

13 May 1990 'Comeragh' international railtour
The tour concluded with diesel haulage. Once again MV loco
No 108 and the RPSI set Belfast Central–Lisburn–Antrim–
Londonderry–Antrim–Belfast (York Road)–Whitehead.

8 June 1990 4 Light engine
Light engine Inchicore–Connolly, and Empty carriages
Connolly–Mullingar–Athlone–Athenry–Ennis. No 4 was first
steamed on 6 June, and passed to travel at 12 noon on
the following day. The former up platform at Athlone was being
demolished, and No 4 sustained a bent step from a protruding
coping stone.

9 June 1990 4 'Ennis 750'
Ennis–Gort–Ennis–Gort–Ennis–Gort–Ennis. The crew
(Paddy Lipper and Martin Cowley with Inspector Mick
Shine) were the men who had crewed No 4 on 11 May. They
were heard to whisper "Will she bite us again?" She didn't!

10 June 1990 4 'Ennis 750'
Ennis–Gort–Ennis–Gort–Ennis–Gort–Ennis–Gort–Ennis.
Then Empty carriages Ennis–Athenry–Athlone–Mullingar–
Dublin. Light engine to Inchicore.

23 June 1990 4 'The Yeats Country' railtour
Dublin (Connolly)–Sligo–Dublin (Connolly). The loco
continued light to Sligo Quay for servicing.

1 July 1990 Satzenbrau advertisement
Coaches posed at Dublin (Heuston) for television commercial
filming.

7 July 1990 4 Bray Seaside Festival
Light engine Dublin (Connolly)–Bray, then with train
Bray–Greystones–Bray–Greystones–Bray–Greystones–Bray–
Dublin (Connolly). Train ran wrong line Pearse–Connolly

because of DART disruption due to an overhead line failure.

21 July 1990 4 'Longford Festival Express'
Dublin (Connolly)–Sligo–Dublin (Connolly). The loco
continued light to Sligo Quay for servicing.

28 July 1990 NIR MV 106 'North West Express'
Whitehead–Belfast (York Road)–Antrim–Portrush–
Coleraine–Castlerock–Coleraine–Antrim–Belfast (York
Road)–Whitehead. Diesel equivalent of the customary
'Portrush Flyer' operation. With No 4 in Dublin for the
summer season, there was no Whitehead-based engine
available for the 'Flyer'. Four diesel Flyers were planned for
28 July, 4 August, 18 August and 1 September, to be hauled
by an NIR Hunslet diesel locomotive. Due to non-availability
of Hunslets, the two trains which did operate were powered
by ex-Irish Rail Metrovicks. Due to poor public response,
two of the four trains were cancelled, and those which did
operate had very much reduced loadings.

11 August 1990 4 'Sea Breeze'
Dublin (Connolly)–Wexford–Rosslare Harbour–Wexford–
Dublin (Connolly). This train carried a sizeable contingent
of English enthusiasts, and Inspector Jack Ahern arranged
with Connolly CTC for the Sealink ferry to be held at Dun
Laoghaire.

18 August 1990 NIR MV 108 'North West Express'
Whitehead–Belfast (York Road)–Antrim–Portrush–
Coleraine–Londonderry–Coleraine–Antrim–York Road–
Whitehead. Diesel equivalent of the customary 'Portrush
Flyer' operation. This was Inspector Frank Dunlop's last
day of railway service – though his connections with the
RPSI continue in various ways down to the present day!
Appropriately Frank's brother George was on duty in
Portrush cabin on the same day and Coleraine Stationmaster
Frank Trainor also came down to Portrush to wish Frank
well. It was rather unfortunate that Frank just missed the
opportunity to supervise 461's inaugural main line run!

22 August 1990 461 Running-in trip
Inaugural trip (in grey undercoat!) following insurance
company inspection, with coach 114 Whitehead–
Carrickfergus–Whitehead. Further mileage had been planned,
but a hot coupling rod bearing called an early halt to the day.

25 August 1990 461 Running-in trip
Further running-in trip with a three coach train Whitehead–
Belfast (York Road)–Whitehead.

8 September 1990 4 'Sea Breeze'
Dublin (Connolly)–Wexford–Rosslare Harbour–Wexford–
Dublin (Connolly). Due to engineering works, the train ran
wrong line Dun Laoghaire to Dalkey. Further bureaucratic
problems – this time new environmental laws banning the
use of bituminous coal in the Dublin area – meant that the
Society had to obtain a special permit for storing coal and
burning it in the engine!

9 September 1990 461 Running-in trip
Further running-in trip with five coach train Whitehead–York
Road–Whitehead–Carrickfergus–Whitehead–York Road–
Whitehead, instead of a planned run to Coleraine.

23 September 1990 4 Enfield shuttle
Dublin (Connolly)–Enfield–Dublin (Connolly)–Enfield–
Dublin (Connolly). The last steam train worked by driver
Tommy Blackwell before his retirement.

4 November 1990 461 Running-in trip
Whitehead–Carrickfergus–Whitehead light engine, then
with two coaches Whitehead–Belfast (York Road)–Larne
Harbour–Belfast (York Road)–Whitehead.

11 November 1990 461 Running-in trip
Further running-in trip with four coach train Whitehead–
Belfast (York Road)–Larne Harbour–Belfast (York Road)–
Larne Harbour–Whitehead.

18 November 1990 461 Running-in trip
Further running-in trip with four coach train Whitehead–
Belfast (York Road)–Coleraine–York Road–Whitehead.

2 December 1990 4 Light engine
Dublin (Connolly)–Whitehead (via Antrim) light engine.

20 January 1991 461 Running-in trip
Whitehead–Belfast (York Road)–Coleraine–York Road–
Whitehead. Further running-in trip with seven coach train.

17 February 1991 461 Running-in trip
Whitehead–Belfast (York Road)–Antrim–Lisburn–Bangor–
Lisburn–Antrim–Belfast (York Road)–Whitehead. Further
running-in trip with a seven coach train.

24 February 1991 461 Running-in trip
Whitehead–Belfast (York Road)–Antrim–Lisburn–Dundalk–
Lisburn–Antrim–York Road–Whitehead. The loco was
scheduled to run to Drogheda to turn, but arrived in Dundalk
(with both big ends carrying heat!) too late to permit this.
Train stopped at Adavoyle for a blow-up on the way back!

17 March 1991 461 Running-in trip
Running-in trip with two bogies Whitehead–Belfast (York
Road)–Whitehead–Belfast (York Road)–Whitehead.

24 March 1991 461 Running-in trip
Running-in trip with seven bogies Whitehead–Belfast (York
Road)–Antrim–Lisburn–Dundalk–Lisburn–Antrim–Belfast
(York Road)–Whitehead.

3 April 1991 461 Light engine
Light engine Whitehead–Dublin for the launching ceremony
mentioned below, crewed by Bobby Quail and George Gaw.
Although NIR Inspector Roy Stanfield was relieved by Irish
Rail Inspector Tony Foley at Dundalk, the other two NIR
men worked the engine to Dublin – the first time George had
ever worked an engine on Irish Rail metals!

6 April 1991 461 Light engine and empty carriages
Dublin (Connolly)–Mullingar–Dublin (Connolly). Test run
to allow Irish Rail's Nicky Moore and Dan Renehan to
familiarise themselves with 461. The loco returned from
Mullingar with four RPSI coaches for the launch ceremony
of 16 April.

16 April 1991 461 Official launch of 461
Empty carriages Dublin (Connolly)–Dublin (Pearse) for the
launch ceremony, then Dublin (Pearse)–Dun Laoghaire–

Dublin (Connolly). The RPSI's first ever Presidential special
conveyed the first ever lady Irish President, Mrs Mary
Robinson, from Pearse to the original Kingstown terminus.

4 May 1991 4 Empty carriages
Empty carriages for 'Decies' international railtour
Whitehead–York Road–Antrim–Lisburn–Dublin (Connolly).

11 May 1991 461 'Decies' international railtour
No 461 Dublin–Gorey, where the engine was failed with
heat in right-hand driving box. IÉ loco 176, at Arklow with a
cement special, came light to Gorey and took over the train.
There was a bit of good fortune here in that, not long after
this disaster, the down Rosslare also became a failure – but
too late to have 176, which was already en route to Gorey!
Their passengers had to await an engine from Dublin. Train
diesel-hauled Gorey–Rosslare–Wellingtonbridge. Due to the
Barrow Bridge having been struck by an Icelandic cargo
ship, tour passengers were bussed to Waterford, and the RPSI
set was diesel-hauled Wellingtonbridge–Rosslare–Dublin–
Kildare–Kilkenny–Waterford – the long way round. No
461 returned Gorey to Dublin (Connolly) light engine. That
night the tour participants were in Waterford, the carriages
somewhere near Kilkenny and Nos 4 and 461 in Connolly
shed! More positively, Dan Renehan worked for the first time
as a passed-out steam driver. He and Tony both passed their
steam driver's examination in 1991.

12 May 1991 4 'Decies' international railtour
IÉ loco 017 worked the special Waterford–Thomastown
where No 4 was waiting, having run light Dublin–Kildare–
Kilkenny–Thomastown. Her axle-loading prevented her
from crossing bridge 114 and coming into Waterford.
Tour organiser Michael McMahon had spent much of the
Saturday evening negotiating some compensation for the tour
passengers, and No 4 thus worked Thomastown–Kilkenny–
Kildare–Tullamore–Dublin (Connolly)–Lisburn–Belfast
Central–Central Service Depot. Fireman Noel Playfair drove
No 4 north from Dublin, having to contend with a broken
snifting valve on one cylinder. The noise of the engine's
restart that night from Balmoral, where railtour organiser
Michael McMahon was set down, could apparently be heard
over most of south Belfast!

13 May 1991 4 'Decies' international railtour
Nominally empty carriages Central Service Depot–Belfast
Central then Belfast Central–Bangor–Lisburn–Antrim–
Belfast (York Road)–Larne Harbour–Whitehead.

16 May 1991 461 Light engine
Dublin (Connolly)–Lisburn–Antrim–Belfast (York Road)–
Whitehead for attention for axlebox repairs and machining of
journal. (Inchicore Works was unable to undertake this due to
pressure of work.)

23 May 1991 4 Light engine
Whitehead– York Road–Antrim–Lisburn–Dublin (Connolly).

26 May 1991 4 Maynooth shuttle
Dublin (Connolly)–Maynooth–Enfield–Maynooth–Connolly–
Maynooth–Enfield–Maynooth–Connolly.

15 June 1991 4 'Sea Breeze'
Dublin (Connolly)–Wexford–Rosslare Harbour. At Rosslare, No 4's pony truck derailed and the train was worked back to Dublin by a 141 class loco. Investigation by Irish Rail confirmed that the problem lay with the track rather than the engine.

18 June 1991 4 Light engine
Rosslare Harbour–Dublin following the incident noted above.

30 June 1991 461 Running-in trip
Whitehead–Belfast (York Road)–Larne Harbour–Whitehead with four coaches.

6 July 1991 461 Stock movement
No 461 ran with coach 114 Whitehead–Central Service Depot and returned with the defunct turntable from CSD mounted on two RPSI bogie flats.

7 July 1991 461 Running-in trip
Whitehead–York Road–Antrim–Coleraine–Antrim–York Road–Whitehead. Further running-in trip with four coaches.

13 July 1991 4 'Sea Breeze'
Dublin (Connolly)–Wexford–Rosslare Harbour–Wexford–Dublin (Connolly).

21 July 1991 461 Running-in trip
Whitehead–Belfast (York Road)–Antrim–Coleraine–Antrim–Belfast (York Road) –Whitehead. Further running-in trip with seven coaches.

3 August 1991 461 'Portrush Flyer'
Whitehead–Belfast (York Road)–Portrush–Coleraine–Castlerock–Coleraine–Portrush–Belfast (York Road)–Whitehead. The locomotive was turned at Coleraine.

17 August 1991 461 'Portrush Flyer'
Whitehead–Belfast (York Road)–Portrush–Coleraine–Castlerock–Coleraine–Portrush–Belfast (York Road)–Whitehead. The locomotive was turned at Coleraine.

24 August 1991 4 'Sea Breeze'
Dublin (Connolly)–Wexford–Rosslare Harbour–Wexford–Dublin (Connolly). A party from the Parnell Society – complete with 19th century costumes – travelled on this train.

8 September 1991 4 Greystones shuttle
Dublin (Connolly)–Greystones–Dublin (Connolly)–Greystones–Dublin (Connolly)–Greystones–Dublin (Connolly). This operation replaced a planned 'Limerick Treaty 300' operation, which failed to attract enough advance bookings to justify its operation. This would have run Dublin–Rosslare–Limerick–Foynes–Rosslare–Dublin with a public excursion from Limerick to Birdhill and back.

13 September 1991 4 Light engine
Dublin (Connolly)–Lisburn–Antrim–York Road–Whitehead.

21 September 1991 4 'Atlantic Coast Express'
Whitehead–Belfast (York Road)–Londonderry–Belfast (York Road)–Whitehead. Farewell trip for driver Bobby Quail. (Other notable 1991 retirees were Inspector Roy Stanfield and driver Alan Robinson.)

2 November 1991 461 Light engine
Whitehead–Bleach Green Junction emergency crossover–Antrim–Lisburn–Dublin (Connolly).

3 November 1991 4 Dept of the Environment charter
Empty carriages Whitehead–Belfast (York Road)–Antrim–Lisburn. No 4 became a failure near Lisburn and the train was hauled by an NIR Hunslet loco to Central Service Depot, Belfast. This was No 4's last movement until 2001. The train was chartered to work two return trips Lisburn–Portadown following the reopening of Moira station buildings and signal box (the only ex-Ulster Railway station extant, and a listed building). NIR 80 class railcar operated to Moira in place of the RPSI train.

5 December 1991 461 Empty carriages
Dublin (Connolly)–Mullingar.

7 December 1991 461 Santa specials
Mullingar–Killucan–Mullingar–Killucan–Mullingar–Killucan–Mullingar.

8 December 1991 461 Santa specials
Mullingar–Killucan–Mullingar–Killucan–Mullingar–Killucan–Mullingar.

21 December 1991 NIR MV diesel loco Stock movement
Two return trips Whitehead–Magheramorne Loop with turntable wagons and non-operational coaches to clear the Whitehead sidings for erection of the carriage shed.

1 March 1992 171 Light engine
Running-in trip after overhaul Whitehead–Belfast (York Road)–Larne Harbour–Whitehead.

4 March 1992 461 Empty carriages
Worked eight bogies Mullingar–Dublin (Connolly).

5 March 1992 461 Private charter
Private charter to launch 'Rail Breaks 92' programme. Dublin (Connolly)–Dublin (Pearse)–Dun Laoghaire–Dublin (Connolly). This operation was requested by Mr Gerry Mooney, Business Development Manager (Passenger) with Iarnród Éireann. Those involved in its operation were later entertained to dinner by Mr Mooney at Heuston station.

12 April 1992 171 Empty carriages
Further running-in after overhaul. Whitehead–Belfast (York Road)–Coleraine–Belfast (York Road)–Whitehead.

21 April 1992 461 Training trips
Training trips for Irish Rail trainee steam crews. Light engine Dublin (Connolly)–Dublin (Heuston). Empty train Dublin (Heuston)–Dublin (Connolly)–Rathdrum–Dublin (Connolly).

22 April 1992 461 Training trips
Training trips for Irish Rail trainee steam crews. Light engine Dublin (Connolly)–Dublin (Heuston). Empty train Dublin (Heuston)–Dublin (Connolly)–Rathdrum–Dublin (Connolly).

25 April 1992 171 Empty carriages
Further Running-in after overhaul. Light engine Whitehead–York Road–Whitehead, then empty carriages Whitehead–York Road–Larne Harbour–Carrickfergus–Whitehead.

3 May 1992 461 Guinness wedding charter
Dublin (Connolly)–Maynooth–Mullingar–Maynooth–Dublin (Connolly). One of only two occasions to date when the RPSI has provided a charter train in connection with a wedding reception.

9 May 1992 461 'Grainne Uaile' international railtour
No 461 plus seven Cravens Dublin (Connolly)–Mullingar–Athlone–Westport.

10 May 1992 461 'Grainne Uaile' international railtour
No 461 light engine Westport–Manulla Junction and ran on to the branch. An Irish Rail diesel loco brought the train from Westport to Manulla Junction. At Manulla, 461 was attached and the diesel loco ran on to Claremorris. Then 461, plus seven Cravens, Manulla Junction–Ballina–Athlone–Mullingar–Dublin (Connolly). An Irish Rail diesel and seven Cravens Dublin–Dundalk, whence Belfast passengers continued to Belfast by bus. Bomb crater at Newry prevented the train being steam-hauled between Dublin and Belfast. (As late as 1992 it was interesting to find a Westport driver with steam experience – driver Paddy Cassidy took the train from Manulla to Ballina.)

11 May 1992 171 'Grainne Uaile' international railtour
RPSI set Whitehead–Belfast (York Road)–Larne Harbour–Carrickfergus–Larne Harbour–Whitehead. (A bomb scare at Monkstown prevented a scheduled run to Castlerock.)

16 May 1992 461 Empty carriages
No 461 with two bogies from Connolly to Mullingar.

11 June 1992 461 Empty carriages
No 461 with one bogie from Mullingar to Connolly.

13 June 1992 461 Royal Canal Festival shuttle
Dublin (Connolly)–Maynooth–Enfield–Maynooth–Connolly–Maynooth–Enfield–Maynooth–Connolly.

14 June 1992 461 Royal Canal Festival shuttle
Dublin (Connolly)–Maynooth–Enfield–Maynooth–Connolly–Maynooth–Enfield–Maynooth–Connolly.

20 June 1992 461 'Midsummer Night's Steam'
Dublin (Connolly)–Mullingar–Dublin (Connolly). The first of what became a traditional operation in the RPSI's annual calendar. The idea came from a steam-hauled barbecue special which the RPSI's David Humphries had experienced the previous year, between Durban and Kelso in South Africa!

27 June 1992 171 'Hills of Donegal'
Whitehead–York Road–Antrim–Coleraine–Londonderry Waterside–Coleraine–Antrim–York Road–Whitehead.

4 July 1992 461 'Strawberry Fair'
Dublin (Connolly)–Enniscorthy–Rosslare Harbour–Enniscorthy–Dublin (Connolly).

12 July 1992 171 Brake test special
Whitehead–Belfast (York Road)–Antrim–Londonderry Waterside–Antrim–Belfast (York Road)–Whitehead. This followed an incident when an NIR 80 class DEMU set collided with a car on a level crossing, and was to establish

that a vacuum-braked train running at line speed could stop between any given warning board and the road crossing. Test stops were done at Aughalish, Barmouth, Magilligan and Eglinton going out, and at Ballykelly, Clooney and Kellswater North coming back. An unscheduled event was at Ballyboyland, when the train struck a herd of cows wandering on the line. There were two bovine fatalities!

18 July 1992 171 'Portrush Flyer'
Whitehead–Belfast (York Road)–Portrush–Coleraine–Castlerock–Coleraine–Portrush–Belfast (York Road)–Whitehead.

1 August 1992 171 'Portrush Flyer'
Whitehead–Belfast (York Road)–Bleach Green–Antrim–Portrush–Coleraine–Castlerock–Coleraine–Portrush–Antrim–Bleach Green–Belfast (York Road)–Whitehead.

15 August 1992 171 'Portrush Flyer'
Whitehead–Belfast (York Road)–Bleach Green–Antrim–Portrush–Coleraine–Castlerock–Coleraine–Portrush–Antrim–Bleach Green–Belfast (York Road)–Whitehead.

22 August 1992 461 'Sea Breeze'
Dublin (Connolly)–Wexford–Rosslare Harbour–Wexford–Dublin (Connolly). The Parnell Society – appropriately costumed – again travelled on this train.

2 September 1992 461 Private charter by RTE
Dublin (Pearse)–Wicklow–Greystones–Dublin (Pearse). A special held during the European Broadcasting Union's annual conference, which in 1992 was hosted by RTE.

6 September 1992 171 Television commercial
Northern Ireland Tourist Board filming charter. Empty carriages Whitehead–Belfast (York Road)–Antrim–Downhill (for filming)–Antrim–Belfast (York Road)–Whitehead. NIR gave permission for running between Castlerock–Downhill–Castlerock (including propelling) without having to go through to Londonderry. The train was used for filming along Downhill strand and was propelled back to Castlerock, as necessary, to cross with regular services. A filming platform was bolted outside the tender on the driver's side. This proved of firmer construction than a platelayers hut which it demolished during filming!

13 September 1992 461 Maynooth shuttle
Dublin (Connolly)–Maynooth–Dublin (Connolly)–Maynooth–Dublin (Connolly)–Maynooth–Dublin (Connolly).

6 December 1992 171 Santa specials
First ever mainline Whitehead-based Santa specials and first public steam train from the newly opened Belfast Yorkgate station. Whitehead–Yorkgate–Whitehead–Yorkgate–Whitehead–Yorkgate–Whitehead.

6 December 1992 461 Santa specials
Eight coach train empty from Connolly to the Boston Yard, then Boston Yard–Pearse–Clonsilla–Pearse–Boston Yard–Pearse–Clonsilla–Pearse–Boston Yard–Clonsilla–Pearse–Boston Yard–Connolly. The trips were scheduled for Maynooth, but worked only to Clonsilla to save stress on recently repaired driving axleboxes.

8 December 1992 171 Dept of Environment special
Run in connection with the designation of Whitehead as a conservation area, the special operated Whitehead–Yorkgate–Whitehead–Yorkgate–Whitehead.

12 December 1992 461 Santa specials
Dublin (Connolly)–Pearse–Maynooth–Pearse–Maynooth–Pearse–Maynooth–Pearse–Dublin (Connolly).

13 December 1992 461 Santa specials
Eight coach train empty from Connolly to the Boston Yard, then Boston Yard–Pearse–Maynooth–Pearse–Boston Yard–Pearse–Maynooth–Pearse–Boston Yard–Maynooth–Pearse–Boston Yard–Connolly.

20 December 1992 171 Santa specials
Whitehead–Yorkgate–Whitehead–Yorkgate –Whitehead–Yorkgate–Whitehead.

In 1993 the RPSI Vice-President, Lord Dunleath, died. He was a good friend of preservation in its widest sense, and was mainly responsible for the funding which returned ex-GNR Compound No 85 to main line service.

16 January 1993 461 Light engine
Dublin–Lisburn–Antrim–Bleach Green emergency crossover–Whitehead.

14 February 1993 171 Charter for UFTM
This charter was in connection with the movement of railway exhibits to Cultra. No 171 worked empty carriages Whitehead–Yorkgate–Antrim–Lisburn–Belfast Central. It then hauled ex-GSR B1a 4-6-0 No 800 *Maedhbh* and ex-LMS(NCC) U2 4-4-0 No 74 *Dunluce Castle*, along with an NIR GM loco at the rear, from Belfast Central to the Ulster Folk and Transport Museum, via the short spur direct to the museum. At Cultra 171 uncoupled and ran forward to regain the up line at Rockport crossover, leaving the GM to hold the dead engines on the 1/73 gradient. Two NIR diesel locomotives (used earlier in the day to top and tail the first stock movement of BCDR 4-4-2T No 30 and GNR 2-4-2T No 93) positioned the dead steam engines in the museum, while 171 ran light Rockport–Belfast Central, then empty carriages Belfast Central–Lisburn–Antrim–Yorkgate–Whitehead. A high profile day for the RPSI and for 171's experienced NIR crew of Willie McCaughley and George Gaw. Several thousand people turned out to see the cavalcade proceeding along the Bangor line, pleasantly surprising some museum staff who thought no-one would be interested in the movement of elderly steam engines.

28 March 1993 461 Stock movement
Whitehead–Magheramorne loop–Whitehead to retrieve stored RPSI vehicles (see under 1991 for further details). No 461 and coach 9 ran Whitehead–Carrickfergus–Magheramorne, collecting the components of two turntables (originally from Londonderry Waterside and Central Service Depot, Belfast) and bringing them to Whitehead. It has been suggested that the movement of two turntables by one train was an event unique in Irish railway annals. Due to a misunderstanding, 461 did not return to Magheramorne to collect the RPSI

coaches. These were returned to Whitehead by an NIR diesel at a later date.

25 April 1993 171 BBC charter
Special in connection with filming scenes for the BBC 'Great Railway Journey' series with Michael Palin. Whitehead–Yorkgate–Antrim–Coleraine (turn engine)–Londonderry Waterside–Coleraine–Castlerock–Coleraine –Yorkgate–Whitehead.

27 April 1993 171 Empty carriages
Empty carriages for 'Sean Ri international railtour Whitehead–Yorkgate–Antrim–Lisburn–Dublin

1 May 1993 461 Empty carriages
Two coaches Whitehead–Yorkgate–Antrim–Lisburn–Dublin for further BBC filming and 'Sean Ri international railtour. Passengers carried from Whitehead to Dundalk only, as wooden stock was banned from passenger carrying between Dundalk and Dublin.

2 May 1993 Film train *Derry to Kerry*
Film train for the recording of Michael Palin's 'Great Railway Journey' series *Derry to Kerry*, advertised to the public. Dublin (Connolly)–Wexford–Rosslare Europort–Dublin (Connolly). The Whitehead set was used as the Dublin-based set was not fully ready for operational duties.

8 May 1993 171, 461 'Sean Ri' international railtour
No 461 and the RPSI Whitehead set Empty carriages Dublin (Heuston)–Ballybrophy, then main tour train Ballybrophy–Limerick Check–Foynes–Limerick Check (loco detached at shed, and whole train diesel-hauled from Limerick Check into Limerick station) No 171 and IÉ Cravens set Dublin (Heuston)– Ballybrophy, then Empty carriages Ballybrophy–Dublin (Heuston).

9 May 1993 171, 461 'Sean Ri' international railtour
No 461 and RPSI Whitehead set tender first Limerick–Limerick Junction where the engine was turned chimney towards Waterford using the direct curve. Chimney first Limerick Junction–Waterford–Rosslare. No 171 light engine Dublin (Connolly)–Rosslare and worked the tour train Rosslare Europort–Dublin (Connolly).

10 May 1993 171 'Sean Ri' international railtour
No 171 and IÉ Cravens Dublin (Connolly)–Dundalk, then with RPSI Whitehead-based set forward Dundalk–Lisburn–Antrim–Yorkgate–Whitehead.

22 May 1993 NIR diesel Empty stock movement
Coaches 88 and 1335 hauled by diesel from Whitehead to Dublin (Connolly) in preparation for the heavily patronised Royal Canal Festival shuttle of the following day.

23 May 1993 461 Royal Canal Festival shuttle
Dublin (Connolly)–Maynooth–Enfield–Maynooth–Connolly–Maynooth–Enfield–Maynooth–Dublin (Connolly).

5 June 1993 171 'Hills of Donegal'
Whitehead–Yorkgate–Bleach Green–Antrim–Coleraine (turn engine)–Londonderry Waterside–Coleraine–Antrim–Bleach Green–Yorkgate–Whitehead.

2 July 1993 171 'The Celebration' Steam & Jazz special
No 171 Whitehead–Yorkgate–Whitehead–Yorkgate–
Whitehead to celebrate the official reopening of the carriage
shed and the re-launch of 171; then with the jazz enthusiasts
Whitehead–Yorkgate–Bleach Green–Antrim–Ballymena–
Antrim–Bleach Green–Yorkgate–Whitehead. The Jazz
special was postponed from 18 June.

4 July 1993 461 'The Shannon' railtour
Dublin (Connolly)–Mullingar–Athlone–Ballinasloe–Athenry–
Mullingar–Dublin (Connolly). The train ran into Athlone
MGWR station, then set back into the GSWR station before
proceeding to Ballinasloe. The procedure was reversed on the
return journey. RPSI stock was once more allowed to work
through to Ballinasloe after negotiations with Irish Rail.

17 July 1993 171 'Portrush Flyer'
Whitehead–Yorkgate–Portrush–Coleraine–Castlerock–
Coleraine–Portrush–Yorkgate–Whitehead.

31 July 1993 171 'Portrush Flyer'
Whitehead–Yorkgate–Portrush–Coleraine–Castlerock–
Coleraine–Portrush–Yorkgate–Whitehead.

21 August 1993 171 'Portrush Flyer'
Whitehead–Yorkgate–Portrush–Coleraine–Castlerock–
Coleraine–Portrush–Yorkgate–Whitehead.

21 August 1993 461 'Sea Breeze'
Dublin (Connolly)–Wexford–Rosslare Harbour–Wexford–
Dublin (Connolly). A planned 'Sea Breeze' on 24 July was
cancelled due to an engineers' possession for bridge repairs
near Wicklow.

12 September 1993 461 Greystones shuttle
Dublin (Connolly)–Greystones–Dublin (Connolly)–
Greystones–Dublin (Connolly)–Greystones–Dublin
(Connolly). Pathing had to be revised to take account of
a new 25mph speed restriction for tender-first running,
previously banned.

18 September 1993 171 'Atlantic Coast Express'
Whitehead–Yorkgate–Bleach Green–Antrim–Coleraine (turn
engine)–Londonderry Waterside–Coleraine–Antrim–Bleach
Green–Yorkgate–Whitehead.

26 September 1993 171 Stock movement
Stock movement in advance of the official opening of
the new Railway Gallery at the Ulster Folk and Transport
Museum. Five bogies, including GNR Directors' Saloon
No 50, Whitehead–Yorkgate–Antrim–Lisburn–Bangor, then
saloon No 50 and coach 411 Bangor–Belfast Central–Cultra.
(The journey into Belfast and out again was because Cultra
siding can only be accessed from the down line). The shunt
at Cultra siding included bringing ex-NCC U2 4-4-0 No
74 *Dunluce Castle* into the light of day yet again to make a
space for saloon No 50!

30 September 1993 171 UFTM opening specials
No 171 and coach 411 Cultra–Bangor, then with four bogies
Bangor–Belfast Central–Bangor–Belfast Central. Then empty
carriages Central–Adelaide goods yard (for coal)–Lisburn–
Antrim–York Gate–Whitehead.

5 December 1993 171 Santa specials
Whitehead–Yorkgate–Whitehead–Yorkgate–Whitehead–
Yorkgate–Whitehead.

5 December 1993 461 Santa specials
Dublin (Connolly)–Boston Yard–Pearse–Maynooth–Pearse–
Boston Yard–Pearse–Maynooth–Pearse–Boston Yard–Pearse–
Maynooth–Pearse–Boston Yard–Dublin (Connolly). No
461 carried battery-powered headlamps for the first time in
compliance with new regulations about lamps for 'after dark'
workings.

12 December 1993 461 Santa specials
Dublin (Connolly)–Boston Yard–Pearse–Maynooth–Pearse–
Boston Yard–Pearse–Maynooth–Pearse–Boston Yard–Pearse–
Maynooth–Pearse–Boston Yard–Dublin (Connolly).

12 December 1993 171 Santa specials
Whitehead–Yorkgate–Whitehead–Yorkgate–Whitehead–
Yorkgate–Whitehead.

19 December 1993 171 Santa specials
Whitehead–Yorkgate–Whitehead–Yorkgate–Whitehead–
Yorkgate–Whitehead. Last steam run by driver Willie
McCaughley – the last ex-GNR employee to work an RPSI
special. He retired in the following year.

27 March 1994 171 Running-in trips
Light engine Whitehead–Larne Harbour–Whitehead–Larne
Harbour–Whitehead.

2 April 1994 171 Whitehead Easter trips
Whitehead–Carrickfergus–Larne Harbour–Carrickfergus–
Larne Harbour–Carrickfergus–Whitehead.

4 April 1994 171 Whitehead Easter trips
Whitehead–Carrickfergus–Larne Harbour–Carrickfergus–
Larne Harbour–Carrickfergus–Whitehead.

23 April 1994 461 'Thank you' special
Dublin (Connolly)–Mullingar–Dublin (Connolly) with six
bogies. Running-in for the engine, and a gesture of thanks to
members and outside bodies who worked for, or supported,
RPSI operations. Travel was by special invitation.

30 April 1994 171 Stock movement
Stock movement for 'Lough Atalia' international railtour.
Whitehead–Yorkgate–Antrim–Lisburn–Central Service
Depot. Due to a hot axlebox 171 did not proceed to Dublin as
intended. She returned to Whitehead for repair and the train
was diesel-hauled to Bangor for stabling. The carriages were
diesel-hauled to Dublin on 7 May.

11 May 1994 171 Light engine movement after repairs
Whitehead–Bleach Green emergency crossover–Antrim–
Lisburn–Dublin for 'Lough Atalia' international railtour.

**14 May 1994 171, 461 'Lough Atalia' international
railtour**
Nos 461 and 171 with seven RPSI bogies Dublin
(Connolly)–Enfield. No 461 and seven bogies Enfield–
Edgeworthstown–Mullingar. No 171 light engine Enfield–
Mullingar. Nos 171 and 461 with seven bogies Mullingar–
Athlone–Athenry. No 461 and seven bogies Athenry–Galway.

No 171 light engine Athenry–Galway.

15 May 1994 171, 461 'Lough Atalia' international railtour
Nos 171 and 461 with seven bogies Galway–Athenry, where 171 was removed with a hot big end. No 461 plus seven bogies Athenry–Athlone–Mullingar–Connolly. No 171 light engine Athenry–Athlone–Mullingar–Connolly for examination.

16 May 1994 461 'Lough Atalia' international railtour'
No 461 and IÉ Cravens set Dublin (Connolly)–Dundalk, and RPSI Whitehead-based set Dundalk–Lisburn–Antrim–Bleach Green–Yorkgate–Whitehead. The RPSI Whitehead-based set was worked empty Dublin (Connolly)–Dundalk by a diesel loco.

29 May 1994 171 Royal Canal Festival shuttle
Dublin (Connolly)–Maynooth–Enfield–Maynooth–Dublin (Connolly)–Maynooth–Enfield–Maynooth–Dublin (Connolly).

4 June 1994 171, 461 Stock movement
Run primarily to bring 461 south, and 171 and coaches north, for the summer operating season. No 461 and four coaches from the Whitehead-based RPSI set Whitehead–Yorkgate–Bleach Green–Antrim–Lisburn–Dundalk–Dublin (Connolly). No 171 and three coaches from Dublin-based RPSI set Dublin (Connolly)–Dundalk, then with five RPSI coaches Dundalk–Lisburn–Antrim–Bleach Green–Yorkgate–Whitehead. No 461 and two RPSI coaches empty Dundalk–Dublin. (Due to IÉ crew shortages, an NIR driver worked passenger to Dublin (Connolly) and for the first time a combined IÉ/NIR crew of Dan Renehan and Noel Playfair worked 171 to Dundalk!)

5 June 1994 171 'The Classic Carrick'
Whitehead–Carrickfergus–Larne Harbour–Carrickfergus–Larne Harbour–Carrickfergus–Whitehead.

11 June 1994 171 Charter for Greenisland golf club.
Whitehead–Yorkgate–Greenisland–Larne Harbour–Greenisland–Yorkgate–Whitehead.

11 June 1994 461 'Midsummer Night's Steam'
Dublin (Connolly)–Mullingar–Dublin (Connolly). This was brought forward one week to avoid a clash with Ireland's World Cup game with Italy!

24 June 1994 171 'Midsummer Steam and Jazz'
Whitehead–Yorkgate–Larne Harbour–Carrickfergus–Magheramorne Loop–Yorkgate–Whitehead. At Carrickfergus, prior to a planned second trip to Larne Harbour, it was found that, due to delays on the Larne Line, one platform of the terminus was occupied by a service train, and the other by an extra diesel set with no driver available to move it. This explained the termination of the second trip at Magheramorne.

2 July 1994 461 'Strawberry Fair'
Dublin (Connolly)–Enniscorthy–Rosslare Harbour–Enniscorthy–Dublin (Connolly).
On this day there were to be 'Newry 850' specials, but they were cancelled due to lack of bookings.

16 July 1994 171 'Portrush Flyer'
Whitehead–Yorkgate–Portrush–Coleraine–Castlerock–Coleraine–Portrush–Yorkgate–Whitehead.

23 July 1994 461 'Sea Breeze'
Dublin (Connolly)–Wexford–Rosslare Harbour–Wexford–Dublin (Connolly).

30 July 1994 171 'Portrush Flyer'
Whitehead–Yorkgate–Portrush–Coleraine–Castlerock–Coleraine–Portrush–Yorkgate–Whitehead.

13 August 1994 171 'Portrush Flyer'
Whitehead–Yorkgate–Portrush–Coleraine–Castlerock–Coleraine–Portrush–Yorkgate–Whitehead.

20 August 1994 461 'Sea Breeze'
Dublin (Connolly)–Wexford–Rosslare Harbour–Wexford–Dublin (Connolly).

27 August 1994 171 'Portrush Flyer'
Whitehead–Yorkgate–Portrush–Coleraine–Castlerock–Coleraine–Portrush–Yorkgate–Whitehead.

4 September 1994 85 Running-in trip
Light engine Whitehead–Carrickfergus–Whitehead, then with four Empty carriages Whitehead–Carrickfergus–Larne Harbour–Yorkgate–Whitehead. No 85 was now running with tender No 73, off a 1948 GNR U class 4-4-0, modified by Peter Scott and constructed at Whitehead.

11 September 1994 461 Greystones Shuttle
Dublin (Connolly)–Greystones–Dublin (Connolly)–Greystones–Dublin (Connolly)–Greystones–Dublin (Connolly). Due to problems with coaching stock, this was worked by an IÉ Cravens set, plus RPSI coach 1419.

17 September 1994 85, 171 'Atlantic Coast Express'
No 171 plus seven RPSI bogies, including GNR saloon No 50, Whitehead–Yorkgate. No 85 light engine Whitehead–Yorkgate. Nos 171 and 85 double-headed Yorkgate–Antrim–Coleraine (turn engines)–Antrim–Yorkgate–Whitehead. The first – and for the future probably the only – occasion when these engines were permitted to double-head on the NCC!

19 November 1994 461 Private charter
Dublin (Connolly)–Greystones–Wicklow–Greystones–Wicklow–Greystones–Dublin (Connolly). Private charter by Greystones La Touche Hotel to celebrate their centenary.

4 December 1994 85 Santa specials
Whitehead–Belfast Central–Whitehead–Central–Whitehead–Central –Whitehead. This was the first steam working across the newly opened cross-harbour link between Yorkgate and Lagan Junction over the Dargan Bridge (now easily Ireland's longest bridge, as technically it stretches from Middlepath Street almost all the way to Yorkgate).

4 December 1994 461 Santa specials
Dublin (Connolly)–Boston Yard–Pearse–Maynooth–Pearse–Boston Yard–Pearse–Maynooth–Pearse–Boston Yard–Pearse–Maynooth–Pearse–Boston Yard–Dublin (Connolly).

10 December 1994 85 Santa specials
Whitehead–Belfast Central–Whitehead–Central–Whitehead–Central –Whitehead.

11 December 1994 85 Santa specials
Whitehead–Belfast Central–Whitehead–Central–Whitehead–Central –Whitehead.

11 December 1994 461 Santa specials
Dublin (Connolly)–Boston Yard–Pearse–Maynooth–Pearse–Boston Yard–Pearse–Maynooth–Pearse–Boston Yard–Pearse–Maynooth–Pearse–Boston Yard–Dublin (Connolly).

17 December 1994 171 Santa specials
Whitehead–Belfast Central–Whitehead–Central–Whitehead–Central –Whitehead.

18 December 1994 85 Santa specials
Whitehead–Belfast Central–Whitehead–Central–Whitehead–Central –Whitehead.

8 February 1995 85 'The Kelly Love Train'
UTV Charter Whitehead–Belfast Central–Bangor–Central–Whitehead. An evening operation to celebrate St Valentine, chartered by, and recorded for, the well-known UTV chat show. A baby grand piano was installed in GNR saloon No 50 by removing one window!

?? March 1995 Filming of coaches
Final year students from Dublin Institute of Technology filmed RPSI coaches at platform 1, Dublin (Heuston).

17 April 1995 85 Easter Bunny specials
Whitehead–Belfast Central–Carrickfergus–Central–Lisburn–Central–Carrickfergus–Central–Lisburn–Central–Whitehead.

6 May 1995 85, 171 North Down charter
North Down District Council charter, celebrating the 50th anniversary of VE day. No 85 Whitehead–Central–Bangor–Central, then light engine to Whitehead. No 171 light engine Whitehead–Central then Central–Bangor–Central–Whitehead.

7 May 1995 461 Greystones shuttle
Dublin (Connolly)–Greystones–Dublin (Connolly)–Greystones–Dublin (Connolly)–Greystones–Dublin (Connolly).

13 May 1995 85 Light engine
Whitehead–Dublin Inchicore for the 'William Dargan' international railtour.

18 May 1995 171 Empty carriages
Empty carriages for 'William Dargan' international railtour. Five-bogie Whitehead-based RPSI set empty carriages Whitehead–Dundalk, to be stabled for the Dundalk–Whitehead section of the tour on 22 May. No 171 light engine Dundalk–Dublin (Inchicore). The locomotive became a total failure while running light from Connolly to Inchicore.

20 May 1995 85, 461 'William Dargan' international railtour
No 461 light engine Inchicore–Ballybrophy. No 85 with IÉ Cravens set Dublin (Heuston)–Ballybrophy. Train splitting with 461 Ballybrophy–Limerick Junction, and 85 Ballybrophy–Limerick Junction, overtaken by 461 at Thurles. No 85 worked the recombined train Limerick Junction–Cork, followed by 461, light engine.

21 May 1995 461, 85 'William Dargan' international railtour
No 461 and IÉ Cravens Cork–Cobh–Cork. Nos 85 and 461 double-heading Cork–Mallow. No 85 Mallow–Dublin (Connolly) followed by 461 light engine to Inchicore.

22 May 1995 85 'William Dargan' international railtour
No 85 and IÉ Cravens Dublin (Connolly)–Dundalk then, with RPSI Whitehead set, Dundalk–Belfast Central–Carrickfergus–Central–Whitehead.

23 May 1995 85 'The Big Breakfast' charter
Run for the Ulster Cancer Foundation. Formed by the stock of the previous day's train. Whitehead–Belfast Central–Lisburn–Antrim–Ballymena–Antrim–Bleach Green–Belfast Central–Whitehead.

10 June 1995 85 'Hills of Donegal'
Whitehead–Belfast Central–Lisburn–Antrim–Londonderry (engine turned at Coleraine)–Coleraine–Antrim–Lisburn–Belfast Central–Whitehead.

17 June 1995 461 'Midsummer Night's Steam'
Dublin (Connolly)–Mullingar–Dublin (Connolly).

18 June 1995 171 Engine and stock movement
Light engine Inchicore–Dublin (Heuston), then with coach 91 Heuston–Islandbridge–Central–Whitehead after repairs.

23 June 1995 85 'Midsummer Day Steam & Jazz'
Whitehead–Belfast Central–Poyntzpass–Central–Whitehead.

8 July 1995 461 'Strawberry Fair'
Dublin (Connolly)–Enniscorthy–Rosslare Harbour–Enniscorthy–Dublin (Connolly).

13 July 1995 461 Exhibition display
No 461 on show out of steam at Platform 1, Dublin (Heuston) along with GNR Directors' Saloon No 50. This was part of an exhibition commemorating one hundred years of railway catering in Ireland, and celebrating the re-branding of 'Network Catering'.

15 July 1995 171 'Portrush Flyer'
Whitehead–Belfast Central–Lisburn–Antrim–Portrush–Coleraine–Castlerock–Coleraine–Portrush–Antrim–Lisburn–Belfast Central–Whitehead.

16 July 1995 171 Light engine
No 171 Whitehead–Dublin for film contract work – painted in a kind of lined black!

26 July 1995 171 Film contract for *Michael Collins*
No 171 and train used for filming between Dublin (Connolly) and Drogheda. The full details of this complex operation appear in a most informative article by Peter Rigney in *Five Foot Three* No 42.

29 July 1995 461 'Sea Breeze'
Dublin (Connolly)–Wexford–Rosslare Harbour–Wexford–Dublin (Connolly).

29 July 1995 85 'Portrush Flyer'
Whitehead–Belfast Central–Lisburn–Antrim–Portrush–
Coleraine–Castlerock–Coleraine–Portrush–Antrim–Lisburn–
Belfast Central–Whitehead.

30 July 1995 171, 461 Film contract for *Michael Collins*
Light engines Dublin (Connolly)–Dublin (Pearse) (which was
doubling as 'Kingsbridge'!) for further film work. The heat
of the day was further intensified as the train needed to be
steam-heated for the film sequences.

31 July 1995 Filming of video for The Corrs
Coaches used at Dublin (Pearse) for filming of video for
The Corrs. Diner 88 was used, and coach 1335 also made an
appearance.

12 August 1995 85 'Portrush Flyer'
Whitehead–Belfast Central–Lisburn–Antrim–Portrush–
Coleraine–Castlerock–Coleraine–Portrush–Antrim–Lisburn–
Belfast Central–Whitehead.

26 August 1995 85 'Portrush Flyer'
Whitehead–Belfast Central–Lisburn–Antrim–Portrush–
Coleraine–Castlerock–Coleraine–Portrush–Antrim–Lisburn–
Belfast Central–Whitehead.

27 August 1995 461 Film contract for *Michael Collins*
Train diesel-hauled with IÉ loco 086 and filmed at various
locations between Dublin (Pearse) and Rathdrum, with 461
between Greystones and Wicklow for some sequences (which
in the end were not used!) A long dry spell had already led
to the cancellation of a 'Sea Breeze' excursion on 19 August
due to the fire risk, and this explains why sparing use was
made of 461.

31 August 1995 171 Light engine
Dublin–Whitehead after film contract work. With high
fire-risk conditions still exercising IÉ, 171 was towed in
steam to Dundalk by an Irish Rail locomotive and worked
normally Dundalk–Belfast Central–Whitehead. This was the
last occasion an RPSI locomotive was turned at York Road
before the transverser was installed.

10 September 1995 461 Enfield shuttle
Dublin (Connolly)–Maynooth–Enfield–Maynooth–Enfield–
Maynooth–Dublin (Connolly).

16 September 1995 171 'Atlantic Coast Express'
Whitehead–Belfast Central–Lisburn–Antrim–Coleraine (turn
engine)–Londonderry Waterside–Antrim–Lisburn–Belfast
Central–Whitehead. No 171 was now in proper GNR black
without nameplates as in pre-renewal days.

24 September 1995 85 Light engine
Whitehead–Belfast Central–City Junction–West Link
Junction–Central Junction–Central–Whitehead. Steam
clearance trials for the newly-built Blythefield triangle in
connection with the reopening of Great Victoria Street.

28 September 95 Filming for VISA commercial
RPSI coaches used in filming a VISA television commercial
in Killarney.

1 October 1995 85 'The Phoenix'
Whitehead–Belfast (Great Victoria Street)–Dundalk–Great
Victoria Street–Whitehead. No 85 continued light engine
Dundalk–Drogheda–Dundalk to turn. First steam passenger
from Great Victoria Street following the reopening of the
former GNR terminus the previous day, 30 September.

1 October 1995 461 Film contract for *Michael Collins*
No 461 light engine Connolly–Pearse. No 461 and five
RPSI coaches filmed at various locations between Dublin
(Connolly) and Wicklow. The train ran Dublin–Greystones–
Bray–Greystones–Wicklow–Greystones–Wicklow–
Greystones–Dublin (Pearse). No 461 light engine Pearse–
Connolly. The train was scheduled to run to Rathdrum,
but did not proceed further than Wicklow. Despite extreme
caution by the crew, stops had to be made to deal with
several lineside fires.

18 October 1995 Film contract for *Bookworm*
Coaches provided at Dublin (Heuston) for filming in
connection with *Bookworm*, a BBC/RTE arts production.

3 December 1995 85 Santa specials
Whitehead–Belfast Central–Whitehead–Central–Whitehead–
Central–Whitehead.

3 December 1995 461 Santa specials
Dublin (Pearse)–Maynooth–Dublin (Pearse)–Maynooth–
Dublin (Pearse)–Maynooth–Dublin (Pearse).

9 December 1995 85 Santa specials
Whitehead–Belfast Central–Whitehead–Central–Whitehead–
Central–Whitehead.

10 December 1995 461 Santa specials
Dublin (Pearse)–Maynooth–Dublin (Pearse)–Maynooth–
Dublin (Pearse)–Maynooth–Dublin (Pearse).

16 July 1995 85 Santa specials
Whitehead–Belfast Central–Whitehead–Central–Whitehead–
Central–Whitehead.

17 December 1995 85 Santa specials
Whitehead–Belfast Central–Whitehead–Central–Whitehead–
Central–Whitehead.

23 December 1995 85 Santa specials
Whitehead–Belfast Central–Whitehead–Central–Whitehead–
Central–Whitehead.

24 January 1996 461 Iarnród Éireann programme for steam trainees
No 461 with four Empty carriages Dublin (Connolly)–
Mullingar–Dublin (Connolly). Seven drivers were trained in
this programme. The format was that days one and two were
spent in the training school at Inchicore and examining the
engine at Connolly shed. The remaining three days (24–26
January) were spent on the road, running empty trains to two
locations where turntables existed, as detailed here. Inspector
Tony Foley and drivers Dan and Tony Renehan were all
involved.

25–26 January 1996 461 IÉ programme for steam trainees
No 461 with four Empty carriages Dublin (Connolly)–Mullingar–Dublin (Connolly).

7–9 February 1996 461 IÉ programme for steam trainees
No 461 with four Empty carriages Dublin (Connolly)–Drogheda–Dublin (Connolly).

25 February 1996 171 Empty carriages
Whitehead–Belfast Central–Whitehead–Central–Whitehead. Running-in trip after big end and crosshead repairs to 171. This was the last trip worked by driver George Gaw before the spell of illness which brought a premature end to his railway career.

30 March 1996 171 Private charter
Private charter by Helen's Bay Golf Club. Whitehead–Belfast Central–Bangor–Central–Bangor–Central–Whitehead. The train collected a party of golfers in period costume at Helen's Bay.

4 April 1996 85 Commercial filming
Film contract for Karat (Israeli coffee). No 85 and five bogies Whitehead–Larne Harbour–Whitehead. No 171 and five bogies Whitehead–Larne Harbour–Whitehead–Larne Harbour–Whitehead.

8 April 1996 85 and 171 Easter Bunny specials
No 85 Whitehead–Central–Whitehead. No 171 Whitehead–Central–Whitehead–Central–Whitehead. Two engines were used to provide running-in for the three day railtour.

30 April 1996 171 Empty carriages
IÉ personnel inspected RPSI coaches for operation south of the border, and 171 plus three bogies worked a test train Whitehead–Belfast Central–Lisburn–Central–Whitehead. On this working, Noel Playfair was passed out as a driver and W Gillespie as a fireman.

8 May 1996 171 Empty carriages
Positioning run for the 'Knocknarea' international railtour. Whitehead–Belfast Central–Dublin (Connolly). No 171 ran hot at Dundalk and had to be removed and taken back light engine Dundalk–Belfast Central–Whitehead.

10 May 1996 171 Light engine
Whitehead–Dublin (Connolly) after attention at Whitehead.

11 May 1996 171, 461 'Knocknarea' international railtour
Nos 461 and 171 with eight RPSI bogies Connolly–Enfield, where the train split. No 171 and four bogies Enfield–Longford, followed by 461 and four bogies Enfield–Longford. Nos 461 and 171 plus eight bogies Longford–Dromod. No 461 light engine Dromod–Boyle. (Double-heading was prohibited over the Shannon bridge at Drumsna). No 171 and eight bogies Dromod–Boyle. No 171 plus eight bogies Boyle–Sligo, then engine only to Sligo Quay for coal and water. No 461 light engine Boyle–Sligo Quay–Sligo.

12 May 1996 85, 171, 461 'Knocknarea' international railtour
No 461 and container wagons worked a photographers' false start from Sligo Quay. Nos 171 and 461 worked the train from Sligo to Boyle, and 461 was detached here, following light engine to Longford. (Double heading was prohibited over the Shannon Bridge at Drumsna). The train ran double-headed from Longford to Dublin (Connolly). No 85 ran light engine from Whitehead to Dublin (Connolly) and worked the tour forward to Portadown (rather than Dundalk where extensive engineering work was taking place) with a train of IÉ Cravens stock. IÉ GM loco 231 preceded with the RPSI set, which was not permitted to carry passengers on the ex-GNR main line between Dublin and Dundalk. No 85 then transferred to the RPSI set for the run forward to Great Victoria Street and on to Whitehead. (This replaced a planned double-heading by 85 and 171 between Portadown and Whitehead.)

13 May 1996 85 'Knocknarea' international railtour
No 85 and the RPSI Whitehead set Whitehead–Belfast Central–Lisburn–Antrim–Coleraine–Portrush–Coleraine–Bleach Green–Belfast Central–Whitehead.

26 May 1996 461 Enfield shuttle
Dublin (Connolly)–Maynooth–Enfield–Maynooth–Connolly–Maynooth–Enfield–Dublin (Connolly).

5 June 1996 461 O'Reilly Tours charter
Empty carriages Dublin (Connolly)–Rathdrum, then with charter party Rathdrum–Lansdowne Road–Dublin (Connolly).

7 June 1996 186 Engine movement
No 186 was moved by road to Inchicore for the open day.

9 June 1996 85 Empty carriages
No 85 Whitehead–Dublin Inchicore with coaches 1142 and 91. No 85 was going to Inchicore for display (with 171, 186 and 461, as well as coach 91) at the 'Inchicore 150' open day.

15/16 June 1996 85 'Inchicore 150'
In steam at Inchicore in connection with an open weekend to celebrate the 150th anniversary of the works. Nos 171, 186 and 461 were also on display, along with Westrail 0-6-0T No 90. No 186's tender remained at Inchicore. No 186 was later moved by road to Belfast docks and finally delivered to Whitehead on 2 October 1996.

16 June 1996 85 Empty carriages
Dublin (Inchicore)–Whitehead with coaches 238, 241 and 91.

21 June 1996 85 'Steam and Jazz'l
Whitehead–Belfast Central–Lisburn–Antrim–Ballymena–Antrim–Belfast Central–Whitehead.

22 June 1996 171 'Midsummer Night's Steam'
Dublin (Connolly)–Mullingar–Dublin (Connolly).

30 June 1996 171 Derby Day charter by IÉ
Dublin (Heuston)–Curragh Main Line–Kildare–Curragh Main Line–Dublin (Heuston). The train ran empty from the Curragh to Kildare, and 171 ran Kildare–Inchicore–Kildare to turn, before working empty stock to the Curragh for the

return trip. This was the first ever haulage of IÉ Mark 2d air-conditioned coaches by a steam locomotive.

6 July 1996 85 'Portrush Flyer'
Whitehead–Belfast Central–Lisburn–Antrim–Portrush–Coleraine–Castlerock–Coleraine–Portrush–Antrim–Lisburn–Belfast Central–Whitehead.

6 July 1996 171 'Strawberry Fair'
Dublin (Connolly)–Enniscorthy–Rosslare Europort–Enniscorthy–Dublin (Connolly). No 171 substituted for 461, whose newly-installed brick arch had collapsed.

20 July 1996 85 'Portrush Flyer'
Whitehead–Belfast Central–Lisburn–Antrim–Portrush–Coleraine–Castlerock–Coleraine–Portrush–Antrim–Lisburn–Belfast Central–Whitehead.

27 July 1996 461 'Sea Breeze'
Dublin (Connolly)–Enniscorthy–Dublin (Connolly). The excursion was due to continue to Rosslare, but the train was terminated at Enniscorthy due to injector problems.

3 August 1996 85 'Portrush Flyer'
Whitehead–Belfast Central–Lisburn–Antrim–Portrush–Coleraine–Castlerock–Coleraine–Portrush–Antrim–Lisburn–Belfast Central–Whitehead.

10 August 1996 171 150th anniversary charter by IÉ
No 171 and a Cravens set Dublin (Heuston)–Kilkenny–Dublin (Heuston). This was run to mark the 150th anniversary of the line to Carlow. At Kilkenny 171 was turned using the newly opened Lavistown triangle, running light Kilkenny–Thomastown–Bagenalstown–Kilkenny.

17 August 1996 85 'Portrush Flyer'
Whitehead–Belfast Central–Lisburn–Antrim–Portrush–Coleraine–Castlerock–Coleraine–Portrush–Antrim–Lisburn–Belfast Central–Whitehead.

24 August 1996 461 'Sixties Steam'
Dublin (Connolly)–Mullingar–Dublin (Connolly).

7 September 1996 85 'Atlantic Coast Express'
Whitehead–Belfast Central–Lisburn–Antrim–Damhead Crossing, between Macfin and Coleraine, where the tender became derailed. The passengers were bussed back to Belfast and the train eventually released from section by an NIR 111 class GM loco. No 85 ran light to Coleraine to turn, and then Coleraine–Antrim–Lisburn–Belfast Central–York Road depot for examination.

8 September 1996 85 Engine movement
No 85 towed by NIR diesel loco from Belfast (York Road) to Whitehead.

1 December 1996 171 Santa specials
Dublin (Pearse)–Maynooth–Dublin (Pearse)–Maynooth–Dublin (Pearse)–Maynooth–Dublin (Pearse).

8 December 1996 85 Santa specials
Whitehead–Belfast Central–Whitehead–Central–Whitehead–Central–Whitehead. Following the Damhead derailment, 85 was limited to 25mph for this season's Santa operations, and the Society was asked not to advertise any steam operations

on NIR which would involve running at speeds greater than 25mph until matters were resolved (see 16 November 1997).

8 December 1996 171 Santa specials
Dublin (Pearse)–Maynooth–Dublin (Pearse)–Maynooth–Dublin (Pearse)–Maynooth–Dublin (Pearse).

15 December 1996 85 Santa specials
Whitehead–Belfast Central–Whitehead–Central–Whitehead–Belfast Central–Whitehead.

21 December 1996 85 Santa specials
Whitehead–Belfast Central–Whitehead–Central–Whitehead–Belfast Central–Whitehead.

22 December 1996 85 Santa specials
Whitehead–Belfast Central–Whitehead–Central–Whitehead–Belfast Central–Whitehead.

9 March 1997 O&K No 3 Engine movement
Ex-CSÉ 0-4-0T locomotive No 3 arrived by low-loader at Whitehead for mechanical overhaul. The RPSI engineering department's first 'outside' contract – for the Downpatrick Railway.

10–11 March 1997 171 Further IÉ crew training trips
No 171 with two bogies Dublin (Connolly)–Mullingar–Dublin (Connolly). Scheduled trips on 12 and 13 March were cancelled due to leaking tubes on 171.

18–20 March 1997 171 Further IÉ crew training trips
Two bogies Dublin (Connolly)–Mullingar–Dublin (Connolly).

24–26 March 1997 171 Further IÉ crew training trips
Two bogies Dublin (Connolly)–Mullingar–Dublin (Connolly).

28 March 1997 171 Good Friday special
Dublin (Connolly)–Mullingar–Dublin (Connolly). The first operation of this now traditional season opener for the Dublin Area Operations Committee.

31 March 1997 85 Easter Bunny specials
Whitehead–Belfast Central–Whitehead–Central–Whitehead–Belfast Central–Whitehead. These operations were timed at 25mph maximum speed, as detailed above.

10 May 1997 171, 461 'Slieve Mish' international railtour
No 171 Dublin (Heuston)–Mallow with IÉ Cravens, then light engine to Cork. No 461 light engine Inchicore to Mallow, then Mallow–Tralee. No 461 was a last-minute substitution for 85, failed by IÉ after the detection of a sharp flange.

11 May 1997 171, 461 'Slieve Mish' international railtour
No 461 Tralee–Mallow with IÉ Cravens, then light engine Mallow–Connolly. No 171 Mallow–Dublin (Connolly).

12 May 1997 171 'Slieve Mish' international railtour
No 171 Dublin (Connolly)–Dundalk with IÉ Cravens, then Empty carriages Dundalk–Dublin. Participants returned Dundalk–Whitehead in an NIR 80 class railcar set. The

temporary NIR 25mph restriction for steam was still in place at this time, and it would have been difficult to fit a path into the normal timetable at this speed.

25 May 1997 171 Royal Canal Festival shuttle
Dublin (Connolly)–Maynooth–Enfield–Maynooth–Connolly–Maynooth–Enfield–Maynooth–Dublin (Connolly).

21 June 1997 461 'Midsummer Night's Steam'
Dublin (Connolly)–Mullingar–Dublin (Connolly).

5 July 1997 171 'Strawberry Fair'
Dublin (Connolly)–Enniscorthy–Rosslare Europort–Enniscorthy–Dublin (Connolly). Despite the destruction by fire (accidentally) of Ballygeary signal cabin in December 1996, the train did manage to go all the way.

26 July 1997 171 'Sixties Steam'
Dublin (Connolly)–Mullingar–Dublin (Connolly). The second attempt in two years at a train with this name. Neither was very heavily loaded – the organisers wondered if passengers had got the idea it was a train for old age pensioners!

6 September 1997 171 'Sea Breeze'
Dublin (Connolly)–Wexford–Rosslare Europort–Wexford–Dublin (Connolly).

30 September 1997 171 Light engine
Dublin (Connolly)–Belfast Central–Whitehead, running at 25mph maximum on NIR track.

16-17 October 1997 A39 Film contract for BBC/RTE
Coaches 1916, 1335 and 2421 used at Castlerea for filming of *Amongst Women*. Motive power was the Irish Traction Group's preserved A class diesel loco No A39. Stock had been previously hauled to Westport before the start of filming. As a footnote, it should be recorded that varying film contracts at this time had varying livery requirements. The three coaches used this time had been turned out in crimson for *Michael Collins*, were painted CIÉ green for *Amongst Women*, and finally reverted to red before returning to RPSI main line service.

16 November 1997 85 Test run with two coaches
Whitehead–Belfast Central–Lisburn–Antrim–Lisburn–Belfast Central–Whitehead. This finally rescinded the 25mph steam limit and marked the implementation of NIR Operating Instruction No 60 which governed northern steam movements from 1997 onwards.

29 November 1997 85 'Christmas Shopper'
Whitehead–Belfast Central–Lisburn–Antrim–Coleraine–Ballymoney–Coleraine–Antrim–Lisburn–Belfast Central–Whitehead.

7 December 1997 85 Santa specials
Whitehead–Belfast Central–Whitehead–Central–Whitehead–Belfast Central–Whitehead.

7 December 1997 461 Santa specials
Dublin (Pearse)–Maynooth–Dublin (Pearse)–Maynooth–Dublin (Pearse)–Maynooth–Dublin (Pearse).

14 December 1997 85 Santa specials
Whitehead–Belfast Central–Whitehead–Central–Whitehead–Belfast Central–Whitehead.

14 December 1997 461 Santa specials
Dublin (Pearse)–Maynooth–Dublin (Pearse)–Maynooth–Dublin (Pearse)–Maynooth–Dublin (Pearse).

20 December 1997 85 Santa specials
Whitehead–Belfast Central–Whitehead–Central–Whitehead–Belfast Central–Whitehead.

21 December 1997 85 Santa specials
Whitehead–Belfast Central–Whitehead–Central–Whitehead–Belfast Central–Whitehead.

4 April 1998 461 Running-in trip
No 461 Light engine Inchicore–Kildare–Inchicore .

10 April 1998 IÉ 074 Easter Bunny special
Dublin (Connolly)–Mullingar–Dublin (Connolly). The train was diesel-hauled due to the non-availability of 461.

13 April 1998 85 Easter Bunny specials
Whitehead–Belfast Central–Whitehead–Central–Whitehead–Belfast Central–Whitehead.

6 May 1998 461 Running-in trip
Light engine Inchicore–Sallins–Inchicore to run in axlebox following repairs in advance of the three day tour.

6 May 1998 171 Light engine
Whitehead–City Junction–Belfast (Great Victoria Street)–Dublin for 'Gall Tír' international tour, running via Great Victoria Street to turn.

7 May 1998 171 Engine movement/empty carriages
Positioning run for 'Gall Tír' international tour. Light engine Inchicore–Dublin (Heuston), then RPSI Empty carriages Heuston–Limerick Junction, via the direct curve to turn the train.

7 May 1998 461 Light engine
No 461 light engine for 'Gall Tír' international tour Inchicore–Kildare–Waterford.

9 May 1998 171, 461 'Gall Tír' international railtour
Diesel loco and Cravens set Heuston–Limerick Junction. No 171 and RPSI Dublin eight bogie set Limerick Junction–Clonmel–Waterford. No 461 plus RPSI Dublin set Waterford–Kilkenny–Bagenalstown–Waterford, using the new direct curve to the Waterford line at Lavistown. The train began diesel-hauled from Dublin to give additional time to run the two steam engines, on the itinerary described above, in one day and to offer maximum photo opportunities.

10 May 1998 171, 461 'Gall Tír' international railtour
No 171 light engine Waterford–Rosslare Harbour. No 461 and RPSI Dublin set Waterford–Rosslare Harbour. No 171 and RPSI Dublin set Rosslare Harbour–Wexford–Dublin (Connolly). No 461 light engine Rosslare Harbour–Wexford–Dublin (Connolly)–Inchicore.

11 May 1998 171 'Gall Tír' international railtour
No 171 plus five Cravens Dublin (Connolly)–Lisburn.

No 171 and RPSI Whitehead five bogie set Lisburn–Belfast Central–Larne Harbour–Whitehead. An NIR GM worked the RPSI set Whitehead–Lisburn and IÉ Cravens Lisburn–Dublin (Connolly).

24 May 1998 461 Royal Canal shuttle
Dublin (Connolly)–Maynooth–Enfield–Maynooth–Connolly–Maynooth–Enfield–Maynooth–Dublin (Connolly).

20 June 1998 461 'Midsummer Night's Steam'
Dublin (Connolly)–Mullingar–Dublin (Connolly).

28 June 1998 171 Test train
Whitehead–Belfast Central–Lisburn–Antrim–Castlerock–Antrim–Lisburn–Coleraine.

4 July 1998 461 'Strawberry Fair'
Dublin (Connolly)–Enniscorthy–Rosslare Europort–Enniscorthy–Dublin (Connolly).

25 July 1998 461 1798 Bi-centennial commemoration
Dublin (Connolly)–Wexford–Rosslare Europort–Wexford–Dublin (Connolly).

1 August 1998 171 'Portrush Flyer'
Whitehead–Belfast Central–Lisburn–Portrush–Antrim–Lisburn–Belfast Central–Whitehead. The loco ran forward to turn on Blythefield triangle between arrival at Central and departure for Portrush. Due to operational problems the train took nearly six hours to get to Portrush! The loco was turned at Coleraine during its return journey to Belfast.

15 August 1998 171 'Portrush Flyer'
Whitehead–Belfast Central–Lisburn–Portrush–Antrim–Lisburn–Belfast Central–Whitehead. The loco ran forward to turn on Blythefield triangle between arrival at Belfast Central and departure for Portrush, and light from Portrush to Coleraine and back to turn during the afternoon.

17 August 1998 461 Film contract
Light engine Inchicore–Connolly, then with RPSI coaches, (brought from Heuston by GM No 216), Connolly–Malahide–Connolly for filming work for the film *Her Own Rules*.

18 August 1998 461 Film contract work for *Durango*
Empty stock Dublin (Connolly)–Arklow. To make space for this train, the coaches of the evening Connolly–Arklow local train worked back to Dublin empty rather than being stabled at Arklow overnight.

19 August 1998 461 Film contract work for *Durango*
Arklow–Rathdrum–Arklow. Loco and train stabled at Arklow, due to lack of siding space at Rathdrum.

20 August 1998 461 Film contract work for *Durango*
Arklow–Rathdrum–Arklow. Loco and train stabled at Arklow, due to lack of siding space at Rathdrum. A marathon 14 hour day obviated the need for further filming on 21 August. Since the crew were out of their hours, the train had to be diesel hauled from Arklow to Dublin on 21 August 1998. No 461 remained at Arklow.

22 August 1998 171 'Portrush Flyer'
Whitehead–Belfast Central–Lisburn–Portrush–Antrim–

Lisburn–Belfast Central–Whitehead. Loco ran forward to turn on Blythefield triangle between arrival at Belfast Central and departure for Portrush. Loco turned at Coleraine during its return journey to Belfast.

28 August 1998 461
Light engine Arklow–Dublin (Connolly) after filming.

5 September 1998 461 'Sea Breeze'
Dublin (Connolly)–Wexford–Rosslare Europort–Wexford–Dublin (Connolly). On this date a party was picked up/set down at Arklow.

12 September 1998 171 'Atlantic Coast Express'
Whitehead–Belfast Central–Lisburn–Antrim–Londonderry–Coleraine (turn loco)–Antrim–Lisburn–Central–Whitehead.

3 October 1998 461 Private charter
Private charter in connection with 150th anniversary of the MGWR. Dublin (Connolly)–Mullingar–Killucan–Mullingar–Killucan–Mullingar–Dublin (Connolly).

3 October 1998 171 A 'might have been'
No 171 was to have been used to steam-haul part of an Irish Traction Group diesel tour from Belfast Central to Larne and Bangor. Due to a landslip near the White Harbour (between Kilroot and Whitehead) this proved impossible.

28 November 1998 171 'Christmas Shopper'
Whitehead–Belfast Central–Lisburn–Antrim–Coleraine–Ballymoney–Coleraine–Castlerock–Coleraine–Antrim–Lisburn–Belfast Central–Whitehead.

29 November 1998 461 Film contract for *Angela's Ashes*
Filming at Dublin (Pearse), disguised as Limerick!

6 December 1998 171 Santa specials
Whitehead–Belfast Central–Whitehead–Central–Whitehead–Belfast Central–Whitehead.

6 December 1998 461 Santa specials
Dublin (Connolly)–Greystones–Dublin (Connolly)–Greystones–Dublin (Connolly)–Greystones–Dublin (Connolly). The normal destination of Maynooth was not available due to engineering work. The overhead wires were up, though not yet energised.

13 December 1998 171 Santa specials
Whitehead–Belfast Central–Whitehead–Central–Whitehead–Belfast Central–Whitehead.

13 December 1998 461 Santa specials
Dublin (Connolly)–Greystones–Dublin (Connolly)–Greystones–Dublin (Connolly)–Greystones.–Dublin (Connolly). Greystones replaced the normal destination of Maynooth, as on 6 December.

19 December 1998 171 Santa specials
Whitehead–Belfast Central–Whitehead–Central–Whitehead–Belfast Central–Whitehead.

20 December 1998 171 Santa specials
Whitehead–Belfast Central–Whitehead–Central–Whitehead–Belfast Central–Whitehead.

20 December 1998 461 Film contract for *Angela's Ashes*
Filming at Dublin (Pearse), disguised as Limerick!

6 March 1999 85, 171 Charter and route clearance
South Belfast Scout charter and annual Belfast-Bangor route clearance. No 85 Whitehead–Belfast Central–Carrickfergus (set down)–Whitehead (Empty carriages). No 171 nominally Empty carriages Whitehead–Belfast Central–Bangor–Central–Carrickfergus (pick up)–Central–Whitehead (empty carriages).

2 April 1999 461 Good Friday special
Dublin (Connolly)–Mullingar–Dublin (Connolly).

5 April 1999 171 Easter Bunny specials
Whitehead–Belfast Central–Whitehead–Central–Whitehead–Belfast Central–Whitehead.

21 April 1999 171 Light engine
Whitehead–Dublin (Connolly).

24 April 1999 85, 171 Dundalk Centenary celebrations
No 85 light engine Whitehead–Belfast (Great Victoria Street) then, with an IÉ Cravens set, Great Victoria Street–Dundalk–Drogheda–Dundalk–Dublin (Connolly). No 171 with IÉ Cravens set Dublin (Connolly)–Dundalk–Poyntzpass–Dundalk–Belfast (Great Victoria Street). Light engine to Whitehead.

8 May 1999 85, 461 'St Munchin' international railtour
No 461 with RPSI Dublin set empty Dublin (Heuston)–Ballybrophy. No 85 with IÉ Cravens Dublin (Heuston)–Ballybrophy, then empty to Limerick Junction. No 461 with RPSI Dublin set Ballybrophy–Limerick–Ennis–Limerick. No 461 and empty train, diesel-hauled Limerick–Limerick Junction due to an engineer's possession which was to begin during the night.

9 May 1999 85, 461 'St Munchin' international railtour
Bus Limerick–Limerick Junction. No 85 with IÉ Cravens Limerick Junction–Dublin (Connolly)–Belfast Central. Light engine to Whitehead. No 461 with RPSI Dublin set empty Limerick Junction–Dublin (Heuston). No 461 was stabled overnight at Inchicore.

10 May 1999 171 'St Munchin' international railtour
Whitehead–Belfast Central–Lisburn–Antrim–Castlerock–Antrim–Lisburn–Belfast Central–Whitehead.

23 May 1999 Filming for *Norah Barnacle*
Static filming at Dublin (Pearse), this time representing Galway. Filming involved only coach 1142.

26 May 1999 461 Private charter
Private charter by an incentive group from Holland. Dublin (Connolly)–Greystones–Dublin (Connolly). Return from Greystones Empty carriages.

18 June 1999 171 'Steam and Jazz' special
Whitehead–Belfast Central–Carrickfergus–Central–Bangor–Belfast Central–Whitehead.

19 June 1999 461 'Midsummer Night's Steam'
Dublin (Connolly)–Mullingar–Dublin (Connolly).

27 June 1999 461 Inchicore open day
No 461 in steam for an open day at Inchicore works.

3 July 1999 461 'Strawberry Fair'
Dublin (Connolly)–Enniscorthy–Rosslare Europort–Enniscorthy–Dublin (Connolly).

15 July 1999 461 Private charter
Private charter by the Royal Society of Chemists' annual conference at Trinity College Dublin. Dublin (Connolly)–Rathdrum, then empty train Rathdrum–Arklow–Rathdrum, then with passengers Rathdrum–Dublin (Connolly).

24 July 1999 461 'Sea Breeze'
Dublin (Connolly)–Wexford–Rosslare Europort–Wexford–Dublin (Connolly).

7 August 1999 171 'Bangor Belle'
Whitehead–Belfast Central–Bangor–Central–Bangor–Central–Bangor–Central–Whitehead. (During the summer of 1999 the Belfast Central Railway was severed for engineering work and, since Bleach Green–Antrim was at this stage closed, 'Portrush Flyer' operations were not possible.)

21 August 1999 461 'Sea Breeze'
Dublin (Connolly)–Wexford–Rosslare Europort–Wexford–Dublin (Connolly).

28 August 1999 171 'Bangor Belle'
Whitehead–Belfast Central–Bangor–Central–Bangor–Central–Bangor– Central–Bangor–Central–Whitehead.

4 September 1999 461 'Sea Breeze'
Dublin (Connolly)–Wexford–Rosslare Europort–Wexford–Dublin (Connolly).

18 September 1999 171 'Atlantic Coast Express'
Whitehead–Belfast Central–Lisburn–Antrim–Londonderry–Antrim–Lisburn–Belfast Central. Due to serious delays the engine ran out of coal at Ballymena, and was piloted into Belfast by an NIR '111' class GM diesel.

19 September 1999 171 NIR charter
Charter for Translink staff 'Fun Day' at the UFTM. Whitehead–Belfast Central–Bangor–Central–Bangor–Central–Whitehead. There should have been a third return trip to Bangor but, shortly before its departure on a very wet day, a landslip was reported near Craigavad. The line was closed and the train returned direct to Whitehead.

13 October 1999 85 Engine movement
Light engine Whitehead–Dublin Inchicore.

14 October 1999 85 Engine movement
Positioning run for Private charter for 'Cork 150'. Light engine Inchicore–Limerick Junction.

16 October 1999 85 Private charter for 'Cork 150'
Limerick Junction–Cork–Limerick Junction. One-way Private charter Limerick Junction to Cork. The train returned to Limerick Junction as a public excursion from Cork, diesel-hauled back to Cork. No 85's train of five Mark 2d coaches and generator van was possibly the heaviest load ever handled by an unassisted four-coupled engine out of Cork.

17 October 1999 85 Engine movement
Light engine Limerick Junction–Dublin (Connolly)–Whitehead.

31 October 1999 171 'Broomstick Belle' specials
Whitehead–Belfast Central–Whitehead–Central–Whitehead–Belfast Central–Whitehead.

31 October 1999 461 'Ghost train'
Light engine Dublin (Connolly)–Enniscorthy and then attached five flat wagons with open sided containers and a goods brake van. The 'ghost train' worked Enniscorthy–Wexford Quays–Rosslare Europort. Three of the wagons were equipped with stage sets, and the other two with a generator and sound desk. The train made three stops along Wexford Quays for a series of ghostly acts involving vampires, demented scientists and assorted ghouls! Following a spectacular firework display, the actors detrained and the now empty wagons and brake van worked to Rosslare to stable.

1 November 1999 461 Light engine
Rosslare Europort–Dublin (Connolly).

2 November 1999 3 *R.H.Smyth* Engine movement
The LPHC engine was in steam to assist with the loading of the Downpatrick Railway's ex-CSÉ Orenstein and Koppel 0-4-0T. The Sugar engine's two year overhaul was complete.

13 November 1999 A39 Coach charter by the ITG
Two RPSI coaches with an IÉ heating van, hauled by preserved A class diesel A39, were used to work a special Dublin (Heuston)–Islandbridge–Dublin (Connolly)–Wicklow and back in connection with the Irish Traction Group's AGM.

27 November 1999 171 'Christmas Shopper'
Whitehead–Belfast Central–Lisburn–Antrim–Coleraine–Castlerock–Coleraine–Ballymoney–Coleraine–Antrim–Lisburn–Belfast Central–Whitehead.

5 December 1999 171 Santa specials
Whitehead–Belfast Central–Whitehead–Central–Whitehead–Belfast Central–Whitehead.

5 December 1999 461 Santa specials
Dublin (Connolly)–Greystones–Dublin (Connolly)–Greystones–Dublin (Connolly)–Greystones–Dublin (Connolly). Electrification of the line to Greystones was completed and the wires energised, but regular DART services had not yet commenced beyond Bray. Watering was done at Greystones with the current switched off, and with permit to work issued by the Electrical Engineer.

12 December 1999 171 Santa specials
Whitehead–Belfast Central–Whitehead–Central–Whitehead–Belfast Central–Whitehead.

12 December 1999 461 Santa specials
Dublin (Connolly)–Greystones–Connolly–Greystones–Connolly–Greystones–Dublin (Connolly).

1999 marked the retirement of Loco Inspector Tony Foley, the last Irish Rail driver to have worked his way through the old grades of cleaner, fireman and driver in steam days.

18 December 1999 85 Santa specials
Whitehead–Belfast Central–Whitehead–Central–Whitehead–Belfast Central–Whitehead.

19 December 1999 85 Santa specials
Whitehead–Belfast Central–Whitehead–Central–Whitehead–Central–Carrickfergus–Belfast Central–Whitehead.

25 March 2000 171 Light engine
Whitehead–Larne Harbour–Belfast Central–Dundalk–Belfast Central–Whitehead. Returned to Whitehead with a hot bogie axlebox.

27-28 March 2000 461 Film contract for *Rebel Heart*
Two evenings' filming at Dublin (Pearse) platforms 1 and 2.

15 April 2000 85 'Steam Enterprise'
Light engine Whitehead–Belfast (Great Victoria Street). Train Great Victoria Street–Dublin (Connolly)–Great Victoria Street. Light engine Great Victoria Street–Whitehead. The train was formed of Cravens.

21 April 2000 461 Good Friday special
Dublin (Connolly)–Mullingar–Dublin (Connolly).

22 April 2000 171 'Bangor Belle'
Whitehead–Belfast Central–Bangor–Central–Bangor–Central–Bangor–Belfast Central–Whitehead. This run saw 171's reappearance in blue livery.

24 April 2000 171 'Bangor Belle'
Whitehead–Belfast Central–Bangor–Central–Bangor–Central–Bangor–Belfast Central–Whitehead.

8 May 2000 461 Light engine
Positioning movement for 'American Mail' international tour. Dublin–Limerick Junction. The locomotive failed at Limerick Junction with a hot big end, and took no part in the tour.

8 May 2000 85 Light engine
Positioning movement for 'American Mail' international tour. Whitehead–Belfast (Great Victoria Street) (to turn engine)–Belfast Central–Inchicore.

10 May 2000 171 Light engine
Positioning movement for 'American Mail' international tour. Whitehead–Belfast (Great Victoria Street) (to turn engine)–Belfast Central–Inchicore.

13 May 2000 85, 171 'American Mail' international railtour
No 171 light engine Inchicore–Cork. No 85 plus IÉ Cravens Dublin (Heuston)–Cork. No 171 plus IÉ Cravens Cork–Cobh–Cork–Cobh–Cork. The second trip to Cobh was at first cancelled due to lateness, but reinstated again – I must record personal thanks to the signalman at Little Island who shouted this news after us, as we were preparing to abandon photography for the afternoon! The itinerary outlined above replaced the original plan to run the main tour with 171 to Limerick Junction, 85 to Cork and 461 to Cobh.

14 May 2000 85, 171 'American Mail' international railtour
No 85 and Cravens Cork–Limerick Junction and light engine to Dublin (Connolly). No 171 light engine Cork–Limerick

Junction and worked the tour Limerick Junction–Waterford–Wexford–Dublin (Connolly).

15 May 2000 85 'American Mail' international railtour
No 85 and Cravens Dublin (Connolly)–Portadown and light engine Portadown–Belfast (Great Victoria Street). The empty Cravens set was worked Portadown–Dublin (Connolly) by NIR GM locomotive 112, which had earlier run Belfast (York Road)–Whitehead and brought a five bogie RPSI Whitehead set empty Whitehead–Great Victoria Street then continued light engine to Portadown. The tour passengers travelled Portadown–Great Victoria Street in an NIR three-car '80' class set, then joined 85 and the RPSI train which ran Great Victoria Street–Larne Harbour–Whitehead.

26 May 2000 85 'Steam and Jazz'
Whitehead–Belfast Central–Whitehead–Carrickfergus–Central–Lisburn–Belfast Central–Whitehead.

28 May 2000 GM 085 and 171 Greystones shuttle
Dublin (Connolly)–Greystones–Dublin (Connolly)–Greystones–Dublin (Connolly)–Greystones–Dublin (Connolly). Due to brake problems, the first round trip was worked by IÉ GM No 085. No 171 worked the other two.

18 June 2000 onwards 3 *R.H.Smyth* Bleach Green contract
The start of the hire of No 3 by Henry Boot Ltd, contractors for the Bleach Green–Antrim relay. 'Harvey' was moved on this day by low-loader to the level crossing at Dunadry, following the RPSI's success in winning a huge contract to move ballast in connection with the total renewal and re-opening of this section of railway by Northern Ireland Railways.
The little engine was steamed for a total of 90 days, and shifted some 50,000 tons of ballast in the course of running nearly 1000 miles. Her stabling points included Antrim, Dunadry, Muckamore, Kingsmoss East and Kingsmoss West.
As the line was totally in the possession of the contractors, it was possible for the first time to have one of our engines handled on a main line railway by properly qualified non-railwaymen. Some 22 people were involved in driving and firing on the contract – 19 RPSI members (some of them NIR employees who generously spent their days off, driving and firing steam) and one each from the Downpatrick Railway and the Bluebell Railway. Further details of the end of the contract appear below, and a very full account of the whole operation can be found on the RPSI Website.

22 June 2000 171 Light engine
Dublin (Connolly)–Belfast Central–Whitehead.

23 June 2000 85 'Steam and Jazz'
Whitehead–Belfast Central–Whitehead–Carrickfergus–Central–Lisburn–Belfast Central–Whitehead.

24 June 2000 171 'Belfast Lough Express'
Charter by Laganside Corporation. Whitehead–Carrickfergus–Belfast Central–Bangor–Central–Carrickfergus–Belfast Central–Bangor–Belfast Central–Whitehead.

24 June 2000 171 'Midsummer Night's Steam'
Dublin (Connolly)–Mullingar–Dublin (Connolly).

25 June 2000 171 'Belfast Lough Express'
Charter by Laganside Corporation. Whitehead–Carrickfergus–Belfast Central–Bangor–Central–Carrickfergus–Central–Bangor–Belfast Central–Whitehead.

1 July 2000 IÉ 071 'Strawberry Fair'
Dublin (Connolly)–Enniscorthy–Rosslare Europort–Enniscorthy–Dublin (Connolly). No 461 ran hot during her positioning run for the three day tour, and 171 had to cover both Belfast and Dublin operations in this part of 2000. A bomb scare at Meigh prevented 171 from coming south to cover this tour, which had to be diesel substituted.

? July 2000 171 Light engine
Whitehead–Dublin (Connolly). Precise date unclear. The movement was scheduled for 30 June 2000, but on this date the line was closed due to bomb scare at Meigh.

15 July 2000 171 'International Bachelor Festival'
Dublin (Connolly)–Mullingar–Mostrim–Mullingar–Mostrim–Mullingar–Dublin (Connolly).

26 July 2000 171 Light engine
Dublin (Connolly)–Whitehead.

27 July 2000 85 'Save our Railways' charter by NIR
Whitehead–Belfast Central–Larne Harbour–Belfast Central–Whitehead. The train ran empty Larne Town–Larne Harbour–Larne Town for the engine to run round.

29 July 2000 461 'Sea Breeze'
Dublin (Connolly)–Wexford–Rosslare Europort–Wexford–Dublin (Connolly).

26 August 2000 171 'Bangor Belle'
Whitehead–Belfast Central–Bangor–Central–Bangor–Central–Bangor–Belfast Central–Whitehead.

9 September 2000 171 'Atlantic Coast Express'
Whitehead–Belfast Central (loco to Great Victoria Street and back, to turn)–Lisburn–Antrim–Londonderry Waterside–Antrim–Lisburn–Belfast Central–Whitehead. This was possibly the first nonstop run from Derry to Ballymena since the end of steam. The afternoon short working to Coleraine proved that there was a considerable local market in Derry. Unfortunately, timetable and pathing difficulties have made it impossible to exploit that market adequately.

14 September 2000 461 Rolling stock test run
Inchicore–Sallins–Inchicore. Test run for the restored State Coach 351 and the refurbished bogies on coaches 1142 and 1335, postponed from June. IÉ provided an ex-BR brake van. The train was to have run to Portarlington but was terminated at Sallins due to warm bearings on coach 1142.

17 September 2000 461 Private charter
Private charter by a Dutch enterprise group. No 461 and train diesel-hauled Inchicore–Dublin (Connolly), then empty stock Connolly–Arklow–Rathdrum to pick up passengers (who had been led to believe they were waiting for a service train to Dublin!). It ran with passengers Rathdrum–Connolly, and the whole train diesel-hauled back to Inchicore. Coach 351 was included in the train.

23 September 2000 171 'September Steam Saunter'

Running-in trip Whitehead–Belfast Central (light engine to Great Victoria Street to turn)–Lisburn–Antrim–Coleraine–Castlerock–Coleraine. Light engine Coleraine–Portrush–Coleraine for clearance purposes. (Following the implementation of the Halcrow Transmark Report into the safe operation of RPSI trains on NIR, it now became necessary to run a proving trip if a steam train has not run over any section of line in the previous six months.) Train Coleraine–Antrim–Lisburn–Belfast Central–Whitehead.

30 September 2000 85 'Steam Enterprise'

Light engine Whitehead–Belfast (Great Victoria Street). Train, composed of Cravens, Great Victoria Street–Dublin (Connolly)–Great Victoria Street. Light engine Great Victoria Street–Whitehead.

7 October 2000 171 'The Connor Pilgrim'

Private charter by Connor Diocese of the Church of Ireland. Whitehead–Belfast Central–Lisburn–Antrim–University Halt, then empty to Portrush and back to University. University Halt–Antrim–Lisburn–Belfast Central–Whitehead. The engine ran light from Portrush to Coleraine and back to turn. It was many years since a steam passenger train had worked into Portrush as late as the month of October.

14 October 2000 Clearance test for coach 351

Diesel-hauled Inchicore–Dun Laoghaire–Inchicore. Run to test clearances in the bay platform at Dun Laoghaire.

18 October 2000 461 Official launch of State Coach 351

Empty train Inchicore–Dublin (Pearse) for the official ceremony, then a special working Dublin (Pearse)–Dun Laoghaire, followed by a '071' class locomotive to assist with the run-round. Return special Dun Laoghaire–Dublin (Pearse), then empty stock to Inchicore. This was the second time the RPSI had carried an Irish President, and indeed the second lady President – Mrs Mary McAleese – in the history of the State!

28 October 2000 461 Private charter

Chartered to Leixlip Town Commissioners. Dublin (Connolly)–Leixlip–Enfield–Leixlip–Clonsilla–Leixlip–Enfield–Leixlip –Connolly. Two return trips between Leixlip and Enfield, with the train continuing empty to Clonsilla for the engine to run round. This was the last steam train to use the single track from Clonsilla to Maynooth before commissioning of the double track in December 2000.

29 October 2000 85 'Broomstick Belle'

Whitehead–Belfast Central–Whitehead–Central–Whitehead–Belfast Central–Whitehead.

25 November 2000 3 R.H.Smyth Bleach Green charter

The last day of the Henry Boot Ltd contract for the Bleach Green–Antrim relay, which began on 18 June 2000. The engine worked almost the full length of the Bleach Green to Antrim section and steamed onto a low loader. She steamed off again at Whitehead and, after 90 days, the adventure was over. Not one day was lost through mechanical failure either!

3 December 2000 461 Santa specials

Dublin (Connolly)–Dun Laoghaire–Dublin (Connolly)–Bray–Dublin (Connolly)–Bray–Dublin (Connolly). Due to commissioning of double track, Maynooth was not a permissible destination for this year's Santa trains. The first train ran to Dun Laoghaire only, due to engineering works south of Dalkey.

10 December 2000 85 Santa specials

Whitehead–Belfast Central–Whitehead–Central–Whitehead–Belfast Central–Whitehead.

10 December 2000 461 Santa specials

Dublin (Connolly)–Dun Laoghaire–Dublin (Connolly)–Dun Laoghaire–Dublin (Connolly)–Dun Laoghaire–Dublin (Connolly). All trains terminated at Dun Laoghaire due to a landslip at Killiney.

16 December 2000 85 Santa specials

Whitehead–Belfast Central–Whitehead–Central–Whitehead–Central–Carrickfergus–Belfast Central–Whitehead.

17 December 2000 85 Santa specials

Whitehead–Belfast Central–Whitehead–Central–Whitehead–Central–Carrickfergus–Belfast Central–Whitehead.

17 December 2000 461 Santa specials

Dublin (Connolly)–Bray–Dublin (Connolly)–Bray–Dublin (Connolly). The second trip was a Private charter by the Inchicore Works Sports and Social Club.

23 December 2000 171 Santa specials

Whitehead–Belfast Central–Whitehead–Central–Whitehead–Central–Carrickfergus–Central–Yorkgate. The train ran empty to York Road depot. The Larne line was closed due to a landslip.

12 January 2001 NIR diesel loco Stock movement

The engine and stock of the Santa specials on 23 December 2000 were towed dead from York Road yard to Whitehead by an NIR locomotive.

3 March 2001 NIR GM 111 Cancer Research charter

GM 111 light engine York Road depot–Whitehead and empty carriages Whitehead–Belfast Central–Great Victoria Street. Special Great Victoria Street–Whitehead–Great Victoria Street, then Great Victoria Street–Whitehead. This train was to be hauled by 85, which failed at Whitehead with a blown superheater element. No 85 was marginally involved in the operation, being used to steam-heat the stock during the lie-over at Whitehead.

20 March 2001 4 Steaming at Whitehead

Following its overhaul, No 4 was steamed and operated within the Whitehead RPSI site. This was the first movement of No 4 under its own steam since 3 November 1991.

25 March 2001 171 Private charter

Charter for the British Fertility Society. Empty carriages proving run Whitehead–York Road–Bleach Green–Ballymena–Antrim–Lisburn–Belfast Central–Great Victoria Street. Private charter Botanic–Cultra, continuing Empty carriages Cultra–Bangor–Cultra. Special Cultra–Great Victoria Street. Empty carriages Great Victoria Street–Whitehead. The morning trial run was to have been to Ballymena via Lisburn and Antrim, but there was considerable disruption due to a security alert at Finaghy. (This working coincided with a notable modern traction 'first'. Because the GNR main line was blocked, GM 230 and an empty eight-coach De Dietrich set was worked to Ballymena via Bleach Green and thence back to Lisburn via Antrim and Crumlin, so as to have a set based south of the blockage, as well as to officially clear De Dietrich stock to Ballymena via Bleach Green. As it turned out, the security alert was cleared by the time the set reached Lisburn.)

13 April 2001 461 Good Friday special
Dublin (Connolly)–Mullingar–Dublin (Connolly). No 461's last Dublin-based revenue earning trip to date.

14 April 2001 461 Light engine
Light engine Dublin (Connolly)–Belfast Central–Bangor–Belfast Central–Whitehead. Return from Dublin and proving run on the Bangor line.

16 April 2001 461, NIR GM loco Empty carriages
Whitehead–Central–Bangor–Central. There were problems with the water supply, so an NIR GM loco hauled the second trip to Bangor, while 461 went to York Road depot for water, then light engine York Road–Central–Bangor. No 461 took over the train and worked Bangor–Central–Whitehead. This was 461's final operation before the start of her overhaul.

26 April 2001 171 Proving run
No 171 plus RPSI stock Whitehead–Central–Coleraine. No 171 light engine Coleraine–Portrush–Coleraine. No 171 and train Coleraine–Londonderry–Central–Whitehead.

28 April 2001 4 Running-in trips
Five return light engine workings Whitehead–Carrickfergus. A projected gauging trial with empty stock to Antrim, via Bleach Green, was cancelled due to an engineer's possession. On this rather historic day of No 4's return to the main line, the crew was driver Noel Playfair, fireman Willie Gillespie and Inspector Barry Pentland.

8 May 2001 4 Gauging trial
Gauging trial in advance of a Translink Private charter. Empty carriages Whitehead–York Road depot–Antrim–Yorkgate–Whitehead–Carrickfergus–Larne Harbour–Whitehead.

11 May 2001 4 Running-in trips
Running-in trips, carrying passengers, to complete running-in before the 'Belfast and Northern Counties' railtour. Whitehead–Carrickfergus–Whitehead–Yorkgate–Carrickfergus–Yorkgate–Whitehead. During this afternoon there were five engines in steam at Whitehead: *R.H.Smyth* and Nos 4, 85, 171 and 461. It was the first time a public steam train terminated at Yorkgate since it became a through station. These trips were arranged at the last moment, and greatly delighted some cross-channel visitors who came to Whitehead the day before the big tour!

12 May 2001 4, 85 'Belfast and Northern Counties' railtour
Our first completely northern two-day tour, rearranged from Galway due to Foot and Mouth restrictions, which resulted in Iarnród Éireann withdrawing permission for the tour

to operate. No 4 worked Whitehead–Belfast (Great Victoria Street)–Bangor–Belfast Central–Lisburn–Antrim–Ballymena–Antrim–Lisburn–Larne Harbour–Whitehead–Whitehead RPSI. No 85 worked Whitehead RPSI–Yorkgate–Bleach Green–Ballymena–Antrim–Lisburn–Great Victoria Street–Whitehead. This was the last occasion when RPSI wooden-bodied stock carried passengers on any part of the Belfast–Dublin main line. Since 1996 the operation of wooden stock on this section was confined to Belfast–Lisburn only, under special operating conditions. (Wooden stock was permitted into Lisburn from the Antrim branch on 29 June 2003 but only into the back of the island platform at Lisburn.)

13 May 2001 171 'Belfast and Northern Counties' railtour
Whitehead–Belfast (Great Victoria Street)–Portrush (The first ever nonstop steam run from Great Victoria Street to Portrush)–Coleraine–Londonderry–Great Victoria Street–Belfast Central–Whitehead.

20 May 2001 171 Light engine
Whitehead–Belfast Central–Dublin (Connolly).

25 May 2001 85 'Steam and Jazz' special
Whitehead–Belfast (Great Victoria Street)–Central–Whitehead RPSI–Lisburn–Whitehead.

27 May 2001 171 Dublin area shuttle
Dublin (Connolly)–Maynooth–Dublin (Connolly)–Greystones–Dublin (Connolly)–Maynooth–Dublin (Connolly).

9 June 2001 4 Private charter by Translink
Whitehead–Belfast (Great Victoria Street)–Antrim–Mossley West–Great Victoria Street–Whitehead. Translink invited the Society to provide a train for VIPs to sample the newly reopened NCC main line and attend the opening ceremony of Newtownabbey Council's offices at the former Mossley Mill.

10 June 2001 4 Private charters to Translink
Whitehead–Central–Antrim–Central–Antrim–Central–Whitehead. Run for Translink employees and their families in connection with the reopening of the Bleach Green line.

22 June 2001 4 'Steam and Jazz'
Whitehead–Belfast Central–Whitehead RPSI–Lisburn–Whitehead. (The train due to operate to Great Victoria Street to suit operational convenience for running-round, but due to a delayed departure from Whitehead, was able to run round at Belfast Central.)

23 June 2001 171 'Midsummer Night's Steam'
Dublin (Connolly)–Mullingar–Dublin (Connolly). The train stopped at Maynooth to shunt and remove dining car 88 from the train with a hot axlebox.

1 July 2001 Film contract work
Coach 1463 filmed at Inchicore for *Cake*, a television production for TG4. The film was shot digitally, with a green sheet hung outside the coach window. Passing countryside scenes were added in the post-production stages!

7 July 2001 171 'Strawberry Fair'
Dublin (Connolly)–Enniscorthy–Rosslare Europort–
Enniscorthy–Dublin (Connolly).

4 August 2001 4 'Portrush Flyer'
Whitehead–Belfast Central–Portrush–Coleraine–Castlerock–
Coleraine–Portrush–Belfast Central–Whitehead.

11 August 2001 171 'Sea Breeze'
Dublin (Connolly)–Wexford–Rosslare Europort–Wexford–
Dublin (Connolly).

18 August 2001 4 'Portrush Flyer'
Whitehead–Belfast Central–Portrush–Coleraine–Castlerock–
Coleraine–Portrush–Belfast Central–Whitehead.

25 August 2001 4 'Portrush Flyer'
Whitehead–Belfast Central–Portrush–Coleraine–Castlerock–
Coleraine–Portrush–Belfast Central–Whitehead.

2 September 2001 171 Dublin area shuttle
Dublin (Connolly)–Maynooth–Dublin (Connolly)–
Greystones–Dublin (Connolly)–Maynooth–Dublin
(Connolly). Diner 88 again ran hot and was once again left at
Maynooth.

3 September 2001 171 Incentive group private charter
Dublin (Connolly)–Greystones–Dublin (Connolly)–Inchicore.
The train included State Coach 351.

15 September 2001 85 'Steam Enterprise'
This train consisted of IÉ Cravens, worked empty from
Dublin (Connolly)–Belfast (Great Victoria Street) by an IÉ
diesel. No 85 light engine Whitehead–Great Victoria Street,
then Belfast (Great Victoria Street)–Dublin (Connolly)–Great
Victoria Street. The Cravens were returned to Dublin
(Connolly) by the IÉ diesel and 85 ran light Great Victoria
Street–Whitehead.

29 September 2001 4 Light engine
Whitehead–Belfast–Londonderry Waterside–Belfast–
Whitehead. Annual route clearance run.

30 September 2001 4 'Atlantic Coast Express'
Whitehead–Belfast Central–Londonderry–Coleraine–
Londonderry–Belfast Central–Whitehead.

14 October 2001 171 Private charter
Private charter by Leixlip Town Commissioners.
Dublin (Connolly)–Leixlip–Enfield–Leixlip–Clonsilla–
Leixlip–Enfield–Leixlip–Clonsilla–Leixlip–Enfield–Leixlip–
Connolly. There were three return trips between Leixlip and
Enfield, with the train continuing empty to Clonsilla for the
engine to run round. A similar operation to 2000 – except that
the double track from Clonsilla to Maynooth was now fully
commissioned!

28 October 2001 85 'Broomstick Belle'
Whitehead–Belfast Central–Whitehead–Central–Whitehead–
Central–Whitehead–Belfast Central–Whitehead. No 4 was to
have worked this train but her steam heating equipment was
not fully commissioned.

November 2001 Display of coach 351
A two-week exhibition of State Coach 351 at Pearse station.

Restored TPO 2977 was coupled to 351 and acted as a ticket-
selling and display area.

1 December 2001 4 Empty carriages
Nominally empty carriage Whitehead–Central–Londonderry.
The NIR crew stayed overnight at Londonderry – the first
time in many years that a steam crew lodged in Derry!

2 December 2001 4 Santa special
Londonderry–Castlerock–Londonderry and nominally Empty
carriages Londonderry–Belfast Central–Whitehead.

9 December 2001 4 Santa specials
Whitehead–Belfast Central–Whitehead–Central–empty to
Great Victoria Street to turn–Central–Whitehead–Central–
Whitehead. The third train was made necessary by a large
party organised by the Sargent Cancer Care Charity for Sick
Children.

9 December 2001 171 Santa specials
Dublin (Connolly)–Bray–Dublin (Connolly)–Bray–Dublin
(Connolly)–Bray–Dublin (Connolly).

15 December 2001 171 Santa specials
Dublin (Connolly)–Bray–Dublin (Connolly)–Bray–
Dublin (Connolly). The first train was a Private charter by
Inchicore Sports and Social Club. Paths available for only
two trips, due to the more intensive Saturday DART service.

16 December 2001 4 Santa specials
Whitehead–Belfast Central–Whitehead–Central–empty to
Great Victoria Street triangle to turn–Central–Whitehead–
Central–Carrickfergus–Belfast Central–Whitehead. As in the
previous two years, the Carrickfergus 'short working' was a
good way of taking up excess demand from trains earlier in
the day, which were fully booked.

16 December 2001 171 Santa specials
Dublin (Connolly)–Bray–Dublin (Connolly)–Bray–Dublin
(Connolly)–Bray–Dublin (Connolly).

22 December 2001 4 Santa specials
Whitehead–Belfast Central–Whitehead–Central–Whitehead–
Central–Carrickfergus–Belfast Central–Whitehead.

23 December 2001 4 Santa specials
Whitehead–Belfast Central–Whitehead–Central–Whitehead–
Central–Carrickfergus–Belfast Central–Whitehead.

28 December 2001 3BG Engine transfer
The Guinness engine returned to Whitehead by low-loader
from Downpatrick after 12 years on the Downpatrick
Railway.

*In 2002 some problems with our operating agreement with
NIR meant that the northern-based steam operating season
began later than usual.*

29 March 2002 171 Good Friday special
Dublin (Connolly)–Mullingar–Dublin (Connolly).

21 April 2002 171 Greystones shuttle
Dublin (Connolly)–Greystones–Connolly–Greystones–
Connolly.

7 May 2002 85 Light engine
Whitehead–Belfast Central–Great Victoria Street–Dundalk.
This was a precaution against the possibility of bomb scares
north of Portadown on the day of the tour. The crew returned
by service train to Whitehead and worked No 4 (below).

7 May 2002 4 Light engine proving run
Whitehead–Bleach Green emergency crossover–Antrim–
Lisburn–Belfast Central–Whitehead. Engine fitted with
Macminder. On this day also the new operating agreement
with NIR was signed, and normal operation resumed.

11 May 2002 85, 171 'Corrib' international railtour
Six Cravens plus a heating van Empty carriages Dundalk–
Belfast (Great Victoria Street) (the train started as a 3.00am
Empty carriages ex-Dublin) for the Corrib International
Railtour. No 85 then worked the special forward to Dublin
(Connolly). No 171 light engine Inchicore–Connolly, then
worked the tour Connolly–Galway. The last steam visit to the
Galway line before the replacement of semaphore signalling
and, more significantly, the removal of the connection to
Galway turntable in 2003.

12 May 2002 171, 85 'Corrib' international railtour
No 171 Galway–Athlone–Knockcroghery–Dublin
(Connolly), then light engine to Inchicore. No 85 Dublin
(Connolly)–Belfast (Great Victoria Street), then light engine
to Whitehead. The Cravens were worked Great Victoria
Street–Dublin (Connolly) by an IÉ diesel.

13 May 2002 4 'Corrib' international railtour
Whitehead–Belfast (Great Victoria Street)–Central–Bleach
Green–Ballymena–Bleach Green–Yorkgate–York Road
depot–Whitehead.

**19 May 2002 171 'The Donnybrook Scout' private
charter**
Empty carriages Connolly–Booterstown, then with
passengers to Wicklow and return to Bray. Testing of signals
between Pearse and Sydney Parade, following flooding of a
signal relay room the previous day, caused delays and meant
that passengers transferred to a six car DART at Bray. The
empty train returned later in the evening to Inchicore via
Connolly.

30 May 2002 171 Private charter
A Private charter by Iarnród Éireann in connection with the
European Railway Human Resource Managers' Convention.
Empty Dublin (Connolly)–Lansdowne Road, then with
passengers to Wicklow. Empty to Arklow and back to
Wicklow, then with passengers to Lansdowne Road. Empty
to Inchicore. A rare occasion when steam heat was required
so late in the year!

1 June 2002 4 'Hills of Donegal'
Whitehead–Belfast Central–Londonderry–Central–
Whitehead. Slightly unusual in that the engine ran bunker
first for the whole of the outward journey.

8 June 2002 171 'Sea Breeze'
Dublin (Connolly)–Wexford–Rosslare Europort–Wexford–
Dublin (Connolly). This replaced a planned Dublin–
Dundalk–Dublin operation which would have been used to

exchange engines between Whitehead and Dublin, but had to
be cancelled due to non-availability of Cravens. No 171 was
burning coal supplied by Eagle Energy fuels, and its quality
obviated the previous necessity of taking on additional coal
supplies at Gorey en route.

15 June 2002 85 Jubilee charters
Whitehead–Yorkgate–Mossley West–Ballymena–Mossley
West–Belfast Central–Mossley West–Ballymena–Mossley
West–Yorkgate–Whitehead. These were charters by
Newtownabbey and Ballymena Borough Councils to
celebrate the Golden Jubilee of Queen Elizabeth II, offering
a series of short round trips. No 85 deputised for No 4, which
was having work done to damaged firebars before going
south to replace 171. Good crowds were carried, despite
the rival attraction of England playing in the World Cup at
the same time! (A planned Jubilee charter by North Down
Borough Council on 4 June was cancelled due to delays in
engineering work on the Bangor line.)

21 June 2002 4 'Midsummer Jazz' special
Empty train Whitehead–York Road depot (two hour lay-
over)–Central–Ballymena–Central. This was a fraught night
of torrential rain in the greater Belfast area. The Larne line
was closed by flooding, and the Society's Whitehead depot
itself deep in water to rail level. The train was terminated at
Belfast Central – see further entry for 26 June.

22 June 2002 171 'Midsummer Night's Steam'
Dublin (Connolly)–Mullingar–Dublin (Connolly). The last
passenger-carrying operation for 171 before the expiry of her
ticket.

26 June 2002 4 Stock movement
No 4 and seven bogies hauled from York Road depot to
Whitehead by NIR GM 111 due to the unavailability of a full
steam crew. Since there was only one passed-out steam driver
on the whole of NIR at this time, it was remarkable that
occurrences like this were so rare!

28 June 2002 4 'Midsummer Jazz' special
Empty train Whitehead–York Road depot (two hour lay-
over)–Belfast Central–Ballymena–Central–Whitehead.

1 July 2002 4, 171 Engine movements
Exchange of locomotives. No 4 light engine Whitehead–
Belfast Central–Dublin Connnolly and 171 light engine
Dublin (Connolly)–Belfast Central–Whitehead. This ended
(for the meantime) 171's active main line career.

6 July 2002 4 'Strawberry Fair'
Dublin (Connolly)–Enniscorthy–Rosslare Europort–
Enniscorthy–Dublin (Connolly). The locomotive and train
were diesel-hauled Connolly–Inchicore at the end of the day.

27 July 2002 4, 85 'Steam Enterprise'
This tour operated to facilitate an exchange of locomotives.
No 4 and Cravens worked Dublin (Connolly)–Belfast
Central–Whitehead (possibly the first time a Cravens set
has arrived steam-hauled in Whitehead) and 85 Whitehead–
Belfast Central–Dublin (Connolly). No 85 was detached from
the train at Central and turned on the Blythefield triangle
before resuming her journey to Dublin.

The usual Dublin crew of Dan and Tony Renehan, with trainee fireman Shamie Brennan and a pilotman, worked through to Belfast and back, prompting someone to suggest that this was the first time in 92 years that an Inchicore man had worked a steam engine into Belfast. (No 322 had worked into the old Great Victoria Street during the 1911 locomotive exchange, and Dan Renehan reckoned that the crew involved then may have been driver Jack Moloney and fireman Barty Cummins. Dan could find no record of Moloney's name in the Seniority List the GSR first compiled in 1924 – perhaps he had retired or been made a Locomotive Inspector. Cummins was one of three brothers who were all footplatemen. Barty started at Inchicore in 1897, and passed out as a driver in 1930.)

28 July 2002 4 Bangor line gauging and clearance working
Whitehead–Belfast Central–Bangor–Central–Whitehead. Empty six-coach train, supervised by an NIR civil engineer's representative, to clear No 4 for operation on the relaid Bangor line. The whole train was turned on the Blythefield triangle to reverse the turning of the train on the 'Corrib' railtour and to turn No 4 (at the crew's request) to be bunker-first for the outward 'Portrush Flyer'.

31 July 2002 4 Official press launch of No 4 following overhaul
VIP and press reception at Whitehead, followed by No 4 and three coaches working Whitehead–Carrickfergus–Whitehead. The guests were transported by road to the Quality Inn for lunch.

3 August 2002 4 'Portrush Flyer' and Ballymoney extension
Whitehead–Belfast Central–Portrush–Ballymoney–Portrush–Central–Whitehead. This year's 'Flyer' offered, for the first time, an alternative venue to Castlerock for the afternoon extension.

17 August 2002 4 'Portrush Flyer' and Ballymoney extension
Whitehead–Belfast Central–Portrush–Ballymoney–Portrush–Central–Whitehead. The Ballymoney trip this season was advertised as the 'Dalriada' extension.

24 August 2002 4 'Portrush Flyer' and Ballymoney extension
Whitehead–Belfast Central–Portrush–Ballymoney–Portrush–York Road depot–Whitehead. The locomotive sustained damage to a valve head and piston rings and, after slow running from Cullybackey to Antrim, the train was terminated here and most passengers transferred to the following 20.05 service train ex-Portrush. The locomotive and stock ran at reduced speed to York Road and thence to Whitehead, arriving in the early hours of 25 August.

26 August 2002 NIR GM 8113 and 111 'Bangor Belle'
Charter by North Down Borough Council. No 8113 Whitehead–Belfast Central–Bangor–Central–Bangor–Central. No 111 Belfast Central–Bangor–Central–Whitehead. A last minute diesel substitution following No 4's failure on the 'Portrush Flyer'.

15 September 2002 Cancelled working
An 'Atlantic Coast Express' working was cancelled due to the non-availability of No 4. No 85 was in Dublin, but by this time banned from working north of Ballymena.

22 September 2002 4 Running-in trip following repairs
No 4 and four RPSI bogies Whitehead–Belfast Central. No 4 ran light to Great Victoria Street to turn, then with train Central–Antrim–Lisburn–Antrim–Central–Whitehead.

25 September 2002 85 Film contract
No 85, out of steam, with coaches 1142 and 1196, was used for film sequences at Connolly station, Dublin, in connection with a Tesco Ireland Charity of the Year event.

27 September 2002 4 Private charter by Stena Company
No 4 and four RPSI bogies empty Whitehead–Belfast Central, then with passengers Central–Cultra, then empty Cultra–Bangor–Cultra, then with passengers to Central, then empty to Whitehead.

6 October 2002 85 Light engine
Dublin (Connolly)–Belfast Central–Whitehead. A Leixlip Town Commissioners' charter due to run on 13 October 2002 was cancelled as 85 was not cleared to run to Maynooth.

19 October 2002 85 'Steam Enterprise'
No 85 light engine Whitehead–Belfast (Great Victoria Street). Train Great Victoria Street–Dublin (Connolly), formed of IÉ Cravens, which were worked empty from Dublin (Connolly). Less than 24 hours before the operation, Translink informed the Society that the return journey would be outside the driver's hours, hence 85 returned light Dublin (Connolly)–Whitehead in the early afternoon. NIR diesel loco 8208 ran light York Road–Dublin (Connolly) to work the train back to Belfast. (Almost certainly the first Society public excursion to be hauled by a '201 class' loco.) More happily, before departure from Great Victoria Street, a 70th birthday cake for No 85 was cut by chairman Norman Foster in the presence of driver Noel Playfair and dining car supervisor Mrs Rita Henderson.

27 October 2002 4 'Broomstick Belle'
Whitehead–Belfast Central–Whitehead–Central–Whitehead–Belfast Central–Whitehead.

30 November 2002 4 Coleraine Santa specials
Whitehead–Belfast Central–Coleraine–Castlerock–Coleraine–Castlerock–Coleraine–Londonderry. The crew lodged in Derry for the second Christmas in succession.

1 December 2002 4 Londonderry Santa specials
Londonderry–Castlerock–Londonderry–Central–Whitehead.

2 December 2002 4 Light engine
Whitehead–Belfast Central–Dublin (Connolly), for use on the Dublin based Santa specials.

3 December 2002 IÉ '201 class' locomotive Coach test run
The engine hauled RPSI diner 88 and a 'Dutch' van Inchicore–Hazelhatch–Inchicore.

6 December 2002 4 Gauging trial
No 4 was hauled, out of steam, by a 071 class locomotive from Connolly to the new Grand Canal Dock station to test clearances for running round a train here.

7 December 2002 85 Private charters
Private charters for Sense NI and the Sargent Cancer Care Charity. Whitehead–Belfast Central–Whitehead–Central–Whitehead–Belfast Central–Whitehead.

7 December 2002 4 Santa specials
Empty carriages Dublin (Connolly)–Dublin (Pearse), then Dublin (Pearse)–Maynooth–Pearse–Maynooth–Pearse–Maynooth–Dublin (Pearse). On each trip the train continued empty from Dublin (Pearse) to the newly opened station at Grand Canal Dock station for the engine to run round.

7 December 2002 85 Santa specials
Whitehead–Belfast Central–Whitehead–Central–Whitehead–Belfast Central–Whitehead.

8 December 2002 4 Santa specials
Empty train Dublin (Connolly)–Dublin (Pearse), then Pearse–Maynooth–Pearse–Maynooth–Pearse–Maynooth–Dublin (Pearse)–Connolly. On each trip the train continued empty from Dublin (Pearse) to Grand Canal Dock station for the engine to run round. The train formation was eight RPSI bogies plus an IÉ 'Dutch' van for auxiliary steam heat.

14 December 2002 4 Santa specials
Empty train Dublin (Connolly)–Dublin (Pearse), then Pearse–Maynooth–Pearse–Maynooth–Pearse–Maynooth–Pearse–Connolly. On each trip the train continued empty from Dublin (Pearse) to Grand Canal Dock station for the engine to run round.

15 December 2002 4 Santa specials
Empty train Dublin (Connolly)–Dublin (Pearse), then Pearse–Maynooth–Pearse–Maynooth–Pearse–Maynooth–Pearse–Connolly. On each trip the train continued empty from Dublin (Pearse) to Grand Canal Dock station for the engine to run round.

15 December 2002 85 Santa specials
Whitehead–Belfast Central–Whitehead–Belfast Central–Whitehead–Belfast Central–Carrickfergus–Belfast Central–Whitehead.

21 December 2002 85 Santa specials
Whitehead–Belfast Central–Whitehead–Belfast Central–Whitehead–Belfast Central–Whitehead.

21 December 2002 4 Santa specials
Empty train Dublin (Connolly)–Dublin (Pearse), then Pearse–Maynooth–Pearse–Maynooth–Pearse–Maynooth–Dublin (Pearse). On each trip the train continued empty from Dublin (Pearse) to Grand Canal Dock station for the engine to run round.

22 December 2002 85 Santa specials
Whitehead–Belfast Central–Whitehead–Central–Whitehead–Central–Carrickfergus–Belfast Central–Whitehead.

22 December 2002 4 Santa specials
Empty train Dublin (Connolly)–Dublin (Pearse), then Pearse–Maynooth–Pearse–Maynooth–Pearse–Maynooth–Pearse–Connolly. The train continued empty from Dublin (Pearse) to Grand Canal Dock station for the engine to run round.

2003 was an important year for southern operations. Following the negotiation of a revised system of communications, the operating range of all RPSI locomotives was codified and published in the weekly operating circular.

9 March 2003 4 Charter for Leixlip Town Commissioners
Dublin (Connolly)–Leixlip Confey–Enfield–Leixlip Confey–Clonsilla (empty train, to allow engine to run round)–Leixlip Confey–Enfield–Leixlip Confey–Dublin (Connolly). This train was postponed from 13 October 2002.

7 April 2003 4 Crew training trips based on Enfield
Inchicore–Dublin (Connolly)–Mullingar–Enfield, where No 4 was based for the dates listed below. This was the first time an engine had been 'shedded' at Enfield for a long period!

8–11 April 2003 4 Crew training trips based on Enfield
The daily itineraries varied slightly but generally involved two return trips from Enfield to Mullingar, or Enfield–Mullingar–Enfield–Killucan–Enfield if the engine required coaling. An RPSI team, led by none other than the Chairman himself, stayed with the train throughout, and a private security firm was also engaged.

14–17 April 2003 4 Crew training trips based on Enfield
As 8–11 April. On the final day of operating, No 4 was worked back Enfield–Dublin (Connolly).

18 April 2003 4 Good Friday special
Dublin (Connolly)–Mullingar–Dublin (Connolly).

20 April 2003 85 Easter Bunny specials
Whitehead–Belfast Central–Whitehead–Belfast Central–Whitehead–Belfast Central–Whitehead.

27 April 2003 4 Greystones shuttle
Dublin (Connolly)–Greystones–Dublin (Connolly)–Greystones–Dublin (Connolly). The empty train continued Connolly–Inchicore.

30 April 2003 4 Clearance testing special
Inchicore–Westport with one Mark 2 coach and a generator van.

1 May 2003 4 Clearance testing special
Westport–Inchicore with one Mark 2 coach and a generator van.

4 May 2003 85 Light engine
Whitehead–Belfast Central–Great Victoria Street–Dublin (Connolly)–Inchicore. Positioning run for the international railtour.

10 May 2003 4 'Plains of Mayo' international railtour
No 4 with an IÉ Cravens set Dublin (Connolly)–
Portarlington–Westport–Claremorris.

11 May 2003 4 'Plains of Mayo' international railtour
No 4 and the IÉ Cravens set Claremorris–Ballina–
Claremorris–Dublin (Connolly). No 85 Dublin (Connolly)–
Belfast (Great Victoria Street), with a second set of Cravens
stock which returned to Dublin that night, diesel-hauled.
No 85 then worked Great Victoria Street–Whitehead light
engine.

12 May 2003 85 'Plains of Mayo' international railtour
Empty RPSI wooden-bodied set worked by NIR GM
8113 Whitehead–Belfast Central–Whitehead (to pick up
the tour passengers). No 85 worked Whitehead–Larne
Harbour–Belfast Central, then Belfast Central–Ballymena.
NIR GM 8113 worked the RPSI train Ballymena–Antrim–
Lisburn–Belfast Central (No 85 was short of water). The
train ran empty Lisburn–Central with passengers following
in a service train (due to the ban on passengers travelling in
wooden stock on any part of the Belfast to Dublin main line.
No 85 ran light Ballymena–Bleach Green–Belfast Central
and then hauled the RPSI set Central–Whitehead.

24 May 2003 4 'Sea Breeze'
Dublin (Connolly)–Wexford–Rosslare Europort–Wexford–
Dublin (Connolly).

31 May 2003 131 Movement 'in parts'
The frames, motion and wheels of ex-GNR Q class 4-4-0
No 131 arrived at Whitehead.

7 June 2003 4 'Sea Breeze'
Dublin (Connolly)–Wexford–Rosslare Europort–Wexford–
Dublin (Connolly). (A northern 'Hills of Donegal' operation
scheduled for the same day was cancelled, due to No 4 being
in Dublin and 85 not permitted beyond Ballymena.)

20 June 2003 85 'Steam and Jazz'
Whitehead–Belfast Central–Bleach Green–Ballymena–
Central–Whitehead. This run continued the tradition of
dancing on the platforms at Antrim and Ballymena to the
strains of the Apex Jazz Band!

21 June 2003 4 'Midsummer Night's Steam'
Dublin (Connolly)–Mullingar–Dublin (Connolly). The final
RPSI train to visit Mullingar before the double junction
between the Galway and Sligo lines was removed and
rationalised in September 2003.

27 June 2003 85 'Steam and Jazz'
Whitehead–Belfast Central–Bleach Green–Ballymena–
Belfast Central–Whitehead.

28 June 2003 4 and 85 'Northern Enterprise'
No 4 Dublin (Connolly)–Whitehead with eight Cravens and
a heating van. No 85 Whitehead–Dublin (Connolly). No 85
ran light from Central to the Great Victoria Street triangle
and back to turn during the lay over at Belfast Central.

29 June 2003 4 Antrim branch farewell
Whitehead–Belfast Central–Antrim–Lisburn–Antrim–
Lisburn–Antrim–Belfast Central–Whitehead. Two return

trips over the Antrim branch (Antrim to Lisburn only,
wooden stock with passengers now being banned on the
Belfast–Dublin main line.)

2 August 2003 4 30th anniversary 'Portrush Flyer'
Whitehead–Belfast Central–Portrush–Ballymoney–Portrush–
Central–Whitehead. Once again, the 2003 season featured a
Ballymoney, rather than a Castlerock, extension.

16 August 2003 4 'Portrush Flyer'
Whitehead–Belfast Central–Portrush–Ballymoney–Portrush–
Belfast Central–Whitehead.

23 August 2003 85 'Northern Enterprise'
Dublin (Connolly)–Belfast Central–Whitehead–Dublin
(Connolly) with six Cravens and a van. This was one of
a number of trains planned to mark the expiry of 85's
main line certification (though by the end of the year an
extension seemed likely until September 2004) and the first
'Northern Enterprise' to feature an out-and-back working
by one engine. During the lay-over at Belfast Central in
the afternoon, 85 was turned on the Great Victoria Street
triangle.

30 August 2003 4 'Portrush Flyer'
Whitehead–Belfast Central–Portrush–Ballymoney–
Portrush–Belfast Central–Whitehead. The final 'Flyer'
season operation worked by RPSI wooden stock, which
appropriately included ex–LMS(NCC) No 91 of the 1930s
'North Atlantic Express' set.

6 September 2003 85 'Farewell to 85' railtour
Dublin (Connolly)–Cork. Details below.

7 September 2003 85 'Farewell to 85' railtour
Cork–Dublin (Connolly). Billed as 85's final working
to Cork and comprising six IÉ Cravens and a van. The
Society's first – and very successful – attempt to market
a simplified two-day tour package, with participants
responsible for organising their own accommodation.

**15 September 2003 4 Charter by the Institute of
Cytologists**
Empty Whitehead–Belfast Central, then with passengers
Belfast Central–Cultra, empty Cultra–Bangor–Cultra, with
passengers Cultra–Central and, finally, empty Central–
Whitehead. As wooden stock on double line sections is
subject to double-blocking, this charter was to have been
formed of Cravens, worked from Dublin (Connolly) by
diesel, and No 4 was to have worked light engine from
Whitehead to Great Victoria Street to collect it. On the day,
the Cravens set was unavailable, and the evening peak on
NIR was paralysed by a major signal failure on the Larne
line. No 4 thus worked with four RPSI wooden vehicles as
noted above.

26–27 September 2003 4 Light engine proving run
Whitehead–Bleach Green Junction–Londonderry–
Whiteabbey–Bleach Green Junction–Whitehead. This
working left Whitehead at 6.00pm, arriving back around
3.00am the following morning. It was the first RPSI
operation scheduled to run through midnight!

28 September 2003 4 'Atlantic Coast Express'
Whitehead–Belfast Central–Derry Waterside–Central–
Whitehead. This replaced a projected Belfast–Dublin–Belfast
'Steam Enterprise' scheduled for 27 September, which was
cancelled following continued problems about the length
of driver's days. The 'Atlantic Coast Express' was billed as
the last working of our wooden stock into Londonderry. Its
run from Ballymena to Derry is one of the longest nonstop
sections covered by an RPSI special!

18 October 2003 85 'Northern Enterprise'
Dublin (Connolly)–Belfast Central–Whitehead–Central–
Dublin (Connolly) with six IÉ Cravens and a van. Due to
engineering work, the train ran wrong line from Newry to
Poyntzpass. Due to delays on the return journey, the train
was looped at Skerries to allow the 18.10 Central–Dublin
to overtake – certainly new track for an RPSI train! This
operation replaced the customary autumn Greystones shuttle.

26 October 2003 4 'Broomstick Belle'
Empty carriages Whitehead–Belfast Central, then Belfast
Central–Whitehead–Belfast Central–Whitehead–Belfast
Central. Empty carriages to Whitehead.

29 November 2003 4 Coleraine Christmas shopper
Whitehead–Belfast Central–Coleraine–Ballymoney–
Coleraine–Castlerock–Coleraine–Belfast Central–Whitehead.
Christmas shopping special to Coleraine with two local
Santa trips. Billed as the final visit of the RPSI wooden-
bodied set to Coleraine and Castlerock.

30 November 2003 4, 85 Light engine workings
No 4 light engine Whitehead–Belfast (Great Victoria Street)–
Dublin (Connolly). No 85 light engine Dublin (Connolly)–
Whitehead. Locomotive exchange for the Dublin and Belfast
based Santa trains.

6 December 2003 4 Santa specials
Eight RPSI coaches plus an IÉ van empty train Dublin
(Connolly)–Dublin (Pearse)–Grand Canal Dock, then Grand
Canal Dock–Pearse–Maynooth–Pearse–Maynooth–Pearse–
Maynooth–Pearse–Grand Canal Dock–Dublin (Connolly).
Each time the train ran empty Dublin (Pearse) to and from
Grand Canal Dock station for the engine to run round.
This was the last Dublin Santa season before the closure
of Connolly shed – itself the last operational ex-GNR
locomotive shed and scheduled to close in early 2004.

7 December 2003 4 Santa specials
Eight RPSI coaches plus an IÉ van empty train Dublin
(Connolly)–Dublin (Pearse)–Grand Canal Dock, then Grand
Canal Dock–Pearse–Maynooth–Pearse–Maynooth–Pearse–
Maynooth–Pearse–Grand Canal Dock–Dublin (Connolly).
Each time the train ran empty Dublin (Pearse) to and from
Grand Canal Dock station for the engine to run round.

7 December 2003 85 Santa specials
Whitehead–Belfast Central–Whitehead–Belfast Central–
Whitehead–Belfast Central–Whitehead. The second round
trip was a Private charter by Sargent Cancer Care.

13 December 2003 4 Santa specials
Eight RPSI coaches plus an IÉ van empty train Dublin

(Connolly)–Dublin (Pearse)–Grand Canal Dock, then Grand
Canal Dock–Pearse–Maynooth–Pearse–Maynooth–Pearse–
Maynooth–Pearse–Grand Canal Dock–Dublin (Connolly).
Each time the train ran empty Dublin (Pearse) to and from
Grand Canal Dock station for the engine to run round.

13 December 2003 85 Santa specials
Whitehead–Belfast Central–Whitehead–Central–Whitehead–
Belfast Central–Whitehead.

14 December 2003 4 Santa specials
Eight RPSI coaches plus an IÉ van empty train Dublin
(Connolly)–Dublin (Pearse)–Grand Canal Dock, then Grand
Canal Dock–Pearse–Maynooth–Pearse–Maynooth–Pearse–
Maynooth–Pearse–Grand Canal Dock–Dublin (Connolly).
Each time the train ran empty Dublin (Pearse) to and from
Grand Canal Dock station for the engine to run round.

14 December 2003 85 Santa specials
Whitehead–Belfast Central–Whitehead–Central–Whitehead–
Central–Antrim–Belfast Central–Whitehead. This was the
first use of Antrim as a destination for Whitehead-based
Santa operations.

20 December 2003 85 Santa specials
Whitehead–Belfast Central–Whitehead–Central–Whitehead–
Belfast Central–Whitehead.

21 December 2003 85 Santa specials
Whitehead–Belfast Central–Whitehead–Central–Whitehead–
Central–Antrim–Belfast Central–Whitehead. This was
possibly the final day of operations for the Whitehead-based
wooden set.

23 December 2003 131 Movement 'in parts'
The boiler of ex GNR Q class No 131 arrived at Whitehead.

18 January 2004 186 Steaming at Whitehead
No 186 was steamed at Whitehead for the first time since 5
July 1980.

20 March 2004 4 'The Marble City'
No 4 light engine Inchicore–Dublin (Connolly), then with
eight Cravens empty to Heuston Platform 10 – certainly new
track for a steam train! The train ran Heuston–Newbridge–
Kilkenny–Thomastown–Kilkenny–Newbridge–Heuston
(Platform 4 this time). The engine was turned on the
Lavistown triangle at Kilkenny. This was the first RPSI
train to pick up and set down at Newbridge, and the last
steam train to work under semaphore signals from Athy to
Thomastown before the commissioning of the Waterford
line Mini-CTC in mid April 2004. No 4 ran light Heuston–
Inchicore.

27–28 March 2004 186 Crew familiarisation
In steam at Whitehead for crew familiarisation and to shunt
the RPSI's new rake of Mark 2 stock.

9 April 2004 4 Good Friday special
Empty RPSI carriages Inchicore–Connolly then the
customary Good Friday special Connolly–Mullingar–
Connolly. Empty train Connolly–Inchicore.

12 April 2004 186 Easter Bunny train rides

First 'public' steaming of 186 on Easter Monday steam train rides at Whitehead. This replaced the cancelled Easter Bunny specials from Belfast to Whitehead.

14 April 2004 85 Gauging trip for IÉ Cravens

No 85 light engine Whitehead–Belfast (Great Victoria Street) to collect IÉ Cravens, worked north by GM 186. Empty carriages gauging run Belfast Central–Bangor–Great Victoria Street. The coaches returned south with GM 186; No 85 ran light to Whitehead. Almost certainly the first steam-hauled Cravens coaches to work into Bangor.

17 April 2004 85 Titanic Commemoration specials

Charter by Belfast City Council in connection with the Titanic Commemorative Exhibition at the UFTM.

No 85 light engine Whitehead–Lisburn to collect IÉ Cravens which once again had been worked north by GM 186. The diesel loco ran light engine to York Road depot to stable. No 85 worked Empty carriages Lisburn–Belfast Central, then Central–Bangor–Lisburn–Bangor–Lisburn–Bangor–Central. All trains stopped at Cultra to set down and pick up. No 85 plus Cravens worked empty Belfast Central–York Road depot then light engine to Whitehead.

18 April 2004 85 Titanic Commemoration specials

Charter by Belfast City Council in connection with the Titanic Commemorative Exhibition at the UFTM.

No 85 light engine Whitehead–York Road depot then, with empty Cravens, York Road–Belfast Central. Two specials Belfast Central–Bangor–Central–Bangor–Belfast Central. All trains stopped at Cultra to set down and pick up. No 85 light engine Central–Whitehead. The coaches returned south with IÉ GM 186. A planned third trip to Bangor had to be cancelled, as the Cravens needed to be in Sligo for the following morning's 5.15 Sligo–Dublin!

1 May 2004 85 Gauging special

Following discussions with NIR, the first main-line working for the five Mark 2 vehicles was an empty-carriage gauging-special hauled by 85. The train ran Whitehead–Yorkgate–Antrim–Ballymena–Antrim–Yorkgate–Whitehead, making gauging stops at station platforms and emergency stops to test the brakes. This was the beginning of a new era in the Society's operational history!

1 May 2004 4 'Sea Breeze'

Dublin (Connolly)–Wexford–Rosslare Europort–Wexford–Dublin (Connolly).

2 May 2004 85 Gauging special

No 85, with the Mark 2 set again, Whitehead–Belfast Central–Bangor–Central–Newry–Central–Whitehead, making gauging stops at station platforms.

8 May 2004 4 'Slieve Kimalta' international railtour

No 4 and IÉ Cravens Dublin (Connolly)–Limerick Junction–Ballybrophy–Nenagh–Limerick. This much-revised tour ran down the Cork main line to Limerick Junction, where the whole train ran round the direct curve from Kyle level crossing to Milltown level crossing and then set back into the station. This was to avoid bunker-first running for the rest of the day. At Ballybrophy the train drew forward on the main line and set back into the Nenagh bay. At Roscrea the engine was coaled – a possible first among the many places where our engines have taken coal.

9 May 2004 4 'Slieve Kimalta' international railtour

No 4 and IÉ Cravens Limerick–Limerick Junction–Dublin (Connolly)–Dundalk–Dublin (Connolly). Once again this tour ran into Limerick Junction so that the engine could run round and operate chimney-first to Dublin. At Connolly shed the engine was turned, watered and coaled before the final leg to Dundalk. As the Cravens set was needed later that evening, the tour returned to Dublin with No 4, and Belfast passengers were scheduled to travel north by a special train formed of a GM loco and the Mk 2 Gatwick set. In the event, the 15.00 Belfast–Dublin failed at Portadown, a three car 80 class DEMU brought its passengers to Dundalk, and IÉ 223 and the Gatwick set were commandeered to work forward to Dublin with the passengers off the 15.00 ordinary service. Belfast-bound railtour passengers travelled from Dundalk to Belfast (Great Victoria Street) in the three car 80 class set which had arrived from Portadown. (This much-travelled set finished its own day working the 21.20 Belfast–Portrush!)

10 May 2004 4 'Slieve Kimalta' international railtour

No 85 ran light engine Whitehead–Belfast Central–Dundalk to collect the same set of Cravens which were used on 9 May, and had been hauled from Connolly by ex-works IÉ 141, after an overnight interlude in regular service! Belfast passengers travelled to Dundalk by special NIR '80 class' diesel railcar. No 85 and IÉ Cravens ran Dundalk–Central–Bangor–Central–Whitehead–Belfast Central. No 85 worked the empty Cravens to York Road depot and then ran light engine back to Whitehead. The Cravens returned south, hauled by IÉ 141 sometime later.

Picture index

(Entries in talics are train names.)